The Paradise Plan

HILTON HEAD ISLAND SWEET ROMANCE & WOMEN'S FRIENDSHIP FICTION, BOOK 2

ELANA JOHNSON

ISBN-13: 978-1-63876-136-5

Chapter One

Cassandra Haslam waved to the woman in the white SUV, keeping her smile clipped in place until she'd gone. All the way around the corner and out of sight. Only then did Cass turn back to her house, a sigh falling from her lips and turning into a darker sound in the back of her throat.

She re-entered her house, the scent of her husband's cologne always lingering just inside the door. He hung his jacket there, along with his scarf, and Cass gave them both a cursory glance as she went by. West was nothing if not regimented. He did the same thing at the same time every day. So tomorrow morning, when the clock struck eight, he'd shrug into his jacket and wrap that scarf around his neck, where both picked up earthy, musky notes of his cologne. Then he'd kiss Cass, who'd barely be out of bed, and head out the door to work.

Weekend mornings found him with the *National Geographic* magazine and coffee until noon. He couldn't drink it past that, he claimed, or he wouldn't be able to sleep at night.

She walked past the couch and all the clean, crisp lines in the living room. She'd just gotten new furniture and new rugs when she and West had put in new flooring. Cass loved updating old things, and she got called in for a lot of renovations around Sweet Water Falls, Beeville, and other surrounding small towns.

As an interior designer, she could see beauty in things most people couldn't. She could repurpose anything, and she could draw up a set of plans for a customer in only minutes. Her new software and tablet helped with that, and Cass glanced at it as she passed the built-in desk in the kitchen.

She paused there and hugged herself as she faced her friends. "So," she said, and that brought Joy's attention to her. Joy was an exceptional listener, and she and Cass had started walking this winter. It wasn't really cold in the Coastal Bend of Texas, not like some parts of the country. Jacket weather for sure, but Cass had never even owned a coat or a snow shovel.

"Guys," Joy said, and that got Bessie and Sage to stop talking about herbs and poultices. Sage loved everything to do with homeopathic healing, crystals, and connecting her spiritual energy to the earth. Bessie had developed a rash, and Sage was *sure* this essential oil or that one would work to clear it up.

Lauren twisted away from Bea, who had a flight out of San Antonio at seven-fifty tomorrow morning. She'd been staying in Cass's guest bedroom for two nights now, and Cass would miss her when she left.

True to her word, she'd come to Sweet Water Falls for their monthly Supper Club though she'd moved to Hilton Head Island over half a year ago. Right now, she shook her head, and Cass nodded, their silent conversation all Cass really needed.

She'd listen to the others too, but she suspected they'd all have the same opinion on Stacy.

She wasn't a fit for their Supper Club.

"I liked her," Sage said, getting up and taking her dessert plate with her. For their February meal, Cass had served Three Kings cake, though the holiday wasn't for another couple weeks. Lauren had found the tiny plastic baby in her piece of cake, and Cass had crowned her queen for the day.

They'd laughed and talked, the food delicious and the wine flowing, all of them speculating what Lauren's good luck would bring her. As Cass watched, she handed her plate —complete with the plastic baby on it—to Sage, who took it along with hers into Cass's kitchen. The tiny toy got thrown away without much fanfare, the fun it had brought over now.

"I like her too," Joy said with some false qualities in her voice. "I just don't think..." She looked at Bessie, who definitely wouldn't say they shouldn't invite Stacy to be a permanent part of their Supper Club.

Bessie blinked at her. "What? What do you want me to say?"

"Do you think we should invite her back?" Lauren asked, her dark eyes blazing with fire. She was a passionate person, and that passion often clashed with Cass's headstrong way of doing things. They both wanted to be right, and they both wanted to matter, and they both wanted to be in control of some things.

As a result, Cass clashed the most with Lauren, though she loved her dearly at the same time. The common ground between them had always been Bea, who brought harmony to their group of six.

"We should just keep the five of us," Lauren said, turning her gaze to Cass when Bessie didn't answer.

Cass walked over to her seat at the head of the table and sank into her chair. "Yeah," she said, her voice carrying wistful qualities she wished it wouldn't.

"I'm sorry," Bea said, something she'd done a million times before.

"Don't apologize," Bessie said. "It's not your fault."

"It kind of is," Bea said. "I want to keep coming. I do. It's just...hard." She stood too, picked up an empty bottle of wine, and went into the kitchen with it.

Cass watched her, her guilt pinching down inside her gut. The last thing she wanted was to cause any unrest in Bea. She'd lived in Texas for her whole life—until last year when she'd fallen in love with her now-husband, Grant, and moved to Hilton Head, South Carolina.

"Six is just so neat," Cass said. "We each host twice a year. It's easy."

"We could have a bye month," Lauren said.

Cass turned her gaze onto Lauren, not sure she'd heard her right. *Yes, you did*, her mind whispered at her. She simply didn't want to have a bye month in their Supper Club. This event on the third Thursday of the month had been the highlight of her friendship with these women, and she adored her evening with them.

Yes, she saw them each outside of the Supper Club, and she could still do that. Cass literally planned changes for a living. But she had a very hard time accepting them in her personal life, especially without a lot of notice.

Bea had fallen in love with Grant in only a couple of weeks, and by her standards, that was very fast indeed.

"A bye month," Joy repeated. "That's actually a good idea."

It was, but Cass didn't say so.

"We're always so busy in December," Lauren said. "We could easily take that month off. And we've already decided we're all going to Hilton Head for the Fourth of July every year, so we could take June off and do our Supper Club there instead."

"Weeks later," Cass said.

"Yes," Lauren said coolly. "Just like you served Three Kings cake, though the holiday is 'weeks later.'"

Cass's jaw clenched, but she nodded. "It's not a bad idea."

"I like it," Bessie said. "Then we don't have to try to find someone new. I did like Stacy, but she..."

Cass wouldn't want to be Stacy either. She wouldn't want to try to come into a solid group of five people, who'd known each other for several years, and try to fit in. She wouldn't even know where to start, and Stacy had worn a half-panicked look for most of the evening. She'd spoken too loudly, and laughed too long, almost a desperate attempt to show she was enjoying herself and everyone at the table.

"She didn't quite fit," Bea supplied, setting a cup of tea in front of Cass. She looked up and met her friend's eyes, then lifted her hand and ran her fingertips along Bea's forearm as she stepped away. Oh, how she missed her. The ache expanded every time they were together, because then Bea always left again.

Thankfully, this time, Cass had the Muller's cabin-slash-farmhouse on her schedule, and she wouldn't have time to wander listlessly around the house, sighing as she ran a duster over dust-free surfaces and thought about what Bea was doing on the beach.

Over the years of raising her children, she'd worked as a secretary on and off, and the last time they'd talked about her job, Bea had mentioned that she might simply go work for her husband in his property management office.

"I don't think anyone will fit," Sage said, settling at the table with her cup of tea. She gave Cass a warm smile, which Cass returned.

"I think you're right." Cass reached for her tea. She took a sip and sighed. "So we'll take June and December off from the Supper Club." She didn't phrase it as a question, and she looked around the table to find everyone nodding.

Everyone except Bea, that was. She didn't really have a vote, and she didn't try to pretend she did.

"All right," Cass said. "That's what we'll do then." She took another sip of her tea, ready to shake off this melancholy that had draped itself over the dining room. "So. I've got the floor plans done for the Mullers. Who wants to see?"

Bea gave her a smile and took a sip of her tea. "You and your plans."

"It's like you and your lists," Cass shot back.

"I didn't make a list with timelines for my life," she said.

Cass waved her hand in dismissal. It wasn't a crime to have plans for one's life. She'd achieved a lot of the things she'd wanted to in her life, and whenever she felt lost, she got out her kitty cat notebook from fifth-grade and reviewed the goals and plans she'd penciled in for her life.

"I need a floor plan for my job," she said.

"But not for Sariah's wedding," Lauren teased. "She's not even engaged yet."

"She will be in the next month or so," Cass said with confidence. Her daughter—her oldest twin—had called to say she and her boyfriend, Robbie, were talking about marriage and for Cass to block off some dates and start making plans. She knew her mother well, as Cass thrived on having a plan.

The evening wrapped up, and Cass hugged each woman as they prepared to leave her house. Joy held her tightly, and Cass said, "Let's go to lunch next week."

"Absolutely," Joy said with a smile as she stepped back. "You don't have to twist my arm."

Cass grinned and said, "Let me check my schedule for the meetings I have next week, and I'll text you." She once again stood on the porch as the women left her driveway, waving and smiling.

She returned to the house, left the dishes for morning—according to her plan, of course—and looked at Bea. "You're okay tonight?"

"Yes," Bea said. "Are you going to get up and see me off?" Her eyes twinkled, as she knew how much Cass hated early mornings.

"I suppose," she said as she rolled her eyes. Bea embraced her, the two of them holding one another tightly. "Can you please book an afternoon flight next time?"

Bea giggled and ducked her head as she stepped back.

But she'd cut her hair last year and she'd maintained the pixie look, so she didn't have a veil of blonde to hide behind the way she had in the past.

Cass wore her straight brown hair clipped back, and she couldn't wait to get everything unbuttoned, unbuckled, and unpinned.

"We have a gala tomorrow night," she said. "Sorry."

"Yes, the *gal-la*," Cass said, really playing out the last syllable. They laughed together again, and then Cass started toward the hall that led to the master bedroom. "See you in the morning, Bea."

"Night, Cass."

Cass went into the master suite. West sat in the recliner in the reading nook, the lamp behind him providing the light he needed for the puzzles and games he did in a booklet.

"How was it?" he asked, looking over his shoulder at her.

Cass bent her head to take out her earrings. She exhaled as she tossed them onto her dresser. "Really fun," she said.

"And Stacy?"

Cass stepped out of her shoes. "Not a fit." She pushed her hands through her hair and tried to shrug off the weight of the world. She unbelted her dress and walked over to West. "Unzip me, hon."

She bent down and he reached up, and the zipper slid down. West let his hands linger on her waist, and Cass sank onto his lap and wrapped her arms around her husband's shoulders.

"Talk to me, sweetheart."

Cass stared toward the closed bedroom door, not really

focused on anything. “I want to start planning a vacation,” she said.

“All right,” West drawled, and Cass loved that he didn’t question her. “Mountains? Beach? Do I need to check my passport expiration date?”

Cass looked down at him, her love for him swelling. “Do you want to leave the country?” He wouldn’t have to check his passport. His job required him to keep it current, as he traveled for work. She thought of what June would be like once he’d retired, as his paperwork was all turned in now.

“No,” West said with a gorgeous smile, his deep voice sending a thrum through her body. “But I think you do.”

“I just want...” Cass couldn’t finish, because she couldn’t say she wanted to go back in time eight months and reset everything. She leaned down and touched her mouth to West’s. “You.”

He kissed her, and Cass let her discontent melt away as she kissed her husband. As long as he didn’t leave, Cass would be fine.

Chapter Two

Cass practically skipped into the kitchen a weekend or two later, her forest green planner clutched to her chest. West had a full pot of coffee ready, but she didn't find him in the kitchen. He stood out on the deck, against the back railing, a pair of binoculars up to his eyes. They lived on the edge of town, with plenty of wilderness around them, and he loved looking for different species of birds out there.

She bypassed the coffee and went outside. "I have the perfect place," she said.

West turned from the railing, his eyes landing on her planner. "Lord have mercy." He grinned at her and lowered the binoculars to his side. He rested against the railing and smiled at her.

"I've finally figured it out." She wagged the planner back and forth. "Do you want to see the rough outline?"

"I do," he said, coming toward her instantly. "I really do." He paused to pick up his coffee mug from the small round table and looked at her with a hint of joy in his eyes. "Saw a Kentucky Warbler out there."

"They must be on their way back from Mexico," she said, as she'd listened to West talk about the birds in this area for two and a half decades.

"Yep." He stepped around her and opened the door. He ushered her inside, and Cass grinned at him as she went past.

"You'll love this trip," she said. "Loads of birds."

West settled at the table and looked at her expectantly. "Did you plan this just for me?"

"Me too," she said. "It's away from here, and it's still warm, and neither of us have been there." Cass shook her hair over her shoulder and sat down. She flipped open the front cover. "The Everglades." She'd written those words at the top of the page. "Florida." She pointed to the golden "FL" in the corner and beamed at West. "The birdwatching for you, and a beach, fruity drinks, and long walks for me."

West studied her planner, where she'd listed some options for dates they could take the trip. "I can check my work calendar. I've got a case that's close to wrapped, but I have to go over everything with the prosecutors." West worked for the state of Texas as a homicide investigator, which meant a lot of moving pieces between law enforcement and the judiciary system. He loved his job, and Cass loved that they could have their small-town life, free from drama and strife.

"That's why I put options," she said. "Once we know those, then I'll start on the rental, and we'll plan from there." She'd taken a leaf from Bea's book and made a list of possible activities.

"What about Conrad?" West asked, sliding his fingers

along hers. "Beryl?"

She looked down at the golden retriever who didn't get too far from her unless she forced him into a room and closed the door. When she came back, he always looked at her like she'd abused him by making him lay on the bed while she hosted the Supper Club.

"My sister said she'd come," Cass said, smiling at West. "Liz is available on any of these dates." She twined her fingers with West's, enjoying the warmth and roughness of his skin along hers.

"Looks like you have it all planned out," he said. "I like that one that says *eat at the best restaurants.*" Food was his love language, and Cass certainly didn't mind the food at the expensive restaurants they'd gone to over the years.

"I ordered you a birdwatching guide for Everglades National Park." She closed the planner, feeling happy about all she'd put together. "So have you eaten breakfast? Or should we go grab something?"

Before her husband could answer, their teenage son—the last child they had at home—Conrad, entered the kitchen. He wasn't wearing a shirt, and the shorts hanging from his skinny hips looked one wash away from disintegrating. Which wasn't really a problem, because Conrad didn't wash his clothes all that often.

Cass slept easy at night knowing her son *could* operate the necessary appliances to take care of himself. He just usually didn't do so without a lot nagging by one or both of his parents.

"Good morning," she said, rising to her feet. "You're up early."

Conrad grunted and opened the cabinet where Cass

kept all their medicines.

Concern spiked through her. "Are you not feeling well?"

"I'm dying," her son said, his voice full of frogs.

Cass stepped over to him and pressed her hand to his forehead. "Go back to bed. I'll get you what you need."

Her son wore a look of misery, and the heat radiated from his skin even after she'd pulled her hand back. She put together a concoction that would bring down his fever, provide him with a plethora of vitamins, and help him go back to sleep. Once she'd delivered those to his room, smoothed his hair off his forehead, and said she and West might leave for breakfast, she returned to the kitchen.

"Will he live?" West asked, meeting her eyes. His concern for their son rode there, he just wasn't as dramatic about things as Cass.

"I think so," she said. "I'm thinking breakfast at White Aspen."

"I'm not going to say no to that." West rose, pressed his lips to her forehead and added, "I can't wait for the Everglades, hon." He focused on her, his dark eyes searching hers, trying to find something Cass didn't know how to hide from him. "Are you going to live? Without Bea?"

"Yes," Cass whispered, though sometimes she wondered why Bea leaving Sweet Water Falls had toppled everything in her life.

"I'm worried about you," he murmured, his eyes dropping to her hand, which he took in hers.

"I'm okay," she assured him. "Really. I am." She drew in a deep breath. "Things are going well at work, and Conrad only has a few more months of high school, and Sariah is nearly engaged."

"Have you talked to Jane lately?"

"Just yesterday," she said, thinking of her younger twin. "She's great too, and you love your job." She reached up and ran her hands along his shoulders and then flattened his collar. "You're almost done besides." She couldn't wait until they could start their next adventure—traveling the country together. She had so many plans for them. "I'm okay, and we're okay, and life is good."

"All right," West said, that sexy drawl that had attracted her from the moment they'd met still prevalent in his voice. "Let's go to breakfast, baby."

CASS STOOD AT THE WINDOW, DUSK COVERING the day beyond the glass. West hadn't come home from work yet, and something needled at her. He should be home by now. As she lifted her teacup to her lips, her hand shook.

"Mom," Conrad said, and she turned from the view of her front yard. A pond sat out front, and Cass had drawn some of her best designs while sitting beside that water, under the Texas sun.

"Yeah, baby?" She flashed a smile at her son and moved toward him. "How was rugby practice?" She swept her fingers along his forehead, swooping his long hair out of his eyes. It was damp, as he'd just showered after his practice. He'd been blessed with West's thick hair, and Cass smiled at her gorgeous son.

"Fine," Conrad said, frowning. "I just called Dad, and he didn't answer."

Cass looked down at his device in his hands. "I haven't heard from him either."

"He said he was going to stop at the sporting goods store and get me new cleats," Conrad said. He lifted his phone, and an ear-splitting noise came out of it. Cass's phone went off with the same alarm in the next moment, and both she and her son hurried to read the alert.

Cass's eyes swept the message, expecting it to be an Amber Alert or something similar. A few times, they'd gotten license plates for cars that had been stolen by dangerous criminals. But overall, Sweet Water Falls experienced a low crime rate and maintained a fairly peaceful lifestyle.

Where Cass and West lived, on the northwest side of town, away from all the main roads in and out of town, they hardly saw any traffic besides the other folks who lived on this road.

This alert made her blood run cold. *There is a dangerous person reported in the area near the Mirabay Shopping Center. Please do not go to this area. If you see any suspicious activity, please call 911.*

"Where was Daddy stopping?" she asked, her voice hollow and far lower than her normal speaking voice.

"Sweetspot," he said, looking up from his phone. "That's in the Mirabay Shopping Center."

Cass spun away from her son, her heartbeat quaking through her whole body. "He'll be home any minute." She parted the curtains and looked outside. In the two minutes she'd been talking to Conrad, darkness had fallen. No headlights cut through the night, and Cass could barely get a full breath.

She needed West to pull up right now. Now. Right now.

"Mama," Conrad said, his voice scared. "Daddy's still there."

A sob filled her throat, and all she could do was lift her arm and let her son step into her side. They stood together, united and strong, while they watched outside. Conrad tilted his phone toward her, and sure enough, West's location pin sat in the strip mall where Sweetspot was—and where all the activity was. She couldn't help thinking perhaps he'd been there as part of his job. He did have to investigate some dangerous people sometimes.

"I'm sure they've just locked everyone down," she said, the words scraping her throat. She sent another text to West—*are you okay? Are you still at Sweetspot? Please let us know you're okay.*

He didn't respond, and according to her phone, he hadn't even read her message. Conrad's fingers flew across his phone, and Cass watched him text his rugby coach, his friends, and seemingly everyone else around town.

No one knew much of what was happening in the area where police had warned everyone to stay away from.

She wasn't sure how long she stood at the window. Long enough that her legs grew tired, and she sank onto the nearby couch. Long enough that her Supper Club text string bulged with messages about the events happening in Sweet Water Falls. Cass hadn't contributed at all, because her fear had paralyzed her.

"Mama," Conrad said, spinning back to her. "Someone just pulled up." He leaped over the couch, and Cass shot to her feet. She went around the couch instead of over it, arriving at the open door as Conrad jumped to the ground.

"Conrad," she called after him, because she knew instantly that the car in the driveway wasn't West's.

The lights on top of the car gave everything away. Strangely, no sobs choked her now. No tears filled her eyes. No feelings filled her mind.

A police officer rose from the driver's side of the car, and one from the passenger side. Cass couldn't move, and she couldn't stop her son from jogging toward the men there to give them the worst news ever.

She pulled out her phone and sent a single message to the group text. *Something's happened to West. The police are here.*

She stared at the bright screen, lost somewhere in her own mind. The world around her had frozen, and she could barely move through the ice now surrounding her. Joy texted, then Lauren, and then Bessie.

Sage sent a message that blurred, and it wasn't until Bea said, *I'll be there in the morning*, that Cass looked up.

The sound of her son sobbing met her ears, and she blinked at the two broad-shouldered men now standing on her porch.

"Ma'am," one of them said, and Cass knew him.

"Hello, Jonathan," she said, the words a mere ghost coming from her mouth. She knew these men. Her husband had worked with local law enforcement for decades. "He's gone, isn't he?"

Jonathan Gerber removed his hat and ducked his head, and Cass dissolved into tears. Thankfully, the two cops were there to catch her, hold her, and take her and Conrad back inside the house.

Three months later

Cass looked over as someone new arrived at the end of the row. Instant tears flooded her eyes, an event that happened often these days. "Momma," she said. "Daddy." She got to her feet and moved past the empty seats she'd been saving in the row to hug her parents.

They both held her tightly, and Momma said, "This is great, Cass. Everyone's graduated now." They'd often joked that Conrad, Cass's youngest child, might not make it to graduation. He had the saltiest personality out of her three children, and he was the only boy. Cass had struggled to raise him during his early teens—all the way to sixteen, in fact. At that age, a switch had been flipped, and he'd gotten better. Regrown his brain. Something.

Since West's death three months ago, Conrad had retreated a bit. Cass couldn't blame him. She herself had done plenty of pulling away from plenty of things as she tried to figure out how to be only half of a whole. How to be who she was without West. How to parent singly. How to go to lunch alone. How to order food for just one. Two, if Conrad elected to come home.

He sometimes needed to be out of the house, where everything still reeked and reminded everyone who came through the door of West.

West, West, West.

He still existed everywhere, even though he wasn't physically on the earth anymore.

"Thank you for coming," she said, finally releasing her mother.

"Of course," she said. "We wouldn't be anywhere else today."

Cass turned to face the other people who'd come to watch Conrad's high school graduation. She hadn't invited all of them, but they'd shown up anyway, and Cass couldn't say she was upset about it.

Bea stepped past her to hug Cass's mom and dad, her face full of bright smiles. She was always so kind and so accepting, and Cass had tried to be more like her. In the end, she hadn't been able to do it. She was who she was, though that morphed on a daily basis.

Bessie, Sage, and Joy edged by her to say hello to her parents, but Lauren stayed next to Cass. "You never did say if you wanted to go to Colorado with me."

Cass watched the floor in the arena below. She'd chosen a row about halfway up, so she could see everything. She didn't want to miss one moment of her baby's life, because she felt like she needed to drink up twice as many details. Some for her, and some for West.

"I don't know," Cass said.

"You've been saying you need a break, Mom," Sariah said.

"Yeah, I know." Cass sighed and looked over to her oldest. Sariah and Jane were twins, with Sariah being born six minutes before her more free-spirited sister. Out of all of Cass's children, Sariah was the most like her. "Then you got engaged, and I really want to be here to help you plan things."

Planning was Cass's specialty. She loved everything about bringing tens, dozens, or hundreds of pieces together to create something really amazing. A luncheon. A Supper Club. A graduation party.

A funeral.

Or a wedding, she thought. She smiled at Sariah and reached for her hand.

"So you're going to blame your summer stress on me?" Sariah teased. She shook her head, and they all laughed. Cass's didn't last as long as the others, and then her mom and dad wanted to see the girls.

They'd met Sariah's fiancé, Robbie, and as they all settled down and took their seats, Cass found herself right in the middle of all of the people she loved most. They'd all come here today for Conrad.

No. The word entered her mind in a near shout. Not for Conrad.

The people sitting in the row that day for what would surely be a boring high school graduation ceremony had come to support her.

Her.

Those blasted tears came again, and Cass sniffled. Bea reached over and took her hand. Squeezing, she said, "You should come to the island for a week after this. Conrad's going on that trip with Jane. Sariah won't plan much without you since the wedding isn't until October."

She finally looked away from the stage below, her bright blue eyes practically burning with fire. "We have three bedrooms, and one is practically begging you to redesign it."

Pure love streamed through Cass. "I'll think about it."

"Why wouldn't you come?" Bea asked.

Cass threw a glance to Lauren, seated on the other side of Bea. "I don't want to hurt Lauren's feelings. She asked me to go on her company retreat with her."

Bea looked at Lauren, who nodded. "It's fine, Cass. I'll be working the whole time anyway. A week on the beach with Bea and Grant sounds far better than being stuck in a lodge in Colorado, alone."

Cass didn't like being alone, that was true. "You'll be there," she said.

"After work," she said. "Really, I just wanted you to be able to get away."

"I'm capable of planning a vacation," Cass said.

"Yeah," Bea and Lauren said together. Unsaid words hung in the air.

"But you haven't," Bea finally said, giving voice to them. "You and West were going to go to that bird refuge, and you cancelled it." By the time she finished speaking, her voice had dropped to a whisper.

"I'm aware." Cass couldn't keep the acidic bite out of her voice. She hadn't even been able to open the package the bird watching guide had come in. She'd stuffed it on a shelf in the living room and left it.

"Liz will take Beryl," Bea said, tilting her phone toward

Cass. Liz leaned forward from down the row too, her head nodding.

Cass pressed her lips together, the words she wanted to say pulsing against them. The ceremony was about to start, and while she'd partially pressured Bea to go to Hilton Head last summer—and she'd love to spend time on the beach with her best friend—Cass didn't like being the one needled to do what she didn't want to do.

"I'm not ready," she finally said, and no one could argue with that. She looked at Bea, then Lauren, and both of them nodded.

Bea tucked her phone under her leg and gave Cass a smile. "Okay." She looped her arm through Cass's. "You'll tell us when you are, and we'll help you plan the most amazing getaway."

"Again, I know how to plan a vacation," Cass said. It was taking it alone she didn't know if she could stomach.

"There he is," she said a couple of hours later. She'd been able to text Conrad and use some very strong words about how everyone was waiting for him. She'd planned a huge luncheon for family and friends at her house, but the guest of honor hadn't showed.

He did now, his smile wide as he enfolded his grandparents into a double-hug. They laughed, and Cass stood out of the way while Conrad went around to his sisters, his aunts and uncles, and even her friends. Finally, he faced her, and Cass could only smile at him.

They'd gotten along fine, but Cass knew Conrad missed

his father a great deal. He engulfed her in a hug, but not before she'd seen the glint of tears in his eyes. He'd never cried in front of her. Not at the funeral. Not at home when it was just the two of them.

"I love you," she whispered. "He loved you so much."

"I know, Mom." Conrad stepped back and sniffed. He put a smile on his face and turned around. "I'm starving. Is there any food here?"

That caused Liz, Bessie, and Bea to go into a near-uprising, as they'd helped Cass with the food that morning before the ceremony. Bea swatted at Conrad with an oven mitt, and he laughed as he danced out of the way. Cass recognized the coping mechanism. Whenever things got too emotional for Conrad, he made jokes.

Cass had her own coping mechanisms, and she let Liz take over in welcoming everyone to the party. She presented Conrad with the biggest greeting card Cass had ever seen—a two-foot by three-foot thing with tons of glitter on the front covering the numbers for the year of his graduation.

"We all pitched in so you'd have some spending money in Europe this summer," she said. Liz opened the card and a gallon-sized zipper bag dropped out of it, weighed down by the wads of cash inside.

A gasp flew through the crowd. "My goodness," Cass's mother said. "If I'd have known he had that much already, I wouldn't have given as much."

Yes, she would've, but Cass said nothing. Her parents had been nothing but generous over the years, and honestly, without Bea here in Sweet Water Falls, Cass had relied on her mother a great deal since West's death.

Conrad's eyes turned glassy again, and he thanked

everyone, hugged Liz again, and hastily took the greeting card back inside the house. When he returned, Cass realized every eye had landed on her. She hadn't wanted any of the spotlight today. She didn't mind being in it from time to time, especially at a party she'd put together so flawlessly.

From the streamers in his high school colors of red, black, and white, to the banners she'd had professionally printed, to all the shade she'd installed over the deck, this party was spectacular. The plastic dishes and cutlery matched everything, and she'd hand-dyed tablecloths to ensure everything was seamless and perfect.

After all, a person only graduated once. She'd hired Joy to be the professional photographer, and they'd gotten amazing shots a month or so ago for the announcements, as well as several yesterday with the letters the school took to the convention center for the ceremony. That way, they hadn't had to stay after today, and they'd been able to come here for lunch faster.

But at the house, West usually welcomed everyone and presented the gifts. Liz had done that. And now...

"Did you want to say grace, honey?" Momma finally prompted her.

Cass startled, her eyes going wide. West did that too, and now that he wasn't here, Cass had to do it. "Yes." She cleared her throat. "Yes, let's say grace, and then we can eat."

"Conrad wanted cake first," Bessie piped up. "Remember?"

"Yes," Cass said, though she'd forgotten. She honestly didn't know where her brain had gone. She usually knew every line item of the overall plan. "Daddy, would you pray for us? Then Bessie will bring out the cake, and people can eat dessert first if they'd like."

Conrad stepped to her side, and Cass put her hand in his elbow as they bowed their heads. He'd be gone in the morning, off on a European adventure with Jane. They hadn't invited anyone else, and Cass had felt left out for a few seconds. Then she'd realized that her son needed this time with his sister, and Jane needed it with him too.

Sariah called Cass every day, and while they primarily talked about the wedding—which Sariah wanted to have right here in the backyard of her childhood home—they always spoke about West too. Cass needed that, and she'd come to realize that Sariah did as well. That was how she was coping with the loss of her father, and coming to terms with the fact that she didn't have him to walk her down the aisle.

"Amen," chorused around her, and she hadn't heard any of the prayer. She felt the love of God in her life in that moment, though, and she felt it pouring from those who'd come to her home to help her celebrate Conrad's graduation.

"All right," Bessie said in a loud voice. Cass stepped away from her son, ducked her head, and wiped her tears. "Here's the cake!" She presented a five-tier chocolate-iced cake, her face made only of sunbeams and joy. Bessie was such an amazing baker, and Cass's heart filled with love for the generosity of her friend.

"Lord have mercy," Conrad said, and Cass's eyes flew to him. He sounded so much like West, who'd said that phrase all the time, his voice inflecting exactly the way Conrad's had. A touch of dryness, the huge smile, everything about her son reminded Cass of West, and no amount of wiping could clear the tears from her eyes without letting some escape down her face.

Her golden retriever sat on her feet, and Cass looked down at Beryl. He always knew when she needed a friend, and she reached down to pat him, hoping to make his baleful eyes shine with happiness again.

"It's got rugby equipment on it," Conrad said, and he laughed afterward. "Thank you, Bessie." He took the cake from her and held it higher as if anyone could miss it. He slid it onto the table and picked up one of Cass's carefully chosen plates. "I'm going for cake first."

Cass laughed along with a few other people, and the swell of activity pushed Cass back to the railing. She stayed there, letting life flow around her. She took nibbles of the energy everyone had brought to her home, knowing that by evening, she'd be alone again. She wanted to soak in everything she could, so she could feed off of it later, once Conrad had gone with Jane, once her friends had gone home, once she had to face the enormity of her future by herself.

Conrad would be gone to college that fall, and Sariah would get married, and then Cass would... Well, Cass had a lot of crossroads coming in her life, and as a round of laughter went up as some of Conrad's younger rugby-playing friends arrived, she felt excited about them for the first time since she'd dropped her white rose onto West's casket.

The next spring

"That's fine, dear," Cass said as she put the sugar bowl back in the cupboard. "I understand." Of course she did. She knew by now that not everyone could do everything or be everywhere. She'd invited her daughter and her husband to Hilton Head this summer, but Sariah had just said they wouldn't be able to make it. "This is an amazing opportunity for you and Robbie."

Their wedding had been amazing, planned down to the minute and with Plans B and C in case of inclement weather or if two particular guests drank too much. Texas in October had cooperated with amazing colors and weather, though it had been hot. Cass and Sariah had planned for the heat, of course, and they'd beaten it with their misters and fans. Cass had added them permanently to the underside of the deck, and that had only added value to the house.

Conrad had done decently well for his first year in college, and he'd opted to stay at Baylor for the summer.

Jane...well, Jane was currently still traveling, living out of a backpack and staying who-knows-where each night. She literally didn't have a single planning gene Cass did, and she'd established a check-in time for her daughter every day just to ensure that she was still alive.

She was back in the States right now, at least as far as Cass knew, and expected to pass through Texas either today or tomorrow. The next day, Cass flew to South Carolina, and Jane probably didn't know where she'd be.

Cass herself lifted her coffee mug to her mouth. "Don't worry about me, Sariah. I'm doing really well." And she was. West had died fifteen months ago now, and every day Cass felt more and more settled. More and more like herself. More and more like she could not only survive, but thrive.

"When are you going to Hilton Head?" her daughter asked.

Cass knew the exact date and time. The planner in her wouldn't allow anything else, and she'd really leaned into that part of herself in the past year. She'd taken on more clients than ever, just to stay busy and surrounded with people. The truth was, she really needed what she'd privately dubbed her "summer sabbatical."

"Friday," she said. "So you'll have to fly to Taiwan with a hug that's a couple of days old." She smiled at the thought of her daughter out there in the world, making a difference.

"I'll survive," Sariah said. "But we're still on for dinner tonight, right? Just us and you?"

"Yes," Cass said.

"I didn't invite Jane," Sariah said, and the words almost sounded like she'd shot them from a cannon. "Does that make me a bad person?" She sighed, and Cass did too.

"No," she said gently. She didn't know what else to say. "Jane is..." She didn't want to make excuses for her daughter, because she understood the grieving process wasn't linear, and it wasn't the same for everyone, and it couldn't be predicted.

"She's Jane," Sariah said, her voice heavy and tired. That about summed it up. They'd been saying that for years about Jane, and Cass should've gotten her into therapy sooner. Sariah didn't know about the therapy, and Cass kept her younger daughter's confidence.

"We're all doing the best we can," Cass said quietly.

"I know." Sariah took a deep breath. "Okay, see you tonight, Mama. I love you."

"Love you too, dear." The call ended, and Cass stood in her kitchen for several long moments. If she listened hard enough, she could hear the birds chattering outside. She went out onto the deck, the very real image of West standing there, binoculars to his eyes as he searched for his beloved birds, entering her mind.

Today, there were no tears. Today, there was no burst of sadness, overwhelming emotion, or the sense of being purely lost.

Today, Cass smiled, but it was sad. Today, she went to stand where her husband always did, and she tried to see what he saw.

Today, she saw the future—and it wasn't filled with crushing loneliness, solitary nights with dinner for one, or unending unhappiness.

Not anymore.

Something bubbled inside her, and Cass had a hard time identifying it. "Excitement," she said aloud, finally getting her fingers around what she felt. She pulled out her phone to text Bea, and then she hurried inside to switch her laundry. After all, she'd be on the beach in a couple of days, and that required the brightest whites and colors a woman owned.

Chapter Three

Beatrice Turner looked up from the open notebook on the table in front of her. Her husband came through the door, laughing. Grant had an outgoing personality, and Bea often found him laughing about something, with someone.

Today was no different, as Harrison Tate, one of his good friends, came into the house behind him. The door closed, sealing out the South Carolina heat, and Bea rose from her chair. She glanced at her list, her stomach weaving itself into knot after knot.

The top item on her list said, *Confirm Harrison is coming on the trip.*

"Hey, sweetheart," Grant drawled, pulling Bea into his body for a kiss. She smiled against his lips, which kept the kiss chaste as they had company.

"Hey yourself," she said. "The meeting must've gone well?"

"They approved the development for rentals," Grant said, grinning. "So yes."

"It's good for him," Harrison said.

Grant released her and faced him. "It's good for you too," he said. "They'll sell far faster—and people will put higher-end stuff in them—if they know they can rent them."

"You'd think so." Harrison sighed as he sank onto the couch separating the kitchen from the living room in the beach house Bea and Grant had bought after their wedding, almost two years ago now. "But you'd be wrong."

"About which part?" Grant walked toward the fridge. He pulled out a couple of bottles of water and took them over to Harrison.

"They put cheap stuff in rentals." He took the bottle of water from Grant. "Think about yours, Grant. Do you put in granite and plush rugs and all the best stuff?"

Grant sat on the couch too. "Sometimes," he said defensively. Harrison started to laugh. "If I'm going to live in it too."

"Sure," he said. Harrison took a long drink of water. "If you live in it part-time. But who's going to buy one and live in it part-time, then rent it other times?"

"Snow birds," Grant said easily. "And they have money."

Harrison hemmed and hawed, but he couldn't really argue with that. Bea pulled a bowl of fruit salad out of the fridge and went to join them. "So, Harrison," she said, handing him a fork. She exchanged a look with Grant, but she hadn't shown him her list for the day before he'd left for his planning and zoning meeting that morning. "Do you think you'd like to join us in Florida?"

"When is that again?" Harrison asked.

"Yeah, I need to get those dates on my calendar too." Grant tapped on his phone while Bea tried very hard not to roll her eyes.

"It's next week," she said. "Cass is coming in a couple of days, and we're surprising her with the trip to the Everglades on Tuesday." So less than a week, but she kept that part to herself. They all knew what day it was. Her stomach rolled. "I'm thinking about telling her about it instead of surprising her. She might not be ready for a surprise."

She might not want to go at all. She'd been planning a trip to the Everglades for her and West, and Bea had given her oodles of time to be ready to go. Cass had been getting livelier and livelier in the past few months, and Bea really felt like she was ready to take this step.

In fact, it might be the last step she needed to take to truly be healed and ready to move forward. Maybe. She wasn't sure, thus all the knots in her gut, the dry throat, and the way her eyes darted from Grant to Harrison and back.

"Oh, right." He glanced up from his phone. "Tuesday. Yeah, I'm ready to go."

"Should I tell her?"

Grant took a moment to consider. "I probably would, yeah. Can you change the destination if she doesn't want to go there?"

"Yes," Bea said. "I have alternates." She jumped up from the coffee table where she'd perched and retrieved her notebook. "I've made a list of places that can take last-minute reservations for four."

"So it's just the four of us?" Harrison asked.

Bea looked up from her lined paper. "Yes," she said. "Is that a problem?"

"Not for me," Harrison said. "I don't know Cass. I've never met her." He looked over his shoulder to Bea. "Will *she* think it's a problem? Like you're setting her up with me?"

"I'm not setting you up," Bea said. The thought horrified her, and it would horrify Cass as well. "We're taking a trip with our friends."

"It kind of looks like a set up," Grant said.

"You've never said that before." Frustration filled Bea. She definitely had to tell Cass about the trip now. She would never want to surprise her best friend with a "blind date" trip to the place she'd been planning to take her now-deceased husband.

Bea's stomach rolled, and she sank into the dining table chair she'd been sitting in earlier. "Maybe I should just plan to go somewhere else."

"Well, I'm in," Harrison said with a groan as he got to his feet. "I need a break, and I don't have to start on the Thompson project until the middle of June." He drained the last of his water and tossed the bottle into the recycling bin. "Thanks, guys. Bill me for what I owe."

Bea flipped a page in her notebook. "I'm changing all of it," she announced.

"Come on, hon." Grant got up too. "Don't do that. Just talk to Cass and see what she says." He came to the table too and put his palm over the notebook. "I don't want to lose you to another list-making marathon."

She looked up, trying to read his expression. "I do not go on list-making marathons."

"How many of those pages are filled?" Harrison asked, coming to her side and peering down at the notebook. Grant laughed as he withdrew his hand, and Bea quickly snapped the covers together so they couldn't see how many pages she'd written on.

"None of your business," she said. She stood and waved the notebook between them. "*This* is why the trip will be amazing." Fire filled her chest, but she wasn't really angry. She knew she made lists; she loved them. "If y'all aren't interested in an amazing, pre-planned trip, fine. I'll go with Cass by myself." She stepped past Grant, giving him an eyebrow-raise that said, *You better stand up for me, buddy.*

"Come on, Bea," he said. "Don't march out. Of course I love your lists, and I'm totally all-in on this amazing, pre-planned trip." He followed her as she left the kitchen, her notebook tucked against her chest. "I just don't want you to start over." He touched her arm, and she turned to face him. He searched her face, and Bea found love and pleading in his eyes.

He had done and said exactly what she'd hoped he would, so she softened.

"Just call Cass and ask her," he said. "Then you'll know if you need to start over or not. That's all I'm saying."

"All right." She nodded and looked past him to Harrison. "And you're in, no matter what?"

"Yes, ma'am," he said. "I won't question anything on your list at all. Just happy to tag along." He'd obviously gotten the message not to make fun of her lists too.

She grinned at him and then Grant. She threw her arms around him and hugged him. "This is going to be so great," she gushed. "Now, I just need to go call Cass..."

She bustled out of the living room and into the small office she and Grant shared. The first thing she did was cross off the top item on her list—she'd confirmed with Harrison.

But a new task got added, one that made snakes coil around the knots in her stomach.

Call Cass and tell her about the trip to the Everglades.

"There she is," Bea said as Cass came past the security checkpoint. Bea tipped onto her toes and waved, but her best friend didn't see her. "She looks thin."

"She looked like that at Christmas," Grant said. He tucked Bea closer to him. "And when you went for Supper Club in March. And now here in May."

"I think she looks thinner," Bea said. Worry ate through her, but Cass had spotted her and Grant, so Bea hitched a good ole Southern smile on her face and waved even harder.

"She sees you," Grant teased.

Bea lowered her hand, because Cass had broken into a jog. She hadn't wanted to text or call her about taking the trip to the Everglades, because it seemed like an in-person conversation. However, now that Cass stood in front of her, Bea didn't have the words.

She stepped away from Grant and into Cass's arms, the two of them laughing and laughing. "Oh, it's so good to see you," Bea said.

"Sorry the flight was so delayed," she said. "I guess there was someone rowdy on the previous flight, and they got delayed coming in from Tennessee."

"It's fine," Bea said.

"Yeah," Grant added, which caused Bea to move back from Cass. "This worked out great, because Harrison drove us so we didn't have to park." He beamed at Bea like this was great news, but her insides had gone a little icy.

"Harrison?" Cass asked.

"Yes." Bea looped her arm through Cass's. "Which claim are you at?"

"I don't know." Cass started to look around, and Bea shot Grant a dark, dangerous look. He gestured at her to *hurry up and ask her*, because Bea's time had run out.

She had no more excuses.

"Cass," she said, her voice pitching up.

Cass looked at her, her dark eyes brighter than the last time Bea had seen her. Her hair had been cut shorter than normal, but it still hung below her shoulders in very straight layers. Bea had cut hers a couple of years ago once her divorce was final. She'd only tried growing it out once to know she didn't want to do that.

"I've planned a trip for us next week," she said, measuring her words.

"Why are you talking like that?" Cass asked, her eyes turning into slits.

"Like what?" Bea asked.

"Carousel four," Grant said, and he took off in the direction of Cass's bags.

Bea followed, albeit much slower.

"Like you're a travel agent trying to sell me a vacation I don't need," Cass said.

"You do need it," Bea said. "It's to the Everglades, and Cass, I've only been to four National Parks. It's on my list, and I *can't* go without you."

Cass paused, but at least her eyes came open a normal width. "The Everglades."

"I know you were planning to go there with West." Bea swallowed, his name almost rusty on her tongue. "But I thought we could go. Me and you and Grant and Harrison."

Cass's eyebrows flew off her face. "Harrison? This man I've met, oh, let's see—never?" She shook her head. "Bea, no."

"Don't say no," Bea said, but Cass got the word out first. "It's not a date. I'm *not* setting you up. I would *never* do that to you. He's just been working like a dog, and he has a break between builds. He's Grant's best friend, and you're my best friend, and I thought it would be fun."

"Bea?" Grant called.

She looked over to him and waved. Cass started to walk, so Bea went with her. She'd gone quiet, and that had changed about Cass. She'd always been so opinionated and loud. She still was, but in some ways, she took more time to contemplate and think through things.

"When is the trip?" she asked.

"Tuesday through Saturday," she said. "We'll be there for three full days. Two days of travel." Bea didn't dare look at her but kept her focus on her husband up ahead. "You'll meet Harrison in like, ten minutes. He's a nice guy. He's divorced, no kids, and has made it very clear to Grant he's not interested in dating. So it's *not* a set-up. I promise."

"I believe you," Cass said quietly. She touched Bea's arm and stopped again. Bea stepped in front of her and faced her. "Bea, what if—?" She swallowed, and Bea hadn't seen her nervous like this in a while. Cass always exuded confidence. She made decisions all the time, and she never looked back.

"What if what?"

"What if I stayed for the whole summer?" she asked.

"Could I find somewhere to rent on the island, do you think?" She spoke faster and faster. "I know the island fills up in the summer. Could Grant work some kind of landlord magic? Or miracle?" She took a big breath, and looked at Bea with earnestness.

Bea searched her face. "You want to stay in Hilton Head for the summer?"

"Yes."

Bea burst out laughing. She did a little dance around Cass and said, "Yes, I'll help you find somewhere to rent for sure." She faced Grant, who looked at her like she'd gone crazy. "She wants to stay for the summer, Grant. You have to help her find a place to rent."

"What about the Everglades?" he asked. The first bag came plunking onto the belt. "Is she coming on the trip with us?"

Bea turned to face Cass, who squared off with both her and Grant. She put one hand on her hip and gave them a look that Bea knew well. This was the look mothers gave to naughty children, and Bea also knew to hold very still and give Cass the time she needed to come to the decision she had to make.

Grant started to say something, and Bea squeezed his hand. "Give her a minute," she whispered. "Just one... more...minute."

Chapter Four

Harrison Tate pulled up to the appointed pick-up spot, easily spotting Grant and Bea—and a beautiful brunette. She stood taller than Bea by several inches, and she had the long limbs and grace of a woman who came from wealth.

Harrison tried not to judge her so quickly, because he'd heard Bea and Grant talk about her plenty. A widow for over a year now. Three kids. Parents and a sister in Texas. A golden retriever, whom he didn't see. So she'd left him with someone, and Harrison found himself wondering who the lovely Cassandra Haslam might trust enough to leave her beloved pet with.

He came to a stop and immediately jumped out of his SUV. He owned a couple of cars, as well as a truck for work, and as he rounded the tailgate and came face-to-face with Cassandra, he was glad he'd brought this vehicle. "Hello," he drawled to her, his face feeling hotter than it should. He reached for her bag at the same time Grant did, and

Harrison found himself wanting to swat his friend's hand away.

For Harrison wanted to help Cassandra.

He pulled, and Grant pulled, and the suitcase went nowhere. "Oof." Grant stepped back, and Harrison still had a grip on the bag. It suddenly came in his direction, and he flinched away from it so he didn't get hurt. He stumbled slightly, catching himself against the brake light, and the suitcase toppled to the ground.

"Sorry." He hurried to retrieve it, then fumbled with the button to get the back hatch to lift. Grant stared at him as if he'd grown an extra eye, and Harrison's whole body flamed with South Carolina heat as he hefted Cassandra's bag into the back of the SUV.

"There's another one, Harrison," Bea said, and he bustled over to the sidewalk like he was Cassandra's personal butler. He told himself to calm down. He shouldn't be acting like an overeager dog to please this woman.

He didn't even like women. He wasn't dating, at least. He amended his thoughts, because he did like women. If he was going to start dating again—which he wasn't—he'd pick a woman.

This woman, his brain shouted at him, but Harrison silenced it.

"Cass," Bea said as he rolled the bag closer to the back of the vehicle. "This is Harrison Tate."

He grunted as he lifted this much bigger and much heavier bag into his car. He dusted his hands as he turned to face the pair of women. "Nice to meet you," he said.

"Harrison," Bea said. "This is Cassandra Haslam. My

best friend in the whole world." She linked her arm through Cass's, and the two of them smiled at one another.

Cass then faced him, her smile staying clipped in place. She had long eyelashes framing her dark eyes, and a maturity in her face that only came with age. Her teeth sat straight and white in her mouth, and she gripped his hand firmly as they shook. "It's great to meet you, Harrison," she said. Even her voice painted pictures in his ears.

Pure adrenaline soared through him, and he couldn't release her hand. She didn't pull back either, and they stood there, looking at one another. He wasn't sure if the charge filling him was adrenaline anymore, but perhaps...electricity.

"You can't park here," someone said, and Harrison startled. He pulled back and Cass did too. He turned to face the airport attendant.

"Yeah, we're going," he said. He glanced back to Cass, but she'd ducked her head and started to move around the corner of the SUV to get in.

Harrison did the same, berating himself for falling into some sort of trance. How old was he? Fifteen?

Starstruck by a beautiful woman. He ground his teeth together and shook his head. "Don't act like a fool," he muttered to himself. Then he yanked open the door and got behind the wheel.

Grant sat in the passenger seat, and Cass and Bea rode in the back, already talking about something. Harrison liked Bea just fine. She complemented Grant perfectly, and he sure did love her.

"Did you get all the bags?" Grant asked, fluttering his eyelashes at Harrison.

Another round of embarrassment drove through Harrison, igniting a flush in his neck, chest, and face. "I think so," he muttered. He gripped the wheel and eased into the pick-up traffic. The drive to Hilton Head would take an hour, and he suddenly had nothing to talk about with Grant, or either woman in the back seat.

Grant never had a problem chatting, but he remained quiet too, and the two of them listened to Bea and Cass talk about their friends in Texas, how their adult children were doing, and who had taken Beryl.

The dog, Harrison assumed.

"You'll have to bring him if you're going to stay for the summer," Bea said.

Harrison perked up. Cass was going to stay for the summer? "Where are you staying?" he asked.

"I don't know," Cass said. "I don't have a place yet."

"It's almost peak tourist season," Harrison said.

Cass met his eye in the rearview mirror, a hint of challenge in hers. "I'm aware. I just decided today. I'll have to start looking when I get to Bea's."

"Grant will help us," Bea said. "Right, Grant?"

"I'm already looking, baby," he said. "All summer?"

"I can move around if I need to," Cass said. Her voice was deeper than Bea's, and it hit all the right chords inside Harrison's head and chest, creating music there he hadn't heard in a while. "Actually, that might be fun. A week in this house, then another week somewhere else."

"You might have to," Grant said, his voice almost a monotone as he studied his phone. "The only way you'll get something for the whole summer at this point would be to buy something."

No one said anything, as if Grant had dropped an idea

bomb and it hadn't gone off yet. After several seconds of silence, he looked up. "What did I miss?"

"Nothing," Bea said, but her tone was the type of forced casual that said her mind was running in circles. Harrison knew, because his ex-wife had spoken like that.

"Maybe we could look at things for sale," Cass said casually. "I have been thinking about selling the house in Texas."

Bea gasped the gasp of the century. "You have? What? When? Why didn't you tell me?"

Cass laughed lightly, and once again it felt like the stars had aligned. Harrison watched her in the rearview mirror, completely forgetting that he should be focused on the road.

"You're drifting," Grant murmured, and Harrison jerked the SUV back into the right lane. The ladies in the back cried out, and he'd most likely be the color of boiled lobster before they made it back to the island.

"It's a new thing," Cass said once they'd settled and everyone knew they weren't going to die in a fiery car accident. "I look around the house in Texas, and...I don't know. It's not *my* house. It's *our* house. Me and West, and he's not there, and it's just a thought I've had."

"We need to expand on this thought," Bea said, but before she did, she leaned forward and placed one hand on Harrison's bicep. "Oh, Harrison, Cass said she's excited about going to the Everglades with us. Isn't that great?"

"Yes," he said, meeting Cass's eyes in the mirror again. She gave him a smile he would classify as kind and a little bit flirty. He hadn't been in the dating pool for a while, though, so perhaps he'd read it wrong. Or maybe he'd read it the way he wanted to read it. "That's great news. Now I won't be the third wheel."

"My fifth National Park," Bea said with obvious happiness.

Harrison refused to look at Grant, because the trip to Florida and Everglades National Park just got a whole lot more interesting for Harrison. Interesting and enticing and exciting—and Harrison hadn't felt any of those things since Claudia had said she was leaving and filing for divorce.

"DINNER TONIGHT?" GRANT ASKED AS HARRISON unloaded Cass's luggage for her. They'd all go inside Grant and Bea's beach house, and Harrison hadn't been invited to stay for the afternoon.

"Yes, come to dinner tonight," Bea said. "I'm making shrimp scampi, and you inhaled that the last time I made it."

"I didn't *inhale* it," Harrison said. He shot a look toward Cass. Bea had just made him sound like a vacuum.

Grant started to chuckle. "You ate really fast," he said.

"I hadn't eaten all day." Harrison reached for the smaller, lighter bag. "And your wife is a good cook. So sue me."

Cass looked away right as he looked at her, and Harrison almost felt snubbed. She stood only a few inches shorter than him, and she carried an oversized purse that told him she paid attention to the things she bought. She took care of them. She wore a pair of black shorts that went all the way to her knee, and she'd paired them with a white tank top. Classic beauty.

She sure seemed to know who she was, and Harrison liked that. He could feel the confidence oozing from her, and he wanted to ask her to dinner that night. Just the two of them. He'd take her to a nice place out of the tourist zone, and they'd drink wine and laugh and talk until all hours of the night.

His fantasy dried right up as Grant laughed. "What?" he asked.

"Bea asked if you had that meeting for your HOA tonight, and you just stood there." Grant shook his head and reached to push the button to lower the hatch on the SUV. He moved in close to Harrison and whispered, "You're staring at her, man. Calm down."

"I am calm," Harrison hissed at his friend. Grant had obviously seen Harrison's attraction to Cass, but it sure didn't seem like Bea had. Grant would tell her though, and Harrison's humiliation doubled as he thought of how Bea would react.

"Yeah, I think the HOA meeting is tonight, actually," he said. "I might not be able to do dinner."

"Come by after if you want," Bea said. She turned and started towing the smaller of Cass's bags up the sidewalk. Cass went with her, no backward glance in Harrison's direction.

He watched the women go, and then he looked at Grant. "She's pretty."

"Mm." Grant kept his gaze on the two women as they went up the steps and into the house. They'd left the bigger bag for him, but he didn't seem to mind. Everything about Grant was laid-back and easy-going, and Harrison had liked that during some of the stormier times of his life.

"I know I can't ask her out."

"I'm surprised you want to." Grant switched his gaze to

Harrison. "I mean, it's fine. I'm glad you want to. I'm just a little surprised. You didn't even tell anyone about Claudia leaving for months."

Harrison's ex-wife had taken his still-beating heart from his chest and stomped on it. "Yeah." He toed the ground. "It's been a couple of years though, and I don't know. She's...interesting. I'm interested in talking to her and getting to know her."

"You barely said three words to her."

"This is new for me, all right?" Harrison gave Grant a sour look. "You didn't date after your divorce forever."

"Plus, you can't get in more than three words when Bea's around," Grant said dryly. He chuckled, and Harrison joined in.

"She's awesome, Grant. You're lucky to have her."

"I know," Grant said. "I love her. I didn't mean I didn't. It's just...she and Cass are best friends, and am I being an idiot if I say I'm a little worried about her moving here?"

"No," Harrison said. "It's a valid feeling."

Grant shook his head. "A bridge to cross when I get to it." He grinned at Harrison and clapped him on the shoulder. "Really, come by later. We'll have drinks and dessert after dinner, sitting on the back deck, overlooking the water..." He swept his hand through the sky as if painting a picture. "Very romantic."

Harrison shook his head, but his smile had appeared, and he couldn't make it go away. His best friend had painted a mighty fine picture, and Harrison determined he absolutely would come back after his meeting tonight.

Maybe then he could get in more than three words and learn more about the stunning Cassandra Haslam.

Chapter Five

Cass could sit on this deck, listening to the ocean greet the shore, and sip wine forever. A sense of peace filled the air at how slow life felt here, without a neighbor in sight. Grant and Bea had just taken the dinner dishes inside, and Cass took a deep breath of the sea air, held it in her lungs, and then blew it out.

"It's lovely here, West," she said to the black sky. Dinner had been a four-course affair, and the wine had flowed freely. She felt warm from head to toe, but that could be from the muggy air here in Carolina. The sun had gone down an hour ago, but the heat hadn't lessened much.

"You'd like it," she said. "And I'm going to the Everglades. I'll take so many pictures and look for all your favorite birds." She smiled at the moon, raised her glass with the last swallow of wine in it, and then emptied it.

"Hey," a man said, and Cass twisted around. "Sorry." Harrison came up the steps from the beach. "I thought I heard you talking, but I didn't want to interrupt."

Cass hated that he'd overheard her. "Just talking to myself," she said. She set her empty wine glass on the table and wrapped her arms around herself. "This beach is magical."

"It sure is." Harrison leaned against the railing. "Bea and Grant got themselves a really nice place here."

Cass nodded, but she didn't move any closer to Harrison. He'd likewise left an appropriate gap between them. "You missed a fantastic dinner."

He flashed her a smile but said nothing. In some ways, that reminded her of West. The man had been steady and strong, never over-reacting or even *re*acting to things the way Cass did. "Bea says you own a construction firm here," she said, hoping to break the ice between them.

"Yes," Harrison said.

Her heartbeat fluttered, but she wasn't sure if it was from nerves or excitement. Harrison was easily one of the more handsome men Cass had met in her lifetime. Big, broad shoulders, dark hair, and that full beard. That all checked boxes for her, and he screamed, *Just your type!* to every cell in Cass's body.

So many thoughts filled her head, and she wished she could pluck them out one by one. She'd thought about selling the house a lot. Bea was the first person she'd mentioned it to. She'd thought about moving, but not to Hilton Head. Not until she'd touched down in South Carolina.

Now, it seemed like a good possibility. An avenue she hadn't explored yet, but that she definitely wanted to.

She'd thought about staying for the summer here on the island. She'd thought about dating—something she hadn't told anyone. Almost Bea, for a moment there in the airport. Then Cass hadn't been able to do it, and she'd switched her question to whether she could stay here on the island for the summer.

She stole another look at Harrison. He watched the darkness undulate in front of them, the symphony of the sea rumbling somewhere in it neither of them could see. He was definitely her type, and she'd definitely felt her heartbeat bump against her ribs when he'd taken her hand in his at the airport.

That's called a handshake, she told herself. She shook her head slightly and returned her gaze to the darkness too. Harrison hadn't held her hand. He'd shaken it. Completely different things.

"Oh, I learned something at my HOA meeting tonight," he said.

"Yeah?" She turned and leaned her hip into the railing. "Are you on the board or something?"

"It's really small," he said. "A row of houses on the northeast side of the island. You can see Carter's Cove from my back deck." He smiled, and Cass thought he looked good enough to be on the big screen. She wanted to ask him if he'd ever done any acting, but she refrained.

"So there's maybe ten houses? Eleven?" He straightened and faced her too. "A couple of the houses aren't done yet, even, and tonight, I found out that one of them is for sale."

Cass's eyes widened. Her pulse quickened. "Really?" She wasn't sure she could afford a house in a fancy HOA on the water like he'd described.

Harrison chuckled. "Really. The woman who owns it decided not to move here. Her son and daughter-in-law—or maybe her daughter and son-in-law? I don't know. Someone in her family built a new house and they put in a mother-in-law apartment. So she's moving to Raleigh instead."

"Interesting," Cass said. "I'll have to look up the listing.

"Oh, they won't list it, ma'am," Harrison said. "The houses there—" He cleared his throat. "You have to know someone to get in. They only sell through word-of-mouth."

Cass took a step closer to him. "This sounds like a ritzy, gated community."

"Yes, ma'am," he said.

She cocked her head at him, finding him absolutely wonderful. "Ma'am?"

"Just bein' nice," he said.

"Well, stop it," she said. "You're making me feel old." She trilled out a laugh she hadn't heard herself make in a long, long time. With horror, she realized what was happening.

She was flirting with this man. *Flirting* with him.

Thankfully, before she could embarrass herself further, Bea came outside. "All right," she said. "Oh, Harrison is here." She turned back to the house. "Baby, Harrison is here. Bring another plate, okay?"

Grant yelled from inside, and Cass put more distance between her and Harrison. The world had felt dark and cold since West's death, but standing so close to Harrison had added a bit of warmth and a whole lot of light to Cass's existence.

And she had absolutely no idea what that meant, or how to process it mentally and emotionally. Her fall-back for the past many months had been distance and then therapy, and she still did that one of those now.

"I made your favorite," Bea sing-songed. "Peach pie!" She set the tin down on the table, and a beautifully baked pie looked up at all of them.

"And ice cream," Grant said, plunking down a huge tub of the stuff. "Howdy, Harrison."

"Hey, brother." The two shook hands and did a half-man hug. The scent of Harrison's cologne settled into Cass's nose, and she sure did like it. She'd eventually washed West's things, and the house didn't smell like him anymore. She had such a hard time calling it "her house," because that was simply not what it was.

"Harrison was just telling me about a house in his neighborhood," she said, sliding him a look out of the corner of her eye. "He thinks it might be too glamorous for me."

"I did not say that," he said, his voice full of defense.

She smiled in his direction, almost afraid to make eye contact in case she gave away the rioting, almost traitorous emotions spinning through her right now. "He made it sound very fancy."

"It is," Grant says. "He lives in the exclusive Gateway Plantation community."

Harrison growled at Grant, who frowned at him. "It's not 'the exclusive Gateway Plantation community.'"

"It so is," Grant said while laughing. He didn't seem worried by Harrison's dark look. "Who's selling?"

"Viola," Harrison said.

Grant's eyes widened, and he looked at Cass. "Oh, Cass, that would be perfect for you. The house isn't even all the way done yet."

"It's not?" Cass took the plate of peach pie and vanilla

ice cream Bea had dished for her. "How is that perfect for me?"

"Because you can design the whole thing," Bea said. "Pick out all the colors. Do the floors the way you want. Hang your art, all of it."

Cass sat at the table, glad when the pie got served quickly and the others joined her. She liked that Harrison was here, because now she wasn't the third wheel with Grant and Bea. They'd always been so perfect for each other, and sometimes they could make a person feel left out without meaning to.

Cass felt like that a lot anyway, and she knew the problem was mostly hers. "I do like to design things," she said.

Bea scoffed. "Like it? Cass, you thrive on picking out a paint color or the perfect tile from a pile of fifty of them." She gave a mock shudder while Cass simply took a bite of her pie. The creamy vanilla with the warm peaches, the spices, the flaky pie crust... Cass moaned before she could censor herself.

Bea lit up like the Christmas tree in Rockefeller Center. "How's the pie? Good, right?"

"It's the best thing I've ever eaten," Cass said, already going for a second bite. Moaning right out loud was a touch embarrassing, but then Harrison made an almost identical noise.

Every eye flew to him, but his eyes had drifted closed. He was clearly enjoying the pie too, and Bea should like that. Cass flicked a glance in her direction, and sure enough, she looked giddy.

Harrison opened his eyes and realized they were all staring at him. "Sorry," he said, dropping his chin to his chest. "But Cass is right. This is the best thing I've ever eaten." He scooped up another bite, put it in his mouth, and moaned loudly again.

Cass started to laugh, as did Grant and Bea. She needed this camaraderie in her life. She'd left her golden retriever in Texas, and her sister hadn't sent her daily dog pic yet.

So she needed this laughter. She needed the sound of the ocean over the sound of the wind. She needed a fresh start, and as her eyes met Harrison's again, she couldn't help but wonder if he did too.

And...if they could take the first step together.

CASS LOOKED UP AT THE HIGH CEILINGS IN THE house. "It has good bones," she said.

The realtor who'd accompanied her to the waterfront home said nothing. Cass glanced over to him, and he hugged his portfolio to his chest. She went back to examining the property. She'd been impressed by the entrance—a gate, as she'd assumed.

There'd been a guard house too, with a real gentleman inside, checking credentials. That would likely drive her mad after a few times of coming home, but she did like the security it provided. There was a single road into the community, and one had to exit the same way. Only one road curved along this patch of land, and there were thirteen houses, the realtor had informed her. They'd chit-chatted about Hilton Head, what brought her here, and how she knew Harrison.

She'd given vague answers, because she didn't need the whole island to know every detail of her life. Not only that, but she barely knew Harrison Tate. He'd come to desserts and drinks a couple of nights ago, and she hadn't seen him since.

They were leaving for the Everglades in the morning, and Cass moved toward the wall of windows overlooking that glorious, sparkling blue water. She loved the beach, and she felt it calling to her as she glided toward the glass. She went outside, the breeze tickling along her neck and tugging at her hair.

She gathered her dark locks into her hand and held them as she walked along the stones. Not cement. She doubted such a thing was allowed in a community like this. An outdoor fireplace sat in the middle of the patio, and at the push of a button, Cass could have electric flames. Nothing else sat outside, as no one lived in this house yet. So no furniture inside or out.

Bones was about all the house had, and Cass could admit she liked that. It left everything else an open canvas for her to paint how she'd like. She moved to the edge of the stones, where a set of steps led down to a tiny patch of grass. Then the beach opened up beyond that, the water waving hello as it arrived ashore.

Back inside, she ran her hand along the refrigerator handle. It looked like a cabinet, and she asked, "The appliances come with it?"

"Yes, ma'am," the realtor drawled. "Did you want to see the bedrooms?"

"Yes." Cass toured the whole home, from top to bottom and left to right. Finally, she and the realtor stepped out onto the front porch flanked by two tall pillars that extended to the height of the two-story home. "And the flooring can all be changed?"

"To anything you wish," he said. "Our builders do have a few things the owners have selected from. If you purchase, I can put you in touch with them."

Cass nodded, drew a breath, and went down the few steps to the sidewalk. "I can have them repaint some things?"

"Absolutely," the realtor said. His papers shifted and crackled, and he withdrew one that wasn't a normal sheet of paper. It was glossy on both sides, though one sat blank. The other held all the numbers Cass needed to know. "It's been appraised already. Inspected. Miss Gladstone will pay closing costs. She wants this home to go to someone who'll love it as much as she did, and I have to say, Miss Haslam, that seems like it might be you."

Cass looked at the paper and then the man. "I'll let you know."

He nodded, very proper and respectful, and they left the property. Cass drove out ahead of him, and she had nowhere else to go that day. She drove through a coffee spot, got her favorite hot drink, and headed for the beach.

With June days old now, the sun shone brightly. Families had gathered that afternoon, and dogs ran through the sand as owners threw balls for them to retrieve. The wind whipped harder the closer to the ocean Cass went, and she wrapped her arms around herself as she gazed across the water.

She closed her eyes, and suddenly she could feel the movement of the earth beneath her feet. She let it tilt her right and left as she tried to balance against the astronomical speed of the spinning.

Her thoughts collided, and then she opened her eyes. She focused on the horizon, the truth of what she wanted right in front of her. She tugged her phone out of her pocket and dialed.

"No more second-guessing," she told herself. "Move forward with purpose."

The line rang, and Cass turned away from the undulating water...the rest of her life in front of her.

Chapter Six

Harrison lifted his bag into the back of Grant's truck. "Are you going to cover this?" he asked.

"Yeah, and you're helping." Grant unfolded a brand new tarp and he and Harrison spread it over the luggage in the bed. Then Grant pulled down the cover, and they headed for the cab.

"Hey, Harrison," Bea said from the front seat as Harrison boosted himself up into the truck.

"Mornin', Bea." He landed on the seat and looked over to Cass. "Mornin', Cass."

"Good morning, Harrison." She held a to-go cup of coffee for him, and he quickly buckled his seatbelt before taking it.

"Who's ready for eight hours of driving?" Grant boomed, a laugh immediately following.

"You're too chipper for this early in the morning," Bea complained. "Some of us are still waking up." She lifted her coffee to her lips and glared at her husband.

Harrison concealed his smile behind his own coffee cup, and it was Cass who said, "I can't wait to drive for eight hours."

Bea scoffed and snorted. "Don't let her fool you," she said. "She doesn't like a road trip that much."

"I do too," Cass said. "For about half of eight hours."

Everyone laughed, Harrison included, and Grant eased out of Harrison's driveway. "We'll stop as much as anyone wants," he said.

"Yes, you promised me lunch in Daytona," Bea said.

"That's right." Grant reached over and took her hand in his. Harrison watched them, and they were just so pathetically cute. He knew the sting in his chest came from jealousy, and he swallowed and looked over to Cass.

"Did you look at Viola's house?"

"Yes." She nodded and placed her coffee cup in the holder between them. "It's very nice."

"I've walked through it a couple of times," he said. "It is nice. She's up a bit higher than mine, so her patio is spectacular."

"I did like that part of it," Cass said with a smile.

"What are you going to do?" Bea asked, twisting to look at Cass, who rode directly behind her.

Cass drew in a big breath and then pushed it out in an exaggerated way. "Well, waiting is always the hardest part, so I'm going to have to wait."

"On what?" Bea asked.

Harrison caught the glint in Cass's eyes, and one look at Bea told him that drove her nuts. "Cass, you better start talking."

"I put in an offer on the house yesterday," she said. A

girly giggle escaped her lips. "So now I have to wait and see if I can get my loan approved."

Bea blinked, her eyes growing wider and wider. "You better not be playing with me right now."

"I'm not," Cass said. "I put in an offer on that house. The realtor said I'd know if 'Miss Vi-o-la' will accept my offer by five p.m. tonight."

Harrison smiled, because having Cass only three doors down sounded like heaven to him. He looked up to the front seat, and Bea still seemed like she'd been hit with an alien tractor beam. Grant met his eyes in the rearview mirror, and Harrison caught the concern there.

"I think that's great, Cass," Harrison said, and he tapped the drink holder between them. "I hope you get it."

Bea looked at him, still shocked, and Grant said, "Yeah, Cass. Maybe you'll give Bea something to do during the day. I think she's been bored."

Bea whipped her attention to Grant. "Bored? I am not bored."

"You're showing up at my office all the time."

"Your secretary quit," she said. "I'm *helping* you."

Grant grinned at her, and Bea huffed. "I'm teasing, sweetheart."

Harrison looked over to Cass, who watched the exchange in the front seat in a similar fashion as he did. They'd talked a little the other night, over peach pie and ice cream, but he knew very little about her.

He didn't know how to start a conversation with a woman like her. His chest vibrated in a strange way, and his phone buzzed, drawing his attention. Thankful for the distraction, he busied himself with answering texts from one of his workers, and then he dove into his email. As the drive went into the second hour, he finally looked up from his phone.

Bea read something on her tablet in the front seat. Grant drove, humming along to the song playing over the radio. Cass looked over to him at the same time he looked at her. He nodded to the lap desk across her legs. "Working?"

"Yes," she said. "Just doing some final sketches on a house I'm redesigning in Texas." She tilted the pages toward him. "Do you think you'd like a refrigerator with antlers on it?"

Harrison almost burst out laughing. By some miracle, he didn't. "I don't rightly know," he said. "Feels...Texan?"

Their eyes met again, and Cass's smile brightened the whole back seat. "It does feel Texan. And this family owns a cattle ranch. I think it fits."

"Then it probably fits." Harrison hadn't brought work or anything else to do. "Will you move your design business here?"

"Maybe," she said, glancing toward the front seat. "Depends on how bored I get, I suppose." She flashed him a smile that Harrison felt dive right into his heart.

He nodded and looked out his window. "Looks like a pretty day." He didn't have much else to say, and no one else seemed to either.

They stopped for gas and snacks, and Harrison found himself in the convenience store alone with Cass. She picked up a bag of peach-o's, and he said, "Oh, my brother loves those."

Cass looked at the bag for a moment longer. "We used to always get these for the kids on road trips." She seemed so sad. It poured off of her for a moment. Then she blinked, and it boxed right up and went away. She smiled. "I'll get some and text them."

"How many kids do you have?" he asked as she reached for another bag of candy.

"Three," she said. "Twin girls, Sariah and Jane. Sariah is married, and she and her husband moved to Taiwan for the summer."

"Taiwan, wow." He followed her like a puppy dog, but at least Grant and Bea weren't around to see.

"Jane's...somewhere. I think this morning she was arriving in Montana."

"You don't know where she is?"

"She's traveling right now," Cass said, her voice a tad cooler than it had been before. "And Conrad is at Baylor." She gave him a tight smile. "You don't have kids, right?"

"No," he said.

Cass ducked her head and then reached for a bag of chips. "Did you ever want any?"

"Uh, I don't know?" he guessed. "I suppose I would've been happy if we'd had kids, but I was okay without them too."

"Your wife didn't want any?"

"She did," he said, his throat turning narrow. "The timing never felt right, and she really wanted to be the best veterinarian in the world, and...yeah. Then I was growing my construction business, and I think time just slipped away like smoke."

Cass nodded, her eyes filled with compassion. "It has a way of doing that."

"Yeah." He picked up some honey-barbecue chips. "Have you ever had these?"

She wrinkled her nose. "No, thank you."

"Oh, come on," he said with a laugh. "If you haven't had them, how do you know you don't like them?"

She eyed the bag like it might strike. "I just know."

They moved to check out, and when they went outside, Bea and Grant had moved the truck away from the gas pump. "Boiled peanuts," Bea announced as they arrived at the truck.

"What?" Cass asked, also eyeing the peanuts like they'd done her a personal wrong.

"Boiled peanuts, Miss Picky," Harrison teased. He took a couple from the cup in Bea's hand. "They're delicious."

"He's not wrong," Bea said.

Cass still looked riddled with doubt, and Harrison went to get back in the truck. When Cass climbed up next to him, she had a single boiled peanut in her hand. She met his eyes and lifted her perfectly sculpted eyebrows.

"Just try it," he said, his hormones firing on all cylinders. "You might like it."

She peeled one-half of the nut out of the softened shell and put it in her mouth. He knew the moment she tasted it —and liked it—as her eyes brightened again. "Oh, I like that. It's salty." She took the rest of the peanut out and ate it. "Mm, yeah. I like those."

"We need more boiled peanuts back here," Harrison said, and Bea turned around and offered Cass the cup. She smiled at Cass and then Harrison, her eyes narrowing slightly.

He wasn't sure what he'd done, but Bea's bright eyes had

a way of slicing through a man who already felt like he was perched on the edge of a knife.

The trip continued, and Cass laughed quietly once, then twice, before Harrison looked over to her. She passed him her phone, and while surprise darted through him, he took it. "My daughter," she said. "The free-spirited one."

He looked at the phone at a girl in her early twenties. She had the same dark hair and eyes as Cass, with plenty of life flowing from her expression. She wore hiking clothes—shorts and a tank top both in bright colors that clashed. That wasn't anything like Cass, at least from what Harrison knew and had assumed, and the girl wore a lightweight jacket tied around her waist.

She beamed at the camera with one finger pointed up, and Harrison had to look hard to see the mountain goats there.

"Jane," Cass said. "She's holding up the mountain goats. See them?"

"Just now," he said. He grinned and handed her back the device. "She looks like she's having fun."

Cass sighed as her smile softened. She studied the picture for a moment longer. "Yeah," she said. "She does." She tucked her device under her leg and picked up another boiled peanut. Her last one. "She has her father's adventurous spirit."

"You're not like that?" Harrison cast a glance toward the front seat, but Bea had pulled out a pillow at some point and propped it against the window. She leaned into it, eyes closed and unmoving.

"A little, I guess," Cass said. She shrugged her shoulders the tiniest bit. "I mean, I suppose I just put in an offer on a house that's a little bit out of my price range, and about a thousand miles away from anything and anyone I know."

Harrison let her words sink in for a moment. Then he said, "Feels adventurous to me."

She brushed her hair back out of her face. "Bea is on the island."

"That she is."

"I won't be totally alone." She looked at him then, pure electricity flowing from her. "Right?"

"You know three of us on the island," he said. Before he could think about what he was doing, he reached past their sodas and slid his hand into hers. "You'll be fine." The buzzing shock from the touch of her skin told him what he'd done, and he quickly pulled away. Fire burned in his veins, and he gave her another smile and looked out his window.

Everything around him blazed, from the sight beyond the glass to the floorboards under his feet to the breath in his lungs. Had he just made a critical error? Cass hadn't pulled away, gasped, or done anything to indicate she didn't welcome the touch.

Still, he shouldn't have done it.

"Tell me about your ex-wife," she said.

Harrison swung his attention back to her. "Really?"

"Yeah," she said. "Then I won't feel weird that I like to talk about West."

Harrison watched her for a moment, trying to decide if her cheeks were more or less flushed than they'd been a few moments ago. "It's different," he finally said. He couldn't tell if she was blushing or not. Perhaps she was just so naturally beautiful that she carried that pinkish hue in her face all the time. "You loved West. Love him. You didn't...uh, losing a loved one to death is far different than a divorce."

Cass nodded slightly. "You're right. I'm sorry."

"It's fine," he said. "But I don't want to talk about Claudia." He had the strangest inclination to take her hand again. Instead, he fisted his fingers and covered them with his left hand. "But I don't mind if you talk about West. You know, if you want to."

Cass flashed a smile in his direction and said, "Thanks, Harrison." She didn't immediately launch into a story about her husband, and the backseat fell into silence again.

Harrison didn't mind, because his fingers kept burning. He told himself he better be satisfied with the pace Cass set, because she would definitely be the one to decide if he could hold her hand, go to dinner with her, or kiss her.

Honestly, he was a little surprised he wanted to do those things with her. He'd been protecting himself for a while now, but as Grant pulled up to a house in a quaint suburban neighborhood, Harrison found himself ready to get out there again, dating-wise.

He also really needed to get out of this truck before he did something he couldn't take back.

Chapter Seven

Cass let the pristine blue sky flow over her and around her. She breathed it in, the crispness of the morning long gone. She'd gotten up before the sun, something she didn't normally do, and she'd been walking fast on the beach when the first rays of light had touched the sand. The air had been cool then. Now it went down heavily, like part of it was water.

The binoculars around her neck weighed on her, and she reached up to take them off.

"I'll carry them," Harrison said in his throaty voice. Cass shivered internally, ever-so-glad that she didn't let the tremors come to the surface.

She handed him the binoculars with a grateful smile, but she said nothing. They'd been in the Everglades for two days, and today was their last one of adventure. She'd gone on a few solo walks. She and Bea had gone to lunch alone together yesterday. She'd spent most of her time with the whole group, and she liked listening to Bea and Grant talk, and Harrison and Grant, and she enjoyed chatting with Bea about her two sons and her daughter. They were all doing well, and Cass had kept Jane's downward spiral on the down-low.

Lord knew she had enough to talk about of her own to keep Bea happy. She and Harrison had gone on a walk alone last night, but nothing of note had happened. She felt like he was holding something back. After that initial contact in the truck on the drive here, he hadn't touched her again.

He was a quiet man, but Cass knew how to deal with those. West had been quiet too. His mind was always working, though, and Cass had the distinct impression that Harrison's did the same.

"Look over there," Bea said from ahead of Cass. She pointed to the right, where a flock of Roseate spoonbills waded in the water. Maybe "flock" was being a bit generous, but Cass loved the pink and white birds, and she'd been fascinated by them the first time she'd seen one a couple of days ago.

"West would've loved those," she said again. They'd gone on a guided canoe tour yesterday morning and seen flocks and flocks of birds. Cass had never made it that far in her planning for the trip to the Everglades, and while she usually liked being the one in charge of the day's activities, she'd been fine to sit back and let Bea dictate where they went, what they did, and at what time.

She and West would've stayed in a different hotel, and eaten at different restaurants, but what Bea had planned had been wonderful.

"I love those," Bea said.

"I do too," Cass said.

"They're beautiful," Harrison said as he pressed in beside her on the trail.

"This says they feed near the boardwalk during high tide," Grant said, as he'd been their trail guide for the past three days. For how often he quoted something from his book, Cass thought he'd been memorizing it for weeks.

"There are some flamingos," Bea said. The spoonbill had a beak similar to the flamingo, but not as curved. They were whiter on top, with bright patches of pink on the sides, while flamingos were various shades of pink all over. They seemed bigger than flamingos to Cass, but they hadn't gotten so close enough for her to measure.

"And what's that one called?" Cass asked, pointing out into the glades.

"That's a plover," Harrison said. "The gray and white one? With the black ring around his neck?"

"Yep." Cass leaned against the railing on the boardwalk and watched the wildlife. She'd never found the same joy in it that West had—until now. She'd appreciated that he loved it. That he'd burst into the house all excited about whatever he'd seen through his lenses.

"West kept a diary of all the birds he'd seen," she said. A soft smile accompanied her words. "He'd flip through it at night sometimes, just to remind himself of the birds he'd managed to coach close enough to our house."

"He used to put out feeders, didn't he?" Bea asked.

Cass knew she tiptoed around the conversation whenever Cass brought up West. She wished people wouldn't, but she'd probably do the same to them. No one knew how to talk to someone after a loved one died, and Cass had likely been guilty of saying the wrong thing—or nothing at all —herself.

"Yes," she said. "He'd read about what migrated over the area, and he'd put out food for them. He'd build poles to look like tree branches." She'd thought the trees grew close together in Texas, but on some of the walking and biking trails, tours, and canoe avenues they'd done the past couple of days, Cass had seen trees growing out of other trees. They leaned over the water, creating a murky shade that apparently wildlife loved. From birds to alligators to both fresh and saltwater fish, Cass felt like she'd been educated on wildlife extensively during this trip.

"He'd look up pictures of the birds," she said. "So he knew their names when he saw them." She smiled again as a spoonbill took off, its great wings flapping. She watched it go, her heart soaring with it. "I should make a journal for what we've seen here." She hadn't been keeping track, though, because writing down minute details was West's specialty.

Cass was detailed in other ways, but not noticing all the details that made one bird different from another.

Another couple came back down the trail, and everyone in her party shifted and shuffled to let them go by. She stepped backward, right onto Harrison's foot, and he put his hand on her hip and slid his foot out of the way. "Got you," he said, his hand there for a moment, burning into her, and then gone.

She twisted to look at him. "Sorry," she murmured.

He grinned at her. "No problem." He nodded to the couple as they went by, and then indicated she should get walking again. She turned and found Bea and Grant had gone ahead, and she hesitated for another moment.

She wasn't sure why she wanted to be alone with Harrison. He comforted her in a way she hadn't anticipated, and as Bea slipped her hand into Grant's and they went around a curve in the glades, Cass wondered if she could hold Harrison's hand.

Her heartbeat thundered in her chest, and the same question that had been haunting her since she'd met Harrison once again paraded to the front of her mind.

Is this okay?

Can I date again?

Am I being disloyal to West?

She wasn't sure who she could talk to about this. Bea would have too many questions. Lauren wouldn't know what to say. Joy would tell her to trust her heart. Bessie would give similar advice, but she'd probably tell Cass to eat a bunch of awesome Southern food while she did.

Cass had been doing that for a long time. When Harrison spoke of him and his ex-wife focusing on their careers instead of having a family, she understood that. She and West had waited five years before having their twins, because he needed to finish school and have some way of supporting them.

She'd put her interior design on the back-burner, only pulling it out as motherhood allowed her more time as the children grew and left the house. She'd been nearly full-time in the year before West had died, and frankly, the only reason she hadn't gone insane in the fifteen months since was because of her job.

Her nerves rattled at her, and she rounded the bend in the path too.

A glorious sight opened up before her, and Cass paused and sucked in a breath. "Look at that," she whispered. Harrison stopped beside her, and they both looked at the edge of the world.

Blue met blue—the bluest of blues Cass had ever seen—on the horizon. Green fell away on both sides, and Grant and Bea were nowhere to be seen. It honestly felt like Cass and Harrison were the last two people on earth, and that the water was coming for them. Slowly, but surely, it would cover all the dry ground and they'd be left to figure out how to survive with all the warblers, spoonbills, and gators in the Everglades.

"This is stunning," Harrison said. He lifted his phone and took several pictures. "Do you want to be in one?"

"Yes." She moved down the trail a few feet, turned, and cocked her hip. She grinned at him, and his smile in return came instantly.

"Beautiful," he said, and Cass startled. Surely he meant the view, because he bent his head to study the picture he'd just taken. She went back to him to see it, and she did find such beauty in the world around her.

She looked up into his dark eyes, noticing that they weren't brown as she'd originally thought. She put her hand on the side of his face, and time froze. He didn't blink; he didn't breathe.

"Your eyes are green," she whispered. In that moment, she got an answer to one of her questions.

Her feelings for Harrison were real, and they were okay.

Sudden embarrassment flooded her, and she dropped

her hand and stepped back an appropriate distance. "I'm sorry." She shook her head. "I don't know..."

"It's fine," he filled in for her. "Things aren't always what they seem until we get up close, you know?" He gave her a smile cloaked in something she couldn't name and stepped by her. "Come on. We don't need Bea and Grant gossiping about us."

Cass spun around. "They're gossiping about us?"

"No," he said. "And we don't need them to start."

She caught up to him quickly, what with her legs being long and all. Her pulse now pounded out the question, *Is there an us?*

Grant had said Harrison wasn't dating right now. But would he consider going out with her?

Cass knew then that she did want to start dating again—if it was with the right man.

As they continued down the path and caught up to Bea and Grant, Cass searched and searched for the answer to her last question—was she being disloyal to West?

She never found it.

But she did see an American coot, and giddiness filled her. "West loved those," she said, turning to Harrison as if he cared. "They're in Texas year-round, and he loved how chicken-like they are, but also how black."

Harrison chuckled and said, "They're funny little birds."

Yes, they were, and Cass let her happiness expand and flow through her.

Later that night—their last night in the Everglades—Cass stood at the railing on the boat and watched the sun dip into the western sky. "This is gorgeous," she said to Bea, who stood at her side.

"Isn't it? I thought it would be the perfect way to end our trip."

Cass laid her head on Bea's shoulder. "Thank you for doing this. It's been perfect. Exactly what I needed."

Bea nodded, and a Bea who didn't respond right away meant she had something difficult to say. Difficult for her, at least. "You've been talking a lot about West," she said.

"Yes." Cass couldn't deny it, and she didn't want to. "Everyone thinks you don't want to talk about the person who's died, but I like it. It makes him feel more real. He *was* real, you know."

"I know," Bea said quietly. Her divorce had been very hard on her, but Norman still lived on the earth. She'd still see him at her children's graduations and weddings. She could call him and talk to him if she wanted to. Cass couldn't do either of those things.

"You're on the Southern-most tip of the United States," their boat captain-slash-tour guide said over the loudspeaker. "And the sun is going down. Stand by those you love, and enjoy God's glory on the earth."

He fell silent after that, and Cass gazed over the water as it got painted into golds, oranges, silvers, and whites. *West would've loved this*, she thought but didn't say out loud. She didn't want to stop talking about her husband, but as she watched the sun sink lower, lower, lower into the ocean, she felt like today's chapter had ended in a beautiful, perfect display of God's love.

And just like that, she had her answer to her last question.

She wasn't being disloyal to West by going out with someone else. Her chapter with him had been wonderful. Glorious. So much fun, filled with excitement, highs, lows, heartaches, and joys.

Just like the sun had gone, so had West. Cass was still here, and both the Lord and West wanted her to keep living.

Tears pricked her eyes, but this time—for the *first* time since the officers had shown up on her porch that fateful night—they weren't over losing West. They were because Cass held hope in her heart that she could have a fantastic future tomorrow.

With Harrison? her mind whispered, but Cass didn't know the answer to that question...yet.

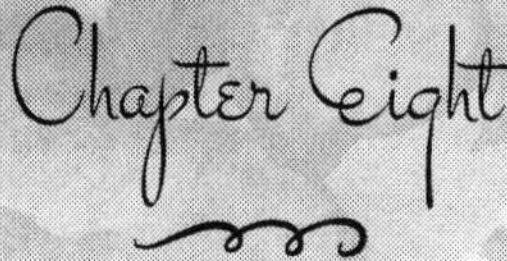

Chapter Eight

Harrison's gaze moved down the curve in the road as he neared his driveway. The house three down sat quiet this afternoon, but he'd seen the carpet guys there this morning. And a cabinetry truck the day before.

He hadn't seen Cass since the day before she'd left Hilton Head about three weeks ago now. Truth be told, he knew it was exactly nineteen days. He'd spent the majority of those days thinking about her while he kept his head down and his hands busy.

He had plenty of work to do now that his build had started, and he'd only come home this early today, because someone had left several pipes out, and he'd stepped on them.

Down he'd gone, and his back ached. He'd ripped his pants, and as soon as he showered and changed, he'd head back over to the construction site.

He made the turn into his driveway and went past the

palms and bushes that concealed the front of his house from the road. As the third house inside the community, almost everyone had to drive past his house to get to theirs, and the landscapers had done a good job at making the front yards as shielding as possible for the residents.

He pulled in front of his porch, parked, and got out. The heat assaulted him, but he barely felt it. Construction was a year-round business here, and he'd lived in Carolina for his whole life so he understood heat and humidity.

He'd seen Grant and Bea a few times over the past nineteen days, so he knew Cass would be back on the island before Independence Day. He had no idea how to do much more than see her by happenstance, and with his work schedule, that would be a miracle.

Frustration moved through him as he tapped in the keycode for his front door. At least the air conditioning worked, and he drew in a deep breath of it. Water. He needed water.

He drank, showered, took some painkillers for his back, and got dressed in the same thing he'd been wearing earlier. A clean pair of jeans and a clean Tate Construction T-shirt, but the same thing. He rarely wore anything different. Sometimes, after work, he put on gym shorts and a clean T-shirt and hung around the house or in the hammock, but sometimes he simply ate and fell asleep on the couch in his construction attire.

Maybe when Cass moved in down the street, he could take her a neighborly gift and welcome her to the community. Mrs. Benson a couple of houses down from Cass certainly would.

Maybe he could find a reason he needed her number and ask Bea for it. He spent the drive back to the construction site obsessing over reasons he might need Cass's number.

"Maybe something with the house," he mused. "Something's wrong with it." If that were the case, Bea would want to come see. She'd want to call herself.

He shook his head. That wasn't going to work. Unless he wanted to confess his feelings for the pretty brunette to her best friend, he had no way to get Cass's number.

"What would you do with it anyway?" he grumbled to himself as he made the turn and bumped down the dirt road to the site.

Of course, a person would call or text another person with a phone number, but Harrison didn't know what to say. Could he ask her when she'd be back?

He already knew that.

He wasn't sixteen years old and couldn't just send a "Hey," to a woman like Cass. Being from Texas, she'd probably say hay was for horses.

Harrison hadn't felt this out of his element since the first few days after Claudia had left. They'd been married for thirteen years, and he was suddenly alone. Things had just...ended.

He'd had no indication that she wasn't happy in their marriage. Sure, they'd had a few conversations about how much he worked, but she had a very busy career too. They'd always had each other to come home to, and he'd been satisfied and happy with that.

Apparently, she hadn't been.

He thought about when Cass had asked him to talk

about her. He hadn't wanted to—and he still didn't—because he didn't have anything to say. He didn't know where Claudia had gone when she'd left. She'd filed for divorce, and he'd signed the papers without contest. He saw no reason to fight her for anything, and he'd sold the house they'd bought together, given her half of the money, and moved into this new house on the coast.

It was far too big for him alone, but he'd gotten it for a screaming deal, as he'd been the general contractor on the build. He'd had a lot of cash to put down, and the financials for his construction firm were healthy and strong.

He wondered if Cass would have any trouble selling her house in Texas, and—

Someone knocked on his window, which ripped Harrison out of his thoughts. He had no idea how long he'd been sitting in his idling truck, and he twisted the key and pulled it out.

He opened the door and got out, saying, "Hey, Reid. Sorry, I was thinking about something."

"No problem." Reid reached up and adjusted his ball cap, his sign of nerves. He had sandy brown hair that curled around his ears and the back of his neck. He worked hard, laughed loud, and always came in for extra hours.

He'd been married for about six months, and his wife was already pregnant. Reid wanted as much money as possible, and he was willing to work for it.

He hooked his thumb over his shoulder now. "We've got a problem over on pad four."

"A big problem or a small problem?" Harrison asked, already weary from the morning. Not only that, but it was

Thursday, and he really needed a weekend. A real one, not a one-day thing where he padded around his house shirtless on Sunday.

"Medium?" Reid guessed. "We hit a water line, and we can't pour the pad until it dries."

Harrison's eyebrows drew down into a frown. "A water line? On pad four?" He looked northeast toward the site. "That's not right."

"It wasn't marked, but it's definitely there." Reid started walking, and Harrison had no choice but to go with him. He'd deal with whatever he found at pad four, because he had to. These beach condos were paying his bills for the next several months, and he'd put in a bid for the newly-zoned rentals-allowed community out at Riverwalk Plantation. That would be a beautiful place to work—full of mature trees and lush, green grasses. He might actually have some shade if he got that job.

"Oh, it's wet-wet," Harrison said as they approached the area. The cement trucks sat waiting nearby, but they weren't needed. Harrison sighed and ran his hands down his face. "Can we pour somewhere else?"

He didn't want to lose the concrete. It. was hard to procure, and if he lost today's pour, it would be at least a week until he could get more. Heck, he'd been waiting for this cement for over a week now.

"I had the guys prep six and seven," Reid said.

"Let's go see." Harrison prayed those sites would be ready, and six very nearly was. "Here," he said. "Maybe we can get seven ready by tomorrow."

Several crew members worked on it, and he whistled

through his teeth to get their attention. His phone chimed at the same time, but he ignored it. "Listen up," he called as his men neared. "We need six cleaned and cleared so we can pour in…twenty minutes." That might be pushing things, but he'd roll up his sleeves and help too. "And seven has to be ready for a morning pour."

Everyone nodded, and then Harrison got to work. He stayed at the site later than normal, because they'd started pouring late and he couldn't leave when he still had men there.

He remembered his phone when he finally waved goodnight to Reid, and he pulled it from his pocket as he took the last few steps to his truck.

Hey Harrison, this is Cassandra Haslam. I got your number from Grant, because I'm going to be moving quite a few things to Hilton Head next weekend, and my house won't quite be ready. He said you have a large garage where I might be able to store my things for a week or two? Feel free to call or text at your convenience. Grant says you're swamped.

His lungs screamed for air, because Harrison had forgotten to breathe while he read the text. He'd gone still at the first line—*Hey, this is Cassandra Haslam*—and he looked up, almost expecting someone to jump out from behind his truck and tell him the text was a prank.

Sweat ran down the side of his face, and he wiped it and got in the truck. With the air conditioner blowing and his phone connected to Blu-tooth, he dialed the number that supposedly belonged to Cass.

The line rang twice before Cass's lovely voice said, "Harrison, you called back."

"Yes." The word sounded like he gargled with glass and

then tried to speak, and he cleared his voice. "Yeah, sorry it's been a few hours. Busy day on-site today."

Cass emitted a sigh, and he could just imagine her pushing her hair out of her face. She'd done that often on the trip to the Everglades. "I understand busy." She laughed lightly. "I put everything in my text, and you can absolutely say no. I'm having a moving company bring my bigger items, but I'm driving a truck full of things to the island next weekend."

"Mm hm," he said. He did have an oversized, three-car garage, and a wide driveway. Depending on what she had, he could probably house it. Then, he'd be helping her, *and* she'd have to come back to his place to get it once her house was ready to move into.

"There's a lot of activity at your place," he said. "I'm surprised it won't be ready."

"Oh, I ordered this fancy bartop," she said with another sigh. "And I'm leaving a lot of furniture here, because it doesn't fit in a beach house. Apparently, I ordered a bed that's on backorder, so I won't have anything to sleep in until that comes in."

"When's that?" he asked, wondering what kind of furniture she had in Texas that wouldn't fit here.

"They've promised me June thirtieth," she said. "But my son and I are coming a few days before that."

"Do you have somewhere to stay?" he asked. Because he had plenty of room.

"Bea said we could stay with her."

"My house is big too," he said, just wanting it out there. "Plenty of room."

Cass hesitated, and Harrison swung his truck toward his

favorite taco truck. This conversation required a lot of shredded chicken and guacamole.

"I'll talk to Conrad," she said. "He'd love a beach house, and he's not very happy with me right now."

"No?"

"He doesn't think I should move to South Carolina." Another sigh, and Harrison wished she was there so he could hold her hand and assure her that she could make her own decisions.

"I'm sorry," he said. "Did your house sell?"

"I decided not to list it right away." Her voice ebbed away from him at the end, and he felt her attention dividing. "I have to go, Harrison."

"Sure," he said. "Listen, I'm a simple guy, and I'm not sure what non-beach-house furniture looks like. Send me a picture of what you've got that doesn't fit in a beach house?"

Cass laughed, and that made Harrison's entire day. Heck, his whole week. "I will. I'll talk to you soon."

The call ended, and Harrison watched the screen on his phone turn dark. Then he grabbed it and assigned Cass's name to the number, feeling like he'd just won the lottery by having her in his contacts.

Days passed, and Harrison's back ached. He went to a physical therapist who gave him some stretches and exercises to do, and one of them was walking as actual exercise, not simply counting his job as his physical activity.

The private beach his property bordered had become his gym, and he was on his way home one evening when he heard someone scream. His attention jerked to the homes along the water, and he found himself about to pass Cass's.

It was too early for her to be on the island yet. She'd told him she and her son would be there on Friday night, and it was only Thursday.

Still, something told him to go check. He'd taken the first step when a crash sounded from somewhere—and it sounded suspiciously like it had come from inside her house. Even if she wasn't there, someone was, and possibly not someone who should be.

Harrison jogged through the sand and up the stone steps to the backyard. He'd removed his, so he didn't have to mow a hundred square feet, but Cass hadn't been in town to do that. Maybe she didn't want to.

"Hello?" he called as he went up another set of steps to the patio. He did like this patio, and as her lot was bigger than his, she had a massive outdoor space that he really liked.

"I'm fine," someone said, and it did sound like Cass.

The back sliding door sat open, and Harrison slowed his step as he approached. "I heard someone scream. I'm going to come in." He peered into the house, but he couldn't see anyone.

The house now held all the finest materials, from the flooring to the cabinetry, as well as a dining room table that could seat eight easily, and a couple of wrapped-in-plastic couches in the living room to his left.

"Hello?" he asked again, committing to entering the house. "Cass?"

"I'm in the kitchen," she said, her voice resigned. "I twisted my ankle, and I'm not sure I can put weight on it."

Harrison strode with purpose then and went around the

dining room table and the island with the fancy lights hanging down from the ceiling.

Cassandra Haslam sat on the floor, one knee bent and that foot planted beside her other leg. She rubbed her left wrist and looked from her limp left foot to him. A gorgeous blush colored her face. “Hey, Harrison.”

Chapter Nine

Cass would never, ever tell Harrison how she'd fallen. Even when he dropped into a crouch and asked, "What happened?" He looked at her with concern in those dark green eyes that played like a chameleon sometimes and made someone think they were brown. Thankfully, he also asked, "What hurts?"

She focused on that question instead of the other one. "My wrist." She indicated it. "My ankle. My hip a little."

What Harrison could do about it, she didn't know. He took her injured wrist in his hands, and while he worked construction, he had the soft, gentle touch of a man who could heal anything.

Cass pulled in a breath, hoping she could play it off as a sharp intake from pain and not from the electricity flowing from him and into her.

"It doesn't feel broken," he said. "I've got a splint at my place." He looked at her, and she nodded.

He moved down and took her foot into his hands. She

hissed at him, and Harrison lifted his head to look at her. "It's not bent oddly."

"I think I just twisted it." She'd been standing on a chair just outside the back door, changing a light bulb, and she'd looked out at the water. She'd lost her balance and her bearings, but she'd managed to find them before she'd fallen.

Then she'd seen him walking on the beach. Shirtless.

That had caused the world to sway again, and she'd toppled from the chair. She'd tried to grab onto it, but she'd failed. Her left leg hit the ground first, and instead of holding her, it had buckled. She'd landed on her hip and then her hand had smashed into the ground.

All around, her ego had—and still was—taken a real beating.

He looked down again, and Cass let her eyes sweep past his dark hair, noting the strands of silver in it, and along the strong muscles in his back. Her mouth turned dry, and the world wobbled again.

He probed her leg, getting closer and closer to ankle. "Tell me when it hurts," he said. He pressed every second, and Cass felt sure she'd run out of leg soon.

Just then, he touched her ankle, and fire shot up to her hip. "There," she gasped.

"I don't think it's broken," he said. "But it's swelling." He looked up at her again. "Let's get you up and onto the couch. We need to ice it."

He stayed low and put his hands under her arms. She'd never be able to tell him that after she'd cried out, she'd tried to get up and hadn't been able to, causing a crash of epic proportions.

Foolishly, she'd thought she could hide in the kitchen

and he wouldn't find her. Of course not. A man like Harrison wouldn't just go by a house when he'd heard someone scream.

"Put your weight on me and your right leg," he said, and he lifted her without her having to do much of anything. She grabbed onto the lip of the cabinets, because her luxury bartop hadn't arrived yet, and took a big breath.

Her left leg didn't want to straighten, and she didn't dare put weight on it.

"All right," he said. "You're up. That's half the battle."

She half-laughed and half-scoffed. "I don't know about that."

He stayed close to her, his hands having burned into her upper arms. One still lingered on the small of her back, as if she might fall backward. And who knew? She might.

"Okay?" he asked. "Your couches aren't uncovered. I'm going to put you at the table."

"I have a couch in the foyer," she said. "I just got here today, and I was getting some things unwrapped."

"The foyer?" he asked. "All the way by the front door?"

She nodded, pain smarting through her hip. She leaned further into the cabinets. "I can make it."

"Mm hm, I'm sure you can." Harrison moved to her side, and the heat and comfort of him behind her dissipated. "Cass." He spoke softly. "I'm going to pick you up."

He didn't wait for her permission. He didn't count down. He simply bent and swept her into his arms.

She cried out again, quieter this time, thankfully. She grasped onto his shoulders and as she settled into the strength of his arms, her adrenaline softened too. Their eyes met, and if Cass had had any doubt about the chemistry and electricity between them, it would've dried right up at the desire swimming in the dark depths of his eyes.

"To the foyer," he said, and it almost sounded like a growl. He moved, and Cass said nothing.

Humiliation drove through her, but she couldn't do anything about the situation. She'd learned to accept things as they were, even if she didn't like that, and she supposed that was one good thing that had come from West's death.

Harrison slid her onto the loveseat in the foyer, and they both sighed. "All right."

"Thank you," she said.

"Do you have medical supplies here?" he asked.

She shook her head.

"Is your son here with you?"

She shook her head again. "No, I came alone, just for a couple of days. I'm flying back tomorrow night, and we'll leave Friday morning to drive."

He nodded again. "Okay, can you stay here while I run to my place and get a few things?"

"Yes," she said. "I'm fine. Really." She didn't necessarily want to be alone, but she'd come to the island alone this morning. She hadn't even told Bea she was coming.

Harrison straightened and looked down at himself, as if just now realizing he was half-naked. Cass did the same, drinking in the flat planes of his abs and then the bulk of muscle in his chest.

"Uh, I'll be right back," he said. He fled like a scared rabbit, and Cass leaned into the loveseat and pressed her eyes closed.

Her only consolation of the past ten minutes was that river of attraction in Harrison's gaze. "River rapids," she murmured, because Cass wasn't twenty and dating her first serious boyfriend. She and Harrison weren't dating at all, but she'd come to accept that she *could* go out with him, and she wouldn't feel guilty about it.

The silence in the house allowed her mind to wander, and she thought through the phone call with Bea a couple of years ago when she'd first met Grant and wanted to take him from island tour guide to boyfriend.

Cass smiled as she thought about guiding Harrison along the same path, but from construction manager-slash-doctor to boyfriend.

"If Conrad is mad about the house," Cass told herself. And he was. "He'll be livid if you start dating Harrison."

She let that thought sink into her head for a moment, and then she brushed it away. Just as she'd told her son, she was an adult, and she had her own life to live. So did he. He'd left the house immediately after his high school graduation, and he'd barely returned in the year since. Was she to waste away there simply because that had once been her plan?

"No," she said aloud, echoing what she'd told him. "Plans change all the time." She hadn't been the most flexible person previous to West's death, but it was definitely a lesson she was learning on a daily basis now.

Sariah said she couldn't come to Texas to help with the move, but she supported Cass in her decision to sell the house, leave Texas, and move to the beach house. So far, at least. Cass suspected her daughter was so overwhelmed with her move overseas that she couldn't be bothered with what Cass had going on.

Jane had barely responded at all, and Cass knew that *was*

her response. And it meant she wasn't happy about the choice, but again, she was never around. She had her own path to trod, and Cass only knew she was still doing her therapy appointments because the charges hit her card when Jane did them.

Cass wanted her to attend those and at least talk to someone, even if it wasn't her.

She often felt like she still needed someone like that, but she'd stopped going to her therapist a few months ago. She'd run things by her Supper Club last week, and the only person who'd seemed even the tiniest bit put out about her departure had been Lauren. Cass understood why, because Lauren needed a lot of personal support, and she didn't have anyone else.

She, Bea, and Cass were close, but Cass had gone to lunch with Joy, who said Lauren would be okay. They went to lunch every week, and Lauren was coping with all the changes in their Supper Club and around Sweet Water Falls.

To Cass, outside of herself, she didn't think Lauren had much change to deal with, but she'd also learned not to judge how another should handle any given situation.

The front door opened again, and Harrison said, "It's just me, Cass."

She opened her eyes and noticed the black T-shirt hugging his arms and chest as he walked in. He might look better in that than he did out of it, and instant heat flooded her face. "Hey."

He held up a tackle box. "Got my first aid kit, so we'll get you all patched up, and then see if you can stand." He looked from her face down to her ankle and back. "I should've put ice on this before I left. Be right back."

He darted back into the kitchen, and she heard him getting ice out of the fridge. He returned iceless to the formal living room, and said, "I need a bag. You've literally got nothing here."

"I know," she said. "I'm staying in a hotel tonight. It was one night."

Harrison had nearly left the room before she'd finished the explanation. "Be right back."

He did return quickly, this time with a plastic wrapper stuffed with ice. He twisted the top and put it on her ankle.

"Brr," she said. "That's cold."

"That's the point," he said. "We want it to numb the pain and stop the swelling." He busied himself with items in the kit, and he wrapped the ice pack around her ankle with a thick, flesh-colored bandage.

He then took her hand and arm and slid her thumb through the splint. "I don't think this needs to be iced." He smiled at her and pulled the straps tight. "We also don't want it to limit blood flow. Too tight?"

Cass bent and stretched her fingers, which had already started to tingle. "Yeah," she said. "A little."

Harrison adjusted it, then picked up a bottle of water and handed it to her. "Pills," he said, dropping them into her palm next. "For the pain."

She swallowed them while he started packing everything up. "Thank you," she said. Her stomach growled, and he'd have had to been deaf not to hear it.

He looked up and asked, "When's the last time you ate?"

"This morning at home," she said. "My home in Texas." A lifetime ago, to be honest.

Harrison's eyes fired concern at her. "You've got to eat

with those pills." He stood and lifted the tackle box. "I'll put this in the truck and be right back."

He left before she could say anything, and when he returned, she held up her phone. "I can order dinner."

"Or..." He stuck his hands in his jeans pockets, and she realized he'd changed his clothes completely. She'd been so focused on his bare chest and then that sexy black T-shirt, she hadn't seen the jeans yet. "I could grill us up something. I was going to make hamburgers and street corn." He didn't look at her until the last word had been delivered, and a keen sense of hope shone there.

Cass didn't want to say no. She just needed to know a few things first. "Harrison," she said, liking the shape of his name in her mouth. "I'm kind of a planner."

"Yeah, I know." He grinned at her. "If you were planning to order something specific, that's fine."

"It's not that." She wasn't quite sure how to say what she wanted to. She hadn't had to consider her words so carefully in a long time. West had known her. She hadn't had to explain anything to him. He knew who she was, and how she operated, and Harrison didn't know either of those things.

"What is it?" he asked.

As she took up the whole loveseat, what with her left leg stretched out in front of her, he stood in front of her, so adorable as he waited for her answer.

"I guess I just need to know... Is this a date?"

A blank mask slid over his face. He blinked, and a new kind of resolve took its place. "Yeah, Cass, we can call it a date if you'd like."

"I want to know what *you'd* like to call it." She'd given him her number a week ago, and he'd texted her a few times.

Nothing over the top. Nothing inappropriate. She found herself enjoying the conversations, even if they'd been superficial and brief.

"Me cooking for you at my house?" he asked, a flirtatious vibe in his voice. "Yeah, I'd like to call it a date."

"Okay," she agreed. "How long until we can eat?"

"Half an hour?" he guessed. "I was going to start dinner when I got home from my walk."

She smiled at him, feeling younger and more like her old self as she said, "Do you normally take slow, evening walks along the beach?"

He laughed, the sound lifting up to the two-story-high ceiling in the house. "No," he said among chuckles. "I fell on the job last week, and I hurt my back. My physical therapist says I need to walk, and the beach is good, because the sand shifts. It forces my core and back to work hard to balance."

Cass couldn't stop smiling. "I see." She looked down at her foot. "How am I going to get to your place?"

He followed her gaze, and then their eyes met again. "Easy," he said, his throat moving powerfully as he swallowed. "I'm going to carry you."

Cass's blood turned to lava at the thought of being in his arms again. "All right, Doctor Tate," she teased. "I think I have all the answers and know the plan for the evening."

"You ready right now?" He ignored the teasing about him being a doctor. "I could help you around here with... whatever you were doing. Unwrapping the furniture or something."

"It can be done later," she said.

"Not if you can't walk."

"After dinner," she said, putting her leg down as if she'd

push to a standing position. "We can come back here, and I'll boss you around. Deal?"

He put his hand under her elbow and helped her stand. She tried a bit of weight on her left toes, and it wasn't terribly painful. Of course, she couldn't really feel her left ankle at all right now.

Her stomach swooped, and that could've been from the pills or the oh-so-nearness of the hardworking, handsome, helpful Harrison Tate.

He swept her into his arms a moment later, sending her adrenaline to the back of her throat. He looked at her, his head only six or eight inches from hers now.

"Deal," he said, but those dark, delicious eyes said so much more.

Cass hoped this brief talk—and her own expression—gave him a good idea of where she currently was regarding a relationship with him, and she held onto him as he took her outside and gently put her in the passenger seat of his truck.

She watched him round the hood, feeling very much like she'd just been rescued by Prince Charming, and she smiled as he got behind the wheel and flashed her that royal grin. "Good?"

"So good," she said, almost giddy for the evening ahead. She'd told no one about her trip today—besides Conrad, and he wouldn't expect her to detail for him all the menial tasks she'd gotten done at the house that day—and the thought of this secret meal with Harrison only added to the excitement coursing through her.

Chapter Ten

Harrison felt like he needed twenty minutes to prep to have Cass enter his house. A few minutes to shower, then a few more to rush around the house and pick up anything he'd left lying out he didn't want her to see. Then he'd make the hamburgers and prep the toppings, and she'd show up in her wide-leg white beachcomber pants, and the navy-and-white striped tank top. She'd comment on the crisp white lines and how citrusy the air smelled.

As it was, he carried her into his house as it had been that morning when he'd gone to work. He had changed his clothes when he'd run home to get the first aid kit, but he'd had to. He wasn't wearing a shirt, and he'd noticed Cass gaping at him.

He couldn't believe he'd told her he wanted this to be a date. He couldn't believe she'd asked.

He'd texted her a few times in the past week, and they'd conversed a little. Nothing of consequence. Nothing he'd worry Grant or Bea couldn't see. If they did, they'd think he was just asking about her travel plans, the size of her plastic bins, and if she needed him to take care of any plants while she waited to get in her house.

"Here you go," he said, placing her on his leather couch. He put a pillow behind her back and she leaned into it.

"Thanks."

"I'm gonna fire up the grill and start working on the corn."

"Bring me the corn," she said. "I once won a shucking competition with my brother and sister." Her dark eyes held a light Harrison hadn't seen yet, and he paused.

"Really?"

"My momma used to make us help in the garden. She *loves* gardening, and we didn't have much money. So we had to shell the peas for *hours*, and I swear, you have no idea how long it takes to fill a bucket with tiny little peas."

Harrison could listen to this woman talk for hours, and he settled on the armrest opposite her. "I bet."

"Corn's the same way," she said. "You shuck it forever, and there was always too much silk for my momma." She laughed, and Harrison grinned at her.

"All right," he said. "I'll bring you the corn."

"She'd do timed contests for us, just to make it fun. I won all the time." She lifted her hands and waggled her fingers—well, the ones on her right hand. "I have deft hands."

He nodded to the splint. "Even with that?"

"I can hold it tight with this hand," she said. "Rip with the other."

"Okay," he said dubiously. "I don't want you overexerting yourself." He pushed himself to his feet and went into the kitchen. As he collected the half-dozen ears of corn from the refrigerator, he told himself he had to talk. He was on a *date*, and he couldn't just go into his chef zone and get dinner on the table as quickly as possible.

He dropped the corn into a big bowl and took it toward her. "How did your other kids react to you selling the house?"

Cass's expression fell slightly. "Fine," she said. "Jane's in her own world, so I didn't get much support from her. Sariah's in Taiwan, and she said it's my house, and I can do what I want with it."

"That you can," Harrison said. He went back into the kitchen and started putting the ground meat together. He seasoned it with salt and pepper and a packet of onion soup mix, then dove in with one hand and mixed it all up.

As he started to shape patties, he asked, "Is Conrad going to stay here with you for long?"

"Just a couple of weeks," she said. "He wanted to make sure I get settled. That I don't need his help moving anything big and don't have it."

"So he's supportive," Harrison said.

"I guess."

He looked up as he patted the meat. "Cass, he is. That's how men show their support. We do things."

She looked over to him, her eyes wide.

"I mean, not *all* men, obviously," he said, his face suddenly growing hot. He dropped his gaze back to his task and put the ready patty down. He picked up another fistful of ground beef. "A lot of men I know, myself included. If you need help, I'm there. You want me to talk about my feelings?" He gave a short laugh. "That's a little harder."

"Conrad was pretty mad when I told him I was going to sell the house in Texas." She spoke quietly, but she wasn't passive. "He wanted me to try living here for the summer first. I decided I could do that if it made him feel better."

"Honey," Harrison said, laying on the Southern drawl as thick as he could. "It's summer here year-round." He laughed, and Cass joined in. He'd not had a woman in this house yet, and it sure did feel good. Like he didn't have to continually come home alone after a tiring day of work.

He kept making patties while she said West's life insurance had paid for the house in Texas, and she could let it sit for a summer if she had to.

"Well, I can't wait to meet Conrad," Harrison said. "He sounds like he's trying, Cass."

"You're probably right," she said. "It felt to me like he rushed right home to make sure I didn't do something he didn't approve of." She spoke with a touch of irritation, and Harrison let her have that moment while he washed his hands.

"I'm going to go start the grill. Be right back." He stepped outside and lit the grill, adjusted the flame, and then grabbed the industrial box of tin foil sheets from the outdoor countertop.

Back inside, he detoured over to her, and sure enough, she'd shucked all of the corn. "Look at you." He handed her the box of tin foil sheets. "Do you want to wrap them too? I usually just drop in some butter, salt, and pepper. I put the cheese on once they come off the flame."

"I can, sure," she said. But she didn't take the box. "I want to come over to the island."

She scooted to the edge of the couch, and Harrison

abandoned the tin foil sheets on the couch in favor of helping her. She got to her feet and took a second to balance.

"I'm going to try to put some weight on it," she said. "And I'm afraid I'm leaking on your carpet."

"It's fine," he said, noticing the water as it turned the beige carpet a darker brown. "It's not the nice stuff like what you've got."

"It's great," she said. "I like your house." She smiled at him, an edge in her eye he hadn't seen yet. He didn't know her well enough to know what that glint meant, but he knew to smile.

"What?"

"I mean, maybe not this *dark brown leather* couch, but overall, the house has a nice vibe."

"Oh, so you'd like a tour later so you can critique my decorating skills, is that it?"

She put one hand against his breastbone and tilted her head back as she laughed. "Yeah." She kept giggling. "I would like a tour later, but not so I can criticize."

"I saw the leather you left in Texas," he said. "I should've let you order food and have it sent to your house." He backed up a couple of steps to give her room to test her weight on her foot.

He kept his hand on her good arm, telling himself it was because he didn't want her to fall. And it was that. He also really liked touching her, and having had her in his arms a couple of times now had broken that physical touch barrier.

She hobbled a bit, but she managed to move. He kept backing up, and she followed him into the kitchen. She slid up onto a barstool, and Harrison rounded the island to get the butter and seasonings.

He retrieved the tin foil sheets from the couch, giving the dark leather the evil eye. Perhaps he should have a lighter couch. Something the color of canvas, with the fabric to match.

"What kind of couches did you get?" he asked. "I saw them in your living room, but I couldn't see through the plastic."

"They're a great taupe canvas," she said, and Harrison burst out laughing. Cass watched him with curiosity on her face.

"Sorry," he said amidst his chuckles. "I'm sorry. I was just thinking I could probably get a couch made out of canvas, and then you said it was canvas."

"Your couch is fine," she said, her voice a touch aloof now. "I didn't mean to comment on your décor."

"Oh, you're getting the whole tour later," he said, pointing a head of Romaine lettuce at her. "*And* I want the commentary. I can't have my beach house looking like Dracula's dungeon."

Cass giggled and shook her head. "It's not a dungeon. One, the windows would never allow that."

"The windows are fantastic," he said.

"What's your favorite part of the house?" she asked.

He nodded behind her, where the floor to ceiling windows showed the ocean beyond.

"The view?"

"Not the view," he said. "You have an amazing patio, but I built out my place to have an outdoor kitchen. That's what I love the most."

Her eyebrows went up, and she stopped wrapping the ear of corn she'd started on. "You have an outdoor kitchen?"

"Yes, ma'am," he drawled.

Cass tilted her head and gave him a wry smile.

"Sorry, ma'am," he teased.

"I want to see the outdoor kitchen."

"Get the corn wrapped, and we'll get the food going."

"Yes, sir." The aluminum foil crinkled as she wrapped it around the end of the corn. Harrison plucked leaves from the head of lettuce and put them on a plate. He got the beef-steak tomato from the basket beside the fridge, and Cass said, "Wow. Look at that tomato."

Harrison looked at her. "Do you like them or not like them?"

"I eat them like apples." She grinned like a kid who'd just been presented with her favorite kind of candy. "And that's a beautiful tomato."

He cored it and sliced off the top. He nudged it toward her with the tip of the knife. "Go ahead then."

She picked up the slice and took a big, juicy bite. Liquid ran down her face, and she laughed as she wiped it. Harrison liked how comfortable she'd become with him, and he wondered what walls she'd had to knock down to do it.

"Wow," he said, chuckling too. "I mean, I like tomatoes on things, but I would never just eat one like an apple."

"You're missing out." She sprinkled salt and pepper on the rest of her slice and polished it off while he sliced the tomato and put those rings on the plate with the lettuce. "I'm not huge into onions, but if you like them, I have one."

"I'm fine without them," she said. "Have you had a hamburger with a fried egg on it?"

His eyes rounded. "Have I? Am I a human being? Of course I have. They're fantastic."

Cass grinned, those white teeth so dazzling. "I love a fried egg on a burger."

"So I'm frying eggs next," he said coyly, and she laughed.

Harrison liked the fun, flirty vibe between the two of them, but it also felt a tad bit fake. He pulled out the jar of pickles, which had already been sliced by the manufacturer. He placed the bottle on the counter, along with ketchup, mustard, and mayonnaise.

He got out the carton of eggs and turned back to her. "Let's head outside."

"Oh, you're going to fry the eggs outside too?"

"Yep. The kitchen is outside."

She looked at the one he stood in. "Do you ever cook in here?"

"Uh." He thought for a moment. "I don't think I have, no. I brew coffee. I eat bowls of cereal. I'm not a cyborg."

"Does your grill bake?" she asked.

"I'm not much of a baker," he said. "Thirty minutes or less is my motto for meals. The grill is great for that." He stepped over to the door and slid it open. "Wait for me, okay? I don't want you to hurt yourself again."

He hurried outside and put the carton of eggs on the shelf beside the grill and the hamburger patties on the counter. He checked the temperature on the grill, and it was nearly ready.

He turned back to the house just as Cass filled the doorway. She carried all six ears of corn in her arms, the shiny silver glinting in the evening sunlight as she hopped outside.

"I said to wait," he said, taking the corn from her.

"It feels okay," she said. "But I'm still puddling everywhere."

"Let me get the food on the grill, and I'll get the ice pack off and the ankle wrapped again."

He did that, then hurried back inside to get a towel and another bandage. Cass had sat at his outdoor table, and she lifted her leg up onto the seat across from her so he could work on her leg.

"The swelling has gone way down," he said.

"It feels a lot better."

He nodded. Dried her foot and ankle, and rewrapped it. She put her leg down and he took the seat it had been in. "What are you going to tell your son?"

"About my foot?"

"Yeah."

"That I twisted my ankle doing something awesome, like saving a mermaid who'd washed up on shore and needed to get back into the surf before anyone else saw her." Her eyes shone with joy, and that made Harrison happy.

"Wow," he said while he chuckled. "I was not expecting you to go there."

"My kids love stories like that," Cass said. "Whenever West or I would get hurt, we'd make up some fantastical story about how we'd incurred the injury."

He nodded, sobering. "I'm sure you didn't do that when West died, though."

Cass pulled in a breath, her eyes turning the size of dinner plates.

"I'm sorry," he said. "I didn't mean to...say that."

Cass shook her head. "No." Her bottom lip wobbled as she said, "It's okay. There weren't any stories of how he'd died saving Santa's reindeer, you're right."

"How did he pass?" Harrison asked. "You don't have to tell me."

"I can." Cass took a big breath. "He was a homicide investigator. Originally, we thought one of the people he'd been investigating had wanted to silence him. He often testified in court cases and whatnot."

Harrison nodded. A story like that would be online, and he could probably find it. He didn't want to; he wanted to hear it in Cass's own voice.

"But really, it was just a case of wrong-time, wrong-place. He'd gone to a sporting goods store to purchase a pair of cleats for Conrad." She ducked her head and smiled. "He played rugby in high school. He plays for Baylor too. Anyway. West was there, and an altercation broke out between a couple of other guys."

Harrison reached over and took her hand in his. "You don't have to," he whispered.

"West intervened when the fighting started," she said. "That's just the kind of man he was. One of the boys—and he wasn't a boy. He was twenty years old—had a gun, and he pulled it out and just started firing." A single tear ran down her face, and she didn't move to wipe it away.

Harrison did it for her, and she raised her gaze to meet his. "I'm sorry," he said. "How unfair life is sometimes."

"Yes," she whispered. "I've learned a lot of things since West died, and that's one of them."

His phone buzzed, telling him it was time to flip the burgers, and he jumped to his feet. He turned his back on Cass so she could compose herself, and as he attended to the corn and hamburgers, he wondered if he should've asked her for that story.

She'd given it though, and as he cracked eggs in the pan on the burner of the grill, he was glad he had. They needed to have a real connection if they were to have a real relationship, and he didn't want another relationship like the one he'd had with Claudia. They'd been more like roommates, coming and going about their own business, only stopping to ask how the other's day was if they happened to run into one another.

He didn't want a repeat of that, but he also didn't have to know everything on date one. He pulled the eggs from the pan and turned to put them on the table. Cass sat there, perfectly composed, and she looked at him.

"Sorry," he said. "I really didn't mean to make you cry on the first date."

She waved her hand. "I cry, Harrison. Sometimes it comes on quickly, and sometimes I think I can control it, but I can't. If you can't deal with a few tears now and then, maybe we shouldn't go out again."

"I want to go out again," he said. He needed to get the other toppings from inside, as well as toast the buns. Instead he crouched in front of her and took both of her hands in his. She had pristine nails, painted the color of the pink spoonbills they'd seen in the Everglades.

"And I'll take you out somewhere nice," he said. "Not try to show off in my outdoor kitchen." He smiled. "All right?"

"I suppose I can be convinced to go to dinner 'somewhere nice' with you." She smiled too, and Harrison's chest tightened in anticipation as she leaned toward him.

He caught a whiff of her peachy perfume as his eyes

drifted closed. He thought for half a second she was going to kiss him—and she did.

Just not on the mouth.

Her lips branded his cheek, and she whispered, "Thanks for letting me talk about West," before she pulled away.

"Yeah." His voice sounded like he hadn't used it in ages, and he stood to get the rest of the food on the table before he ruined it—and the rest of this date.

Chapter Eleven

Well, I think your house is fantastic. Cass's fingers flew across her phone as she waited at the airport. The past couple of days in Hilton Head had been a whirlwind to say the least. The biggest surprise had been how much fun she'd had with Harrison. And that she hadn't texted Bea once.

It'll look so much better with a new couch, Harrison said back. He sent a winking face, and Cass shook her head. She didn't regret saying the couch was too dark—it was—but she could've exercised more tact.

He'd taken it well, and the home tour had been wonderful. Several of his rooms sat empty, which she feared hers would as well. She'd only ordered enough furniture for the main level of living, which included her bedroom. All of the rooms upstairs wouldn't have anything in them until the moving company brought the main contents of the house. Her Christmas decorations, all of West's things, all of the children's mementos from their childhood.

She'd promised Conrad she'd make up one of the bedrooms just for him, so he could come vacation at the beach anytime he needed to. He'd come from at least a little bit of her cloth, because he loved the beach, and she'd told him a house or a geographic location didn't make a home.

It was the people there who mattered, and no matter what any of them did, West would not be walking back through the front door of that house in Texas.

She looked up from her flirt-fest on her phone and let herself gaze at nothing. She could see West on the back deck with those binoculars, making coffee on the weekends before he settled down with the newspaper, or sleeping in his recliner after a long week of work. Those images came easily, as did ones of when he'd taught Conrad to ride a bicycle, and when he'd gone to every one of Jane's dance competitions, rain, shine, health, sickness, no matter what.

Those things stuck in her mind, but she wasn't sure what his voice sounded like anymore. She couldn't place the scent of his cologne either.

Harrison didn't sound or smell like West, she knew that. It was a different kind of good, and only a pinch of guilt accompanied the thought.

Cass wasn't sure what tomorrow would hold, and for a woman who liked to make plans, that scared her. Or at least it had every day for the past sixteen months, since West had died.

But now, it almost felt exciting, like she was on an adventure and tomorrow's could be the best view yet.

A COUPLE OF DAYS LATER, CASS FOUGHT THE URGE to tell her son to slow down. They'd made great time in the drive from Sweet Water Falls to Hilton Head, mostly because Conrad had a lead foot.

He and Cass had alternated the driving responsibilities, and she looked out her window and pressed her lips together. He hadn't killed them yet, and at this rate, they should arrive at her new house in paradise ahead of schedule.

Which wasn't bad, but it also wasn't ideal. She'd asked Bea and Grant—and Harrison—to meet her at the house at seven, not six-fifteen.

She didn't want to unload everything herself, as a new kind of exhaustion Cass hadn't experienced in a while had descended upon her. She bent to withdraw the bottle of pills from her purse, and she took a couple of painkillers in the hopes that by the time they reached the house, they'd have kicked in.

"Right?" Conrad asked.

"Yep." Cass looked at her handsome son. They'd actually had a very good drive, with good conversations. He wasn't as angry today, and Cass's decision to come to Carolina for a couple of days without him had cooled him off.

Her heartbeat thumped against her breastbone. He'd not handled her leaving Texas very well, and she had no idea how he'd take the news of her dating Harrison.

One date, she told herself. *Is one date dating?*

She didn't know anymore, and she cleared her throat. "Are you seeing anyone in Waco?"

Conrad threw her a look. "Really, Mom?"

"Yes, really," she said, drawing strength back into herself.

"College students date, Conrad. It's not illegal or unheard of."

He shook his head. "You freaked out when I went out with Allison."

"You were fifteen." Cass couldn't believe that was who'd he'd brought up. "And she was a senior. And she started dating someone else while you two were still together, *and* she got pregnant like two months later. I was right to be worried about that."

Conrad said nothing, but she noticed his fingers tighten on the wheel. "I'm not goin' out with anyone," he said.

"You post a lot of pictures."

"That's me with my roommates and our floor group," he said. He cut her a glance out of the corner of his eye. "I did take a girl to a movie or something last month or whatever, but it didn't really turn into anything."

Cass nodded. "See? You didn't die by telling me that. Or *whatever*."

Conrad gave her half a smile, and Cass half-relaxed. She still wasn't sure how to tell him *she* was seeing someone, and she continued to sit on the news.

She hadn't told Bea either. Or anyone else in the Supper Club, but once they all arrived next week for Independence Day, to see her house, and for Supper Club—which she was hosting earlier in the month and on her new beachfront patio—she'd tell them.

That was the plan at least, and Cass had started sticking to her plans more and more often lately.

Her plan to keep in touch with her children and make sure they knew where she was and how she was doing. Going okay.

Her plan to decorate and design the beach house how she wanted, without regard to cost. Check.

Her plan to pack most of what she owned and move it to South Carolina. Check.

Her plan to get a fresh start in a new place. In progress.

Her plan to sell the house in Texas. Well, she had a skeleton plan for that, but she hadn't executed hardly any of the bones. Conrad had enough change in his life right now, and she'd promised him the summer before she decided.

"Another right," she said, and Conrad made the turn. He stopped the moving truck at the gate, and Cass gave him the code.

He punched it in, and the gate rumbled to the side, allowing them access to the community. Her eyes flew right to Harrison's, of course, and a blip of panic combined with guilt. It stayed for a moment, and then disappeared.

If things between them didn't work out, she'd forever be looking at his house as she drove by. Trees, shrubs, and bushes concealed the front porch, but her eyes could trace the path of the driveway back to his enormous garage, and she could see most of the second floor.

As Conrad drove past, she finally tore her eyes from the light gray structure.

"Wow, Mama," Conrad said, slipping back into his Texas-boy voice. "This place is *fancy*." He looked at her with wonder in his eyes. "You can afford this?"

"Yes," she said quietly. "It's very nice. Private. Quiet." All of the things she wanted. Sort of. She didn't really like being alone, but she had people here she knew already, and she didn't have to stay in the house all day, every day, by herself.

"There's a private beach," she said. "Walking trails. Bike

trails. Loads of history here. I'm going to get my business going here too. I'll have plenty to do."

Conrad blinked at her. "Yeah," he said. "You will."

She wasn't sure why she'd felt like she needed to tell him that. Probably for her own sanity. "It's this one," she said, nodding to the light blue house. The roof shone like polished oil in the evening sunshine, and Cass did love this house.

Conrad turned into the driveway, now barely giving the truck any gas at all. They bumped into the driveway, and Cass said, "Go all the way around to the front door. I think it'll be easier to get in that way."

He did, easing forward until the back of the truck sat even with the steps. The furniture guys had brought in her things through the garage, but the front door was actually taller and wider than the entrance to the house from the garage.

She'd set the code on her front door while she'd been in town a couple of days ago. She got out of the truck and took a deep breath. The air went down hot and thick, but Cass was used to that.

This still felt like the first breath of a grand adventure, and she stretched her back and legs while Conrad opened the huge doors on the back of the truck.

"Bea and Grant will be here soon," she said. "We don't have to unload ourselves." She extended her hand toward him. "Come see the house."

He looked a tad disgruntled, but he took her hand and faced the house. They stood there together, the two of them, and Cass let herself feel whatever she needed to feel.

Acceptance that West was gone. That was a blessing, as she'd fought it for a long time.

Grief that he wasn't there to see this beautiful home.

Sadness that he'd never see it.

Happiness that she got to live here, and that her children could come and stay with her.

And all-powerful love for the life she'd lived—and the one she got to keep experiencing right here on Hilton Head Island.

"It's really big, Mama," Conrad said.

"Too big," she agreed. "It had the waterfront property I wanted."

His hand in hers tightened. "You've always loved the beach."

"Your dad and I used to have a place on Galveston," she said. "You were a tiny boy, so you might not remember." She took the first step toward the house, and Conrad went with her. "We sold it when you were two and Daddy got moved to the Coastal Bend. It was too far to drive after that."

"I don't remember that," he murmured. "I've seen the pictures though."

She nodded, and they climbed the long, wide steps to the porch. "It has pillars."

"Daddy would've liked that," Conrad said, looking up toward the high roof overhead. "He loved pillars."

Cass was suddenly glad they'd arrived early, because she now realized that her son needed this time to see the house the way she did. To talk about his father and how he would've fit here. And how he didn't.

"Yes," she said. "Daddy loved pillars on houses." She released his hand to tap in the code to unlock the door, and when it disengaged, she opened the door and gave it a little push. She indicated he should go first. Smiling, she said, "Go on. It's just a house."

She was hoping she could make it a home by herself, a task she hadn't done since college when she'd taken her half of a dorm room and made it as cozy as possible. Her space. Her comfort zone. Her happy place.

She wanted this beach house to be that too, and she hoped Conrad could feel it.

He took a step and then paused. "Wait," he said. He pulled his phone out of his pocket. "I told the girls I'd record it for them." He tapped and nodded. "Okay, ready. You narrate it for us, Mama. Show us your new house." He brightened, and Cass put a big smile on her face too.

He loved film and electronics, and she hoped he'd be happy in his career major of digital art, photography, and film. So far, he had been.

"All right," she said. "This is the entryway. The foyer, some people call it, but I think that's stuffy." She grinned and indicated the painting of a great blue whale she'd purchased. "I put a whale here to welcome everyone to the beach respite, because whales are representative of compassion and solitude, and they possess knowledge of both life and death." Her throat tightened, and her eyes met Conrad's. "Your daddy loved whales," Cass said, not caring that her tone pitched up. "Once he retired, we were going to go on a whale-watching trip. We never did get to, but maybe the four of us could go together one day."

"Five," Conrad said. "Sariah has Robbie now."

Cass wiped her blasted right eye, which always got

weepier than the left. "Yes," she said, smiling fully into his phone again. "The five of us."

She didn't know if Jane would have a special someone by the time the whale-watching trip happened. Perhaps Conrad would too.

And Cass might could even bring Harrison...if they were still together.

A COUPLE OF HOURS LATER, SHE SAID, "THAT'S everything that stays here. Now we just have to get the rest of this over to Harrison's and we'll unload there."

"I have pizza too," he said, and Cass gave him a grateful smile. She hadn't hugged him hello when he'd arrived. He hadn't touched her. They'd told no one of their hamburger date from three nights ago, and she hadn't shown her text conversations with the man to anyone either.

"I'm starving." Conrad jumped down from the back of the truck. "Pizza sounds great."

"I brought chocolate chip banana bread," Bea said. "It won't be as good as Bessie's, but it's not bad."

"It's fantastic," Grant said, wrapping his arm around Bea's waist. They grinned at one another, and Cass turned away before they started kissing.

"I'll drive," she said. Everyone loaded up and went down the street three houses, where Cass's larger items and extra storage bins would be stored until the beach house was truly finished. She saw no point in unloading it at her place, hauling it upstairs, and then having to move it all when the flooring for the bedrooms up there finally arrived. The railings had also come out yesterday for a recall, and Cass now didn't know how long it would be before she could really move in. Hopefully before Supper Club.

She reminded herself that she could host a catered dinner on the back patio without rugs and cabinets in the bedrooms upstairs.

At Harrison's, the unloading commenced, but she soon found herself alone with him in the garage. As she glanced around, he came to her side.

"They're all inside," he said quietly. His hand slid down her arm to hers. "Eating."

She squeezed his hand. "Thank you for getting food."

"It was part of the plan, right?" He grinned at her, and Cass had the overwhelming urge to kiss him right there in his garage. With her son and her best friend only a couple dozen feet away, behind closed doors.

His eyes melted into hers, and neither of them moved.

"When can I see you again?" he asked, the perfect thing to say. Cass wanted to feel beautiful and desired. She wanted to feel like this handsome man couldn't wait to be alone with her again.

"I'm not sure," she murmured. "Conrad and I are going to be unpacking what we can, and then hitting the beach. Doing some of the touristy things..." She let her words hang there, because she couldn't commit to anything right now.

Harrison nodded and released her hand. "All right. I can be patient." He didn't sound happy about it, but Cass liked that too. He moved to go up the ramp to the truck, but he stopped and turned back to her. "Where did you decide to stay?"

Cass swallowed and tucked her hands in her shorts

pockets. "Bea's," she said. "Honey, she has real beds." She took a couple of steps to him and put one hand against his chest. "You don't, and I'm an old lady. I can't be getting up and down off the floor and a four-inch air mattress." She grinned up at him, and his stoic expression finally cracked.

"Oh, all right," he said in a sweet-and-sour way. He leaned closer and closer, until Cass thought *he* might kiss her. "But, Cass, you're not that old."

"Older than you," she said, her lips barely moving. "Right?"

"Probably," he said. "But not much."

"How much?" she asked.

"I don't know how old you are," he said.

"Forty-seven," she said.

He nodded as he put a safer distance between them. It didn't matter, because the spicy, ocean-y scent of his cologne had entered her nose and fired up her pheromones. His body heat seeped into hers through her palm, and she dropped it.

"I'm forty," he said. "So not too different." He turned and went up the ramp, leaving Cass cold and alone at the bottom of it.

"Mama," Conrad called, and she spun back to him. How long had he been there? What had he seen?

"Yeah?"

"You've got to come see this guy's outdoor kitchen. Bea says she's never leaving." He laughed, gestured her toward him, and ducked back inside.

Cass looked over her shoulder to Harrison, who chuckled. "Go on," he drawled. "Go see my amazing outdoor kitchen."

"I'm telling my friends at Supper Club next week," she said. "And my kids."

"That's fine with me, sweetheart," he said as he went past her with her mother's antique desk in his hands. "You're in charge here."

Cass did like being in charge, and she started for the door. Now she just had to figure out how to be amazed by something she'd seen before, and it better be a good performance, because Bea had raised three teenagers and could smell a lie from fifty feet away.

Chapter Twelve

Lauren Keller ignored her phone as she guided the minivan off the freeway. She wasn't sure how she'd been designated the driver from the airport to Hilton Head, but she sat behind the wheel.

She had plenty of work emails to answer, and she could've gotten something done on this hour-long drive. She told herself she didn't have to work when she was out of town, on vacation. Yes, she had a busy job, but that didn't mean she had to work it all the time.

Those were the things she'd been trying to tell herself this year, and now that six months of the year had passed, the anxiety over not having her phone in her hand for an hour could easily be reasoned with.

Lauren was keenly aware of the passing of time, and she wished she wasn't. Now that she'd turned forty-five, she'd started the acceptance process that she wouldn't be able to have children.

She'd started seeing a counselor, and she really liked

Lindsey. She asked hard questions, and she posed scenarios for Lauren that kept her up at night. She paid to go every week, though, and she'd been slowly finding some answers to some of the questions and situations posed.

She'd always wanted children, but she'd never found the right man to marry. Her mantra of not having a man if he wasn't the right one stuck with her, and while Lauren hadn't been ready to start dating a year or two ago after her second failed relationship with an ex-boyfriend, she'd told Lindsey only two days ago that she felt ready now.

She drove across the bridge that led them to Hilton Head, and her thoughts moved to a man she'd met two July's ago.

Blake Williams. She barely knew the man, but she'd sat with him at the Fourth of July celebrations here on the island for two years in a row.

She knew men at work too, but she really didn't want to date someone she worked with. Lauren had never been in a relationship that had lasted longer than a couple of years, and that would make things awkward at work once they broke up.

A sigh slipped from her mouth, and Joy, who rode shotgun, looked over to her. "You okay?"

Leave it to Joy to hear the smallest of sounds. "Yes," Lauren said. "Just tired. That flight was so hot."

Joy reached up and ran her hand down the back of her neck. "Yes, it was."

"I'm sleepy." Lauren gave her a smile and tuned into the conversation happening between Bessie and Sage in the row behind them.

"...my grandmother's peach pie recipe," Sage said. "I

think you guys should try it at The Bread Boy. It would sell like hotcakes with the pie shells."

"I can talk to Cherry," Bessie said. "Oh, I was going to talk to y'all about her too." She leaned forward as Joy twisted to look at her. Lauren looked up into the rearview mirror for a moment. "I think she'd be an amazing addition to the Supper Club."

"Who?" Lauren asked.

"Cherry Forrester," Bessie said. "Her family owns Sweet Water Falls Farm. You know, the Coopers? She got married a few years ago, and she's older like us. She might be as old as Sage even."

"You make me sound ancient," Sage said.

"No." Bessie looked at her. "That's not what I meant." She shook her head while Joy gave a light laugh. "I'm just saying she's not in her thirties."

"I know her," Joy said. "She and Jed bought that rescue ranch from Betty Jones."

"Yes," Bessie said. "She said she knew Lauren, because your firm did something for the Forrester's corn maze over the holidays?"

"Oh, right," Lauren said. "Sybil was on that project, not me. But yes."

"She and Jed don't have kids. She works at The Bread Boy as our general manager, and she'd be perfect."

"Does she cook?" Joy asked.

"Is that a requirement?" Lauren glanced over to her.

Joy met her eyes quickly before Lauren had to look back to the road. "I guess not."

"I cater almost every month I have to host," Lauren said.

"Cherry can cook," Bessie said. "She brings in jams all

the time for our customers to taste with the bread samples. They're so good, she's started selling them from the cash register."

"She makes jam?" Sage asked. "We should definitely at least ask her."

Lauren started to laugh.

"What?" Joy asked.

"I'm glad the requirement to be invited is to be a jam-maker," Lauren said, still chuckling.

"It's an odd requirement," Joy said.

Sage tossed her long hair, and Lauren caught the last whip of it. "That's not what I meant. I meant it's hard to make jam, so she's probably a good cook."

"Which we just established wasn't a requirement," Lauren said.

But Joy had already started saying, "I didn't think we were inviting anyone new." She looked to the two ladies in the back seat and then to Lauren. "Bea comes to Texas every month for Supper Club, and she hosts at a restaurant."

Lauren didn't want to be the one to say it, but she knew Bessie and Sage wouldn't. She still gave them a pause to do so, but when neither of them spoke up, she drew a big breath.

"I know Cass says she's just going for the summer, but guys, she cleaned out her whole house."

"No, she didn't," Joy said. "All of the beds are there."

"None of the storage is," Lauren said. "She took her holiday decorations, Joy. All of her clothes, not just her swimwear and fancy vacation clothes." Cass dressed better than anyone Lauren knew, and she worked in the corporate world. She saw good fashion daily, and Cass was above all of that.

"She's moving there permanently, guys. She just hasn't listed her house for sale yet." She cast a look at Joy, who wore an expression of disbelief. Lauren didn't say more. Joy already knew; she just hadn't accepted it.

"Then they'll come together," Bessie said into the silence that had joined them in the minivan.

Lauren gave a small shake of her head, but she didn't make it big enough for Bessie to see behind her. No, Cass and Bea weren't going to keep flying to Sweet Water Falls for Supper Club. Lauren *felt* it deep in her soul.

She hadn't planned on saying anything quite yet, but now felt like the right time. "I'm thinking of coming here to stay with Cass for a few months." She eased her foot onto the brake and came to a stop at a red light.

She looked at Joy, who wore the widest eyes Lauren had ever seen. "Oh, come on, Joy. You could too."

"If you all come for the summer, only Sage and I will be left in Texas," Bessie said.

"Then *you* could fly here for Supper Club," Lauren said, meeting her eyes in the mirror again. "Things are changing again, guys. That's the truth of the matter."

"She just needs a new start," Joy said, speaking of Cass. "She stayed in Texas for a long time, in that house, alone."

"I think she'll be happy here," Lauren said. "And I think I'll stay longer than the summer. My job has offered me a new position in the company, and it's out of Miami, but they're willing to let me work remotely and go to Florida a couple of times a month, or as necessary."

"So you can work anywhere," Joy said.

"Yes." Lauren got the van moving again. "I know Bea's here, but she's with Grant, and their marriage is still new. I can—and want to—be here for Cass."

Joy nodded, but she said nothing. Lauren knew the other woman so well that she knew Joy's mind now ran a hundred miles an hour. She worked as a classroom reading aide, and school was out for the summer. She too could come live on Hilton Head for two months. She didn't have children at home; her divorce had been final for almost eighteen months now.

"Don't say anything to anyone, please," Lauren said. "Cass told us she'd be here for the summer, and I'm just assuming she won't come back."

"I think you're right," Sage said.

"Yeah," Bessie said with a sad sigh. "Me too."

"Let's enjoy the weekend," Lauren said. "Fireworks tomorrow night. Supper Club the day after. And then two days on the beach before we have to go home." She smiled around at everyone, glad when they returned the gesture.

"We won't say anything, right, ladies?" Joy twisted to look at Bessie and Sage, and they all agreed. She faced the front again. "All right. Now." She exhaled in a long breath. "I need to find a handsome man over forty *I'm* willing to relocate for."

She gave Lauren a cat-like smile, and Lauren burst out laughing again. Joy did too, and Bessie and Sage joined in.

"Don't we all?" Lauren asked, and once again, her thoughts traitorously moved to Blake Williams. Why, she didn't know, but she found herself hoping he'd be sitting with Grant at tomorrow night's fireworks.

"LAUREN, YOUR HAT," SAGE SAID THE FOLLOWING evening, and Lauren turned back to retrieve it. She already carried the chair she'd sit in that evening, as well as a beach tote with her eReader, her phone, a portable charger, and sunscreen. She had fairly tan skin normally, and she rarely burned, but they'd already spent a large portion of today out in the sun. Grant had rented a boat, and they'd packed food and fun into several hours together.

He'd brought a friend of his Lauren had met before—Harrison Tate—but Blake had not been present. She hadn't wanted to bring him up with anyone lest they think she was interested, as she wasn't even sure she was.

"Hey," a man said, his voice bright and full of life. Lauren's ribs tingled with the vibrations in that deep tone, and she swiped her beach hat off the top of the minivan and turned around to face the speaker.

Blake Williams stood there, wearing a pair of shorts the exact blue as in the field of stars on the American flag. They too had stars all over them, stitched into the fabric, not just printed on. He wore a pair of loafers with them, no socks, and his shirt was red-and-white striped. He was the personification of the flag, and she scanned him from head to toe one more time before looking into his eyes.

Blake was tall, trim, and tan. He grinned at her. "Lauren, hey. Bea said you'd be here again this year." He touched his chest. "Blake Williams."

"I remember who you are, silly," she said, her blood bubbling in her veins as if she'd poured baking soda into them and it was reacting with vinegar.

So she was definitely interested in him. She'd felt this on both previous occasions she'd been around him. She smiled and moved in to hug him. "How have you been?"

"Good," he said, embracing her lightly in return. That was the appropriate response since they really didn't know one another. She wondered—and hoped. Prayed, really—that he had the same physical reaction to her as she had to him. She had no way of knowing, as his smile stayed hitched in place, and his dark blue eyes fired friendliness at her. She wanted more than that, but she told herself not to be impatient.

The first time they'd met, she'd been kind, but she'd definitely brushed him off. She didn't live here, and she didn't want a long-distance boyfriend.

But her situation had changed. She wondered if his had too. Or what his situation was at all. "Are Bea and Grant here?" she asked.

Blake nodded back the way he'd come. "Same spot as the last couple of years." He looked down the aisle of parked cars.

"Are you leaving?" she asked, noting that the other women had left her behind. Joy would have questions, but Lauren trusted her explicitly. All of the women in her Supper Club, though she did reveal things to them in stages.

"Just for a few minutes," he said with a smile. "I'm going to get my girlfriend and my momma."

Lauren's heart turned into a lump of ice. "Oh, great," she said. "See you back here in a bit then." She turned away from him, not needing to embarrass herself further. She walked away in what she thought was an even stride. Not too fast. Not too slow. Just a walk.

She stepped off the hot asphalt and onto the sidewalk, and then finally under the trees. The shade cooled her face, and since she worked out every day in the corporate gym at her office, she caught up to her Supper Club friends easily.

"Who was that?" Joy asked.

"Blake." Lauren only gave her a cursory look. "I've met him a couple of times. Here. For the fireworks every year."

Joy nodded. "He was handsome. Is he single?"

Lauren shook her head, her smile almost ironic. "Nope. He just told me he's going to pick up his girlfriend and his mother." She linked her arm through Joy's. "Sorry. But surely Blake and Harrison have more male friends on the island."

"Maybe Harrison himself," Bessie said. "He's single."

Lauren looked over to her too, wondering why she saw things no one else did. "Is he?" she asked, vowing she wouldn't say any more than that.

"I asked him this morning," Bessie said, coughing immediately afterward.

"Bessie," Joy admonished. "You did?" She leaned forward to see Bessie past Lauren.

"Yeah," Bessie said, lifting her head and shaking her hair over her shoulders. "If you want a hot summer boyfriend, Joy, I'm going to help you find one."

They all started to laugh, and Lauren kept her vow of silence. After all, Cass deserved to tell everyone that she'd already set her sights on the handsome Harrison Tate.

Chapter Thirteen

Blake Williams glanced over to Lauren Keller as he set up the camp chair for his mother. "There you go, Momma," he said pleasantly. He took her arm and helped her ease into the chair. "Now, I don't want you doin' anything tonight. If you want a drink, tell me and I'll get it for you. We've got food and snacks. Those licorice whips you like."

His mother glared up at him, but she didn't try to stand up again. He might forcibly and firmly push her back down if she did. She'd had a hip replacement only seven weeks ago, and he'd only brought her because she'd threatened to come whether he helped or not. So he figured he better help.

"I'm fine, young man."

"I'm forty-five," he shot back. "Your grandson is a young man." His son was only twelve, actually, so he technically didn't qualify as a young man either. He was a preteen, and Blake had half-custody of him. He had him quite often, as he and Jacinda spoke all the time and had to work out

Tommy's schedule. She traveled often enough to make a regular schedule hard, and Blake had some business trips every now and then too.

This weekend, Tommy had gone to Carter's Cove for the holiday, and Blake would get him back on Monday. The boy had swimming lessons starting next week, and then they had a father-son camping trip on the weekend for his Boy Scout program. Blake loved being outdoors with his son, and he volunteered to go on every camp, every hike, every fishing trip, that fit his schedule.

"Yes," Momma said. "How is Tommy? You've kept him away."

"Only because he's such a klutz right now." Blake set up his own chair, aware of someone watching him. He looked over to Lauren, and she quickly looked away. He wasn't sure what that was about, but his chest grew a bright spot right in the middle of it.

He knew what that was, and he should not be feeling attracted to her. *She probably thinks you're a liar*, he thought. He'd told her he was going to get his girlfriend and his mother, and he'd only returned with one woman.

The older one, still currently glaring at him. "He is," Blake said as he sat. "Every time he goes to your place, he breaks something, and then you'd be left to clean it up."

"Who's watching him while you work then?" Momma folded her arms.

Blake squirmed and then crossed his legs. He didn't want to say, but Momma likely already knew.

"He's twelve, Blake," she said. "He can't stay home alone."

"He can," Blake said, swallowing hard. "He comes into

the office for part of the day, and then I give him work to do at home. He does that, and I'm home in three or four hours. It's fine." He did work reduced hours in the summer, and Tommy hadn't complained one bit about having to clean out the fridge—a twenty-minute job—and then playing video games in the air-conditioned house for a few hours.

Momma pursed her lips. "Where's Camille?"

"She's with her aunt, I guess," Blake said. "I didn't realize she'd said we'd sit with them, and I was already set up here."

"Mm." Momma didn't say anything else, but the humming said it all. *Must not be serious if you can't sit with her family instead of your friends.*

And maybe it wasn't. His relationship with Camille was a few months old, and he didn't feel too terribly much for her. Certainly not the same burning sensation beneath his ribs that flared to life as his eyes drifted over to Lauren again.

He'd met her a few times now, and he'd been happy to see her once again in the parking lot. She had gorgeous dark hair and eyes, with thick eyebrows and beautiful, full lips.

She laughed, further driving his hormones up a notch. He couldn't be feeling this way about her, not when he had a girlfriend. She wasn't here, but that didn't mean Blake could entertain such thoughts about another woman.

He put Lauren out of his mind, which was easy as Grant said, "Miss Linda," in his gushing, salesman voice. Blake knew it, because he'd often used a voice like that when entertaining potential new clients. "Look at you out of the house." He glanced over to Blake, because Grant knew the story behind Blake's mother's presence.

He rolled his eyes, but Momma said, "Yes, the warden approved some released time."

"Momma," Blake started, but his defense got drowned out by Grant's hearty laughter. His daughter Shelby stood next to him, and she laughed too.

Blake glared at his mother, then Grant, who finally stopped laughing.

"Let me get you a lemonade," Grant said. "Mango or strawberry?"

"Raspberry," Blake and Momma said together, and their eyes met. Grant and Shelby moved away, and Blake reached over and squeezed her hand. "I love you, Momma."

"I love you too, son," she said, softening like melting butter in the microwave.

Satisfied that he wouldn't have to endure the evening with a Grumpy Gus, he pulled out his phone and navigated to Camille's name. He didn't know how to break up with her via text. They'd been dating for months. Didn't he owe her a personal, face-to-face explanation?

Listen, he tapped out. *I'm not sure things are working between us. Should we go to dinner and talk about things between us?*

Camille responded lightning-quick, the way she usually did. He really liked that, because he hated being on the hook when he had hard texting conversations. *We don't need to go out just to break up.*

Blake's eyebrows went up. *Do you want to break up?*

Like you said, I'm not really feeling things between us either.

Blake didn't know how to respond to that. Should he

confirm that he'd gotten the text? Like, *Great. We're not together anymore. Thanks for the good times.*

That sounds so ridiculous in his head, and he didn't let his fingers type that out.

Okay, he did type. *Well, no hard feelings?*

None, she said, and just like that, Blake tucked his phone under his leg and looked over to Lauren again. She sat about twenty feet from him, which was close enough to observe without being creepy or too obvious.

She wore almost no red, but plenty of blue and white. Only her shoes were a crimson canvas with a white star on the top, and he found her classic and sophisticated. He hadn't spoken to her much last year, but he knew she worked in the corporate world too, just like him.

He wondered if she had a boyfriend, but she'd never brought anyone to Hilton Head with her. Of course, taking a trip together from Texas to South Carolina would require a very serious boyfriend, and she could have a new boyfriend or one she wasn't ready to take trips with back in Texas.

Someone like her... She could *easily* have a boyfriend back in Texas. Probably two or three.

He stopped his thinking there, because Grant returned with his mother's lemonade, and he pulled his chair up next to Blake. "So," Grant said. "Bea has her Supper Club tomorrow, and I was thinking we should grill at Harrison's."

"Is that what you were thinkin'?" Harrison asked.

"I bought all the food this afternoon," Grant said with a grin. "I have Shelby, so kids are welcome." He looked at Blake.

"Tommy's with his mother," Blake said, to which Grant nodded.

"Just us then," he said.

"I can invite Scott," Harrison said, lifting his eyebrows. "Anderson."

"Sure," Grant said. "I'll text Oliver too. He's usually down for a good barbecue, and he can bring smoothies to keep us cool."

A plan came together, and Blake simply went along with it. Grant was one step away from Bea, who was intimately connected to Lauren, and Blake just needed to figure out how to erase the distance between them without being too obvious.

Chapter Fourteen

Cass stepped over the threshold of the sliding door, her hands full of the biggest bowl of fruit salad she'd ever made. Everything here on the island tasted better, and she wasn't sure if that was really true or was a placebo effect due to the sun, sand, and surf.

It didn't matter. She adored a good fruit salad anyway, and this one had reds, yellows, oranges, greens, and purples. It was gorgeous, and she set it on the table where her friends had already gathered. "That's everything," she said. She didn't take a seat, but instead stayed on her feet, hoping to draw everyone's attention.

Bea looked up at her, saw something Cass couldn't guess at, and said, "Ladies. Ladies! Settle down."

The chatter dried up, and all eyes turned to Cass. She cleared her throat. "I have a few pieces of news."

No one said anything, which was probably a record for them. Someone usually had *something* to say, something snarky or that they had realized something was off. She met Lauren's eyes, who nodded slightly.

Of course Lauren had seen the chemistry between her and Harrison. The woman saw *every*thing. It was why she was so good at her job and why she had never gotten married. Some might call her *picky*, but Cass liked to label her *detailed*. And the details mattered a great deal.

"I, uh, went out with Harrison Tate last week." There. She'd said it. Pulled the pin on the grenade and thrown it. All that was left was to wait for it to explode.

It took one, two, three seconds for Bea to press her palms to the table and stand up. She faced her. "You did what?"

"She went out with Harrison," Lauren said, her voice almost bored.

"It wasn't really 'out,'" Cass said, her hands winding together. "He made dinner for us at his house." She looked at Joy, who looked like she'd seen a ghost. Bessie started to nod, her acceptance coming faster.

"Good for you," Sage said. "You're a good woman and have plenty of life to live." She nodded, her wise eyes smiling at Cass. "Good for you, Cass, and Harrison seems really nice."

"He *is* nice," Cass said, her gaze flying back to Bea's. Why did she look like she'd just sucked on a lemon? "What's wrong with me going out with Harrison?"

"Nothing," Bea said innocently. Her voice pitched way too high, and Cass sank into her appointed chair.

"Sit down," she said to Bea. "We might as well eat while you lecture me."

"I'm not going to lecture you." Bea sat down too. "I'm just surprised."

"Join the club," Joy said almost under her breath. Cass's gaze flew to her. Joy didn't sound very happy about the relationship, and Cass wondered why.

"Why is me going out with someone surprising?" Cass asked.

"Not someone," Bea said slowly. She reached for the platter of sandwiches and plucked one section from the very middle. No one would want the butt of the six-foot sub, not even Cass herself. It was always too dry, without enough mayo and mustard on the meat. Maybe Conrad would eat it.

He'd gone down the street after Grant had told him about a "men's grilling night" at Harrison's, and Cass looked to her right. She couldn't see down the beach, as houses, pools, and backyards sat in her way. Not only that, but the coast curved around to the left, which meant his house actually sat in front of hers geographically.

The thought of her son down the street with her boyfriend—she stalled there. Harrison was not her boyfriend. They hadn't held hands or kissed. They'd been on one date—a really good date, but just the singular one.

"...that's all I'm saying," Bea said.

Cass had missed what she'd said. "Sorry," she said, looking at her friend. "I missed that."

"I said, I don't think Harrison is...quite your type."

Cass blinked at her. "And what type is that?"

"He does have a house in the community," Bessie said.

Cass's eyes flew to hers. "Are you saying he's not good enough for me?" She lifted her chin and glared at Bea. "Because that's ridiculous. The man owns his own construction firm here on the island. Even if he didn't, I wouldn't care. I don't need some rich celebrity to take care of me."

Bea shook her head and reached for the cheddar and sour cream potato chips. "That's not what I meant."

"What did you mean, then?"

"I meant, he's...he is more working class than business class. He's not like West at all."

"What makes you think I want a man like West?" Cass asked.

Silence draped over the table now, and Cass filled her plate with all the things a good picnic should have—potato salad, fruit salad, a hunk of sandwich, potato chips, and sweet tea. She'd spread a red-and-white checkered tablecloth over the patio furniture too, and she'd stopped by a florist that morning to get a vase of fresh flowers for the centerpiece.

She'd bought everything except the salads, which she'd made with Bessie that afternoon. Bea had brought the sweet tea, and Cass lifted her glass to her lips. "I loved West," Cass said. "I love him. Not past tense. But Harrison doesn't have to be like him for me to like him. It's kind of exciting to be exploring something different." She speared a strawberry and looked down the table. Everyone watched her, and she let a somewhat naughty smile touch her face. "It's like an adventure."

Lauren smiled first and shook her head. "I think it's great, Cass."

"Thank you," she said, looking to Joy.

Joy nodded and said, "I'm glad you told us before I made a fool of myself."

Cass frowned. "Why would you have done that?"

"She wants a Hilton Head summer boyfriend," Bessie said, grinning. She giggled, and Joy swatted her arm. "I asked

Harrison if he was single yesterday morning on the boat, and he said yes." Her eyebrows went up.

"We haven't told anyone," Cass said, her gaze moving to Bea. "Sorry, Bea. Don't be mad. I just needed...a day or two."

"A week," Bea said, eyebrows cocked.

"I needed a week," Cass amended.

"She's not mad," Lauren said. "She likes being the first to know, so she's stinging. She'll find a way through it." She popped a green grape into her mouth, and Cass marveled that she could say things so bluntly and act like they didn't also cause a sting.

Bea gave her a sharp look, and Lauren did have the decency to look a tad ashamed. She turned back to Cass and covered her hand. "I am happy for you. It will be a grand summer adventure."

"You got yours," Cass said. "Maybe I'll get a happily-ever-after too." She picked up her sandwich then and took a big bite.

"What about Conrad?" Sage asked, and Cass very nearly choked.

She shook her head and hastily put her turkey and provolone back on her plate. "I haven't told Conrad. Or the girls. Or anyone but the five of you. So, this is something we have to keep between us."

Everyone nodded, but then Bessie said, "No one in Texas will care."

"Are you kidding?" Cass asked. "My parents live there. My sister. My kids know a ton of people." She shook her head. "No. You can't just be casually talking about who I'm dating, even in Sweet Water Falls."

"Who you're dating?"

Cass yelped at the sound of Conrad's voice, and she spun in her chair. Sure enough, her son stood there, his face turning a shade of purple a human face should never be. "Conrad." She shoved her chair back and got to her feet. Her right ankle twinged in pain as she hurried across the expansive patio.

Her son turned and went back inside, his anger floating on the air and slamming into her as she followed him. "Conrad," she said. "Wait."

"Wait?" He spun back to her, and Cass quickly slid the door closed. Her friends could see right through the glass, but maybe the whole neighborhood wouldn't be able to hear the forthcoming conversation. "You're dating? Who? Someone here? Someone online? Who is he?"

Conrad paced back and forth, his long legs eating up the length of the island in the kitchen and he wore the floor between it and the dining room table. He looked over to her with venom in his eyes. She didn't answer but folded her arms and glared back at him.

He finally paused at the opposite end of the table and copied her pose. "Start talking, Mom."

"First." She held up one finger. "I am your mother, and I deserve more respect than you're currently showing me. Secondly." She pulled out her proper grammar and held up another finger. "I am a grown adult, and I do *not* need your permission to do anything. I can sell that house in Texas. I can move here. I can date anyone I want. You're not *my* father, and I do not have to run anything by you for your approval."

Her chest heaved, but Cass needed to get these things out of her mouth. "I call all of you kids all the time. I make sure you're healthy and happy. I ask you how you're doing. I pay for everything you all need." Her voice almost broke, but she drew in a deep breath to cover it. "Have you asked me how I'm doing this year? You left right after graduation, and I stayed. I stayed in Texas by myself! I'm the one who had to live in that house all alone with everything your father owned. The way his clothes smelled. His half of the bed empty." She gestured right and left with every example of the loneliness and abandonment she'd felt. Her. Not him.

Conrad started to cry, but Cass was past that. Pure anger simmered inside her. "I know you miss your father," she said. "I do too. I've gone to counseling too, Conrad. I've taken steps to heal from losing him, and I'm ready to move on. You can't expect me to live in the past forever."

Her son nodded, and Cass flew toward him and gathered him into a hug. "We can never replace him," she whispered as Conrad sobbed into her shoulder. "I'm not trying to do that. I'm trying to find someone to share my life with again. A friend. A companion. You're busy at college—trying to find someone to share your life with too. Sariah has a life with Robbie. Jane's...well, Jane's trying to find herself, just like the rest of us."

"I'm sorry," Conrad said. He stepped back and wiped his face. He went into the kitchen and flipped on the sink. He splashed water on his face and turned away from her to get a towel. He kept his back to her as he said, "I'm sorry, Mama."

"I haven't told the twins," she said. "I just told the ladies in Supper Club tonight too. You were next."

He faced her again. "If you're willing, I'd like to know who it is."

Cass swallowed and re-folded her arms, pressing them

against her stomach to try to calm it. "It's Harrison, son. Harrison Tate."

"The guy down the street? The construction guy I'm eating dinner with tonight?"

Cass seriously didn't get why everyone only saw that about him. She supposed she wouldn't want her son to find Harrison as sexy as she did. Bea either. Still, they acted like Harrison wasn't worthy. "Yes," she clipped out. "The construction guy. He's sweet and strong and sexy and—"

"Gross, Mom, stop." Conrad held up both hands. "I don't need to hear about how *sexy* he is."

Cass grinned at him but didn't say anything else. She and her son looked at each other across the kitchen, and Conrad finally relaxed.

"Why did you come home?" she asked.

"Harrison doesn't have any Miracle Whip for the burgers, and I said we did. Grant asked me to come get it." He opened the fancy fridge. "But I couldn't find it."

"It's not in the fridge," Cass said. "We haven't opened it yet." She moved past the island and the fridge and into the pantry. She plucked the bottle from the shelf there and turned to hand it to her son.

He'd followed her, and she pressed the bottle into his chest. He stood a few inches taller than her, just like West, and she looked up at him. "Conrad," she started, but he shook his head.

"You don't owe me any explanations," he said. "Honest, Mama. I'm sorry." He enfolded her into another hug, this one with less emotion and no tears. She held him as tightly as she could, squeezing her eyes closed in the process. "I'm sorry I abandoned you last year," he said.

"You didn't," she whispered. "I wouldn't have wanted you to do anything different."

He pulled away and peered at her. "Yeah?"

"Yeah," she said. "Of course, Conrad. You're nineteen years old. Your father died. It's terrible and sad, but that doesn't mean you have to live in terrible sadness every day of your life. You don't need to stay here with me. You can go back to Waco and work, find a pretty woman to fall in love with, and make your films. All of that. You have to keep living."

And so did she.

"And so do you," Conrad whispered, to which Cass nodded.

"Yes," she whispered back.

He took the Miracle Whip and backed out of the pantry. "I suppose I have to go back over to that guy's house and pretend like I don't know he's kissing you."

Cass trilled out a laugh. "We're not kissing, Conrad. I've known him for about a month, and we've been on one date."

"So you don't approve of kissing on the first date?" Conrad asked, his eyes twinkling with mischief.

"Conrad, you be nice to the girls in Waco."

He laughed, and Cass found that wildly better than watching her son cry. "I'm nice, Mama." He went toward the front door, and Cass watched him go. She sagged against the couch in the living room as the front door closed, and then she looked up to the vaulted ceiling.

"That could've gone better," she said. But gone it had.

"Cass," Bea said gently. "You okay in here?"

She turned and faced her friend, then the backyard.

"Yes," she said, though she wanted to call it a night. She wouldn't see her Supper Club until the third week of August, and she walked toward Bea. "I'm okay."

Bea drew her into a hug and said, "I didn't mean to imply Harrison wasn't good enough for you. He's a great man."

"Thank you," Cass whispered. She stepped back and looked into Bea's bright blue eyes. "We've been on one date, Bea. One. And I'm not calling you every night to tell you what happened. Or didn't happen."

"Of course not," Bea said. "Though I would like to remind you that I told all of you about me and Grant."

"Not immediately," Cass argued back. "And besides, I'm not you, Bea."

"Leave her alone," Lauren called from the patio. "Come eat, you guys. Supper Club isn't Supper Club if we're not all together."

Cass gestured for Bea to exit the house first, which she did. Cass followed her, pulled the door closed, and rejoined her friends at the table. She cleared her throat and sat up straight and tall. "So Conrad now knows. I'll call the twins in the morning, and then I suppose I'll have to tell my parents and Liz." She looked at her plate and tried to recenter herself in the meal.

She looked up and surveyed her friends. She reached over and took Bea's hand in her right one, and then Bessie's in her left. "I love you guys," she said, a wave of emotion overcoming her. The tears she'd warned Harrison about made an appearance, but this was her Supper Club. If she couldn't cry with them, who could she weep with?

"Thank you for adjusting the date for me this month,

and thank you for coming to Hilton Head for Independence Day."

"It's been amazing," Sage said earnestly. "Right, ladies?"

"I'm staying," Lauren blurted out. Cass wasn't surprised, but she hadn't been expecting Lauren to tell anyone about her summer plans quite yet. "I mean, I have to go back to Sweet Water Falls to tie up a few things in the office there, and get more clothes, but I'll be back by next weekend." She drew in a full breath and looked only at Cass.

"The house is ready for you," Cass said. "Everything was delivered as promised, and your bedroom is ready." She and Conrad had been living in the house since Tuesday, which was by the skin of their teeth, and Lauren and Joy were staying here with them, while Sage and Bessie had bunked with Bea.

Lauren cut a look at Joy, which drew Cass's attention there too. Joy hid behind her mason jar of sweet tea and said nothing, and Cass decided she didn't have to worry about things she didn't know. Not tonight, with everything else going on. Not until Joy confided in her, and Cass had more facts.

"So," Bea said. "When are you seeing Harrison again?"

"I don't know," Cass said. "It's been busy with everyone here, and me and Conrad getting the house set up, and..." She shrugged. "I don't know."

"Maybe breakfast tomorrow," Lauren suggested.

"You guys, I can handle my life," Cass said, annoyed already that she'd told them about Harrison. "Okay? I don't need suggestions, and I don't need you intruding."

"She's lecturing again," Sage said. "Let's talk about something else." She gave Cass a friendly smile and added,

"Like the fact that tomorrow we can sleep in and then spend all day basking in the sun." She spread her arms wide and tilted her head back.

Cass laughed with a few of the others, because they'd been doing that for two days already. Sage loved the beach as well, and the conversation picked up and moved on to other things. Relief flooded Cass, and while she still had to make a couple of calls to her family to tell them about Harrison, she was glad she wasn't keeping secrets from her friends anymore.

As the chatter continued around her, she texted Harrison quickly. *How are things going over there? Conrad knows about us.*

Yes, we've had a little talk about it, Harrison responded. *Nothing's burned down so far. So I'm counting that as a win.*

Cass smiled at her phone, aware of at least one woman watching her. *What do you think about us going to breakfast tomorrow? Even if you only have a couple of minutes, maybe we could grab coffee and pastries from that place you've been telling me about.*

"Who are you texting?" Bessie asked.

"I'm setting up my second date." Cass glanced over to her. She looked down the table to Lauren. "Breakfast, like Lauren said."

Her phone buzzed, and she looked at it. *Gourmet Goods,* Harrison said. *I can swing by about seven? I have to be on-site by eight. Time enough for coffee and pastries?*

What kind of pastries? she teased, hoping he could catch the flirting in the printed text.

Pain au chocolat, he responded. *Almond croissants. Banana bread pudding.*

She laughed and showed her phone to Bessie. "I think he's speaking your love language, not mine."

Bessie smiled at the texts too. "If there's a place with banana bread pudding here on the island, I want to try it." She looked across the table to Bea. "We'll go at say, nine? Then we won't run into Cass on her date."

"She can come too." Bea stretched across the table and snatched Cass's phone. "Because I bet Harrison has to go early." She scanned the device. "Yep. She'll be done with her date at eight. So she can fill us all in at nine."

Cass grabbed her phone back and said, "Maybe." Then she told Harrison she'd see him at seven o'clock in the morning. After that, she was finally able to relax at Supper Club, and she enjoyed it more than she had in a long, long time.

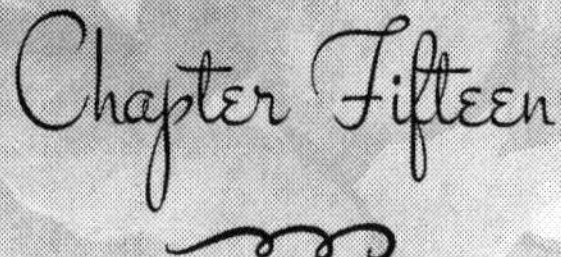

Chapter Fifteen

Harrison pulled into Cass's driveway the next morning before seven. Probably ten or fifteen minutes early, and yet she sat on the top step, her knees tucked almost all the way to her chest as she studied her phone.

He wished his vehicle was silent so he could observe her for a few moments, but she heard his engine or his tires on the stone or both and looked up. A smile popped onto her face, and she got to her feet.

Harrison had no words for a woman as sophisticated as her. She wore a pair of light blue pants that seemed made just for her body. They tapered at the ankle, and she wore a pair of white, strappy sandals that showed off her bright pink toenails.

Her top matched the pants and had obviously come as a set. It looked like a fitted jacket with a bright white zipper up the front, which she'd done up just past her chest. He caught a hint of cleavage as she stood, and he told himself to stop staring and get out of the truck.

He did that, barely meeting her as she reached the bottom of the steps. He couldn't help touching her, because the fabric on these clothes looked like it would be really soft—and it was. He ran his hand along her hip and then up her back. He leaned in and took a deep breath of her hair and skin, saying, "Mm, you look amazing this morning," in a low voice.

She put one hand on his bicep, creating an intimate circle between them. Harrison had forgotten what it felt like to be part of a couple, to be able to move in and have this level of closeness with another human being. His heart beat mighty hard, and happiness flowed through him.

He felt good about himself when he was with someone else. And someone of Cass's caliber...she made him feel like a million bucks.

"Thank you," she said, stepping back. She scanned him down to his work boots and back. "You look great too."

He chuckled and shook his head. "Right. In my company T-shirt and steel-toed boots. I'm sure I'm the sexiest man on the island." He laughed louder and moved to open the passenger door for her. He didn't step back out of the way, but instead reached inside and picked up the bag of boiled peanuts he'd stopped at Claire's to get for her.

He turned and held them out to her. Her smile had faded, but it came roaring back. "Harrison," she said. She took the peanuts and lifted one to her mouth. "I love these things."

"I know you do." He did move out of the way then to allow her access to his truck. "I figured you could snack on them all day. What are you up to today?" He glanced at her house as if Lauren and Joy would be standing there watching. He didn't see them, but that didn't mean they couldn't see him.

He faced Cass again and took the opportunity to put his hand on her back as she got into the truck. She twisted to put the peanuts on the seat beside her, then whipped her attention back to him. "There's a bottle of peach iced tea here."

He grinned at her. "No sugar, sweetheart." He knew what she liked, and as she softened and said, "Thank you," he knew she liked being taken care of too. Harrison really liked doing that for her, which surprised him somewhat. He went around the truck, telling himself that just because he hadn't been terribly romantic with Claudia didn't mean he had to have that type of relationship with every woman.

Cass was a completely different person than Claudia, and she sparked different wants and needs inside Harrison.

He got behind the wheel and looked at her as he pulled his seatbelt across his body. "Ready?"

"We don't need to go to Gourmet Goods if you brought all of this."

"Oh, we're going," he said. He backed up and turned around in her driveway. "Those are for later today, Cass. When your friends are driving you insane and you need a quiet moment." He gave her a smile and pulled onto the street.

"How do you know my friends will drive me nuts today?"

"It's inevitable," he said simply. "It's not a commentary on them." He cut a look at her, suddenly nervous. "It's just... they've been here for two days already, and we're goin' out this morning, and I'm assuming they'll have questions." He swallowed, because he'd had to answer a lot of questions last night once Conrad had come back with the Miracle Whip. Everyone on Hilton Head would know about his relationship with Cass by nightfall, he was sure. Oliver and Grant knew now, and they knew just about every local on the island.

Thankfully, it was summer, and the tourists didn't care about who dated whom, even if one of those people was a widow who'd lost her husband sixteen months ago.

"They will have a lot of questions." She popped another peanut into her mouth. "Sorry about Conrad."

"We already talked about it," he said. "You don't need to apologize again." She had last night, after her Supper Club had ended. After Conrad had gone home. After Harrison had gone to bed. He'd set her notification to something glamorous and glitzy, and when his phone had made that noise close to eleven p.m., he'd rolled over and picked it up.

He and Cass had texted for almost an hour before she'd finally told him to go to bed, and he stifled a yawn right now. "So what are you doing today?"

"The beach," she said. "Bea has a kite she wants to show us. We're going this morning, and then we're going to hit the shopping this afternoon." She smiled, and Harrison nodded.

"You like shopping?"

"I do," she said, though it was a little slow. "We lived in a small town in Texas. Not really a big shopping place, with good fashion or anything."

"You probably got good at doing things online," he said.

"That's what I was going to say." She laughed for a moment or two. "I'm really good at shopping online to get what I like."

"Well, that outfit is gangbusters," he said, looking over to her again. He licked his lips. "You seriously look like a model in it."

She laughed fully then, shaking her head. "That's not true."

"Oh, it's true."

She tucked her dark hair behind her ear, revealing a large gold hoop earring. She had everything together from head to toe, and Harrison did feel completely out of his league in that moment.

"What do you turn to when your friends are driving you insane?" she asked.

"Cheeseburgers," he said. "Chocolate-covered pretzels." He grinned. "I have a full shelf in my pantry filled with chocolate-covered pretzels."

"Wow," she said. "Scandalous."

He laughed. "If you try to take some, I'll know. I have the bags numbered."

"I wouldn't dare." She crossed her legs, and Harrison dang near drove them off the road. "Favorite beverage?"

"Am I driving or not driving?"

"You're driving," she said. "You have to go to work or out dancing with your girlfriend." She gave him a look filled with flirtatiousness, but panic struck Harrison right between the ribs.

"I don't dance," he said. "But if I had to take my girlfriend fishing or to the movies, I'd drink Diet Dr. Pepper."

"Fishing?" Cass sounded horrified. "Do I look like a woman who'd like fishing?"

"Yes," he said without hesitation. "You look like a woman who hasn't given fishing a chance, and if she would, she'd like it." He grinned at her. "I'll bring all the peach iced tea, boiled peanuts, and chocolate-covered pretzels."

She laughed now too, and Harrison reached over and took her hand in his. He drew it all the way to his lips and kissed the back of it as she quieted. "So." He cleared his throat. "Are you my girlfriend?"

"I...don't know," Cass said. "Am I?"

"I'm not seeing anyone else," he said. He wanted to look at her, but he had to drop her hand and keep his eyes on the road as he went around a curve at a speed that was a little too fast. He applied the brakes and prayed he wouldn't whiplash her around.

"I'm obviously not either," Cass said.

Harrison swallowed, but his throat was so dry, the walls of it stuck together slightly. "This is only our second date," he said. "Maybe you'll decide you're out of my league by the end of the hour."

"I doubt it."

"Maybe you won't like any of the things I do." He looked at her now. "Like fishing or movies."

"I adore movies. I could be persuaded to try fishing." She shook her hair over her shoulder as if puffing herself up, prepping to do the dreaded fishing.

"I won't make you bait the hook," he promised.

She grinned at him. "Deal."

"Maybe I won't be a good kisser." Harrison shrugged one shoulder like he really might not be able to land a kiss. He knew with a woman like Cass, it would have to be the most amazing kiss of her life. She wanted—and probably got —the best of everything.

Harrison suddenly needed to know more about her husband. How could he ever compare to West?

You don't need to, he told himself, but it wasn't in a very convincing voice.

"Maybe you won't be," she said in a non-committal tone.

Harrison wanted to defend himself. "I guess we'll find out."

"Will we?" she teased.

"Eventually," he said, not wanting to imply that he'd be kissing her immediately or anything. He'd been thinking about it, of course, but he could control himself. For a while.

Hilton Head Gourmet Goods came into view, and Harrison said, "Here we are," before Cass could respond about when she might allow him to kiss her. He pulled into the lot, which wasn't terribly full for this early in the morning. In a couple of hours, it would be insane, and Gourmet Goods would sell out by noon.

"You get whatever you want, okay?" he asked. "I don't care if we only have one bite. If you want to try it, we get it."

"I like the way you think," she said, already unbuckling her seatbelt though he hadn't come to a complete stop in a spot yet. He did, and they got out of the truck and headed inside.

He reached for her hand, glad when she secured her fingers between his, as if she wanted to hold his hand. "You have nice hands," she said.

Harrison had no idea how to respond to that. "Thanks," he said, not wanting to be unaccepting of the compliment.

Only a couple of people waited in line ahead of them,

and he pointed out the fruit tarts, the almond croissants, and the treasured *pain au chocolat*.

When it was their turn to order, he rattled off a half-dozen pastries he wanted and looked at Cass. Her eyes had gone wide, and he chuckled. "I said whatever you want."

"I think you covered it."

"I didn't get the raspberry mousse tart."

"Then one of those."

He nodded to the woman behind the register—Susan May—and pulled out his credit card. "And two coffees, please." Gourmet Goods had plenty of sugar, cream, and flavored syrups on their coffee bar.

"Oh, and Susie, can I get two dozen beignets for the boys on site?"

"Sure thing, Harry." She smiled at him, twisted, and yelled over her shoulder. "Beignets for Harrison Construction." She faced him again and took his card. She ran it while a teenaged girl started picking their order.

Susie handed his card back, and Harrison said. "We'll be here for a bit. Bring the doughnuts out whenever."

"You got it." She looked past him to the next customer, and Harrison nodded Cass down the counter.

"They'll bring them out when they've got them," he said, guiding her with his hand on her back again. "Let's sit by the window over here. It has an amazing view of the park. You might even see some birds."

They took a table for two that likely wouldn't hold their pastries, and Harrison tucked his wallet back in his pocket and sat across from Cass.

"Harry?" she asked, eyebrows moving up.

"She's a local."

"So do all locals call you Harry?"

"Just the ones I grew up with," he said. Their coffee arrived, and Harrison got up to get sugar and cream. "Do you want flavoring?"

"This might be odd, but if they have coconut, I'd take that."

"I'll look." Harrison brought over the sugar substitute packets and the real cream, and then he studied the syrup bottles. He spied coconut and lifted it from the tray.

Back at the table, Cass stirred cream into her cup and then put in one pump of coconut syrup.

"Coconut cream," he said.

"It's like the beach in a coffee cup," she said.

"Fascinating."

"I suppose you're a coffee purist."

"Lots of sugar," he said. Lifting the real, raw sugar packets. "Not the fake stuff either." He poured in three of them and grinned at her. "If that's a purist move, then yes."

"No cream?"

"No, ma'am." Harrison stirred his coffee and lifted his cup to his lips. Their display of pastries arrived, and Harrison clapped his hands together. "Here we go."

Cass giggled, and when their eyes met, Harrison would've sworn he saw all the way inside her soul. Sure, she was classy and put together. She might be out of his league, but she was also a human being, and she wanted to enjoy good food, good company, and be loved.

Harrison felt himself falling, and he did nothing to stop it. In fact, he gave her the softest smile he'd ever given someone, and nudged the box toward her. "You pick first," he said, his voice almost a whisper.

She brightened and said, "Oh, I'm going in for the *chocolat*."

Harrison grinned and watched her lift the lucky pastry to her lips. She took a big old bite, further obliterating his view that she was picky and prissy, and then her eyes rolled back in her head as she moaned. With her mouth full, she couldn't speak, but she nodded as she chewed, a bright light in her dark eyes.

"Good?" he asked.

She swallowed, but still had plenty of *pain au chocolat* in her mouth when she said, "So good," and extended the bitten-off pastry to him.

He took it and took an equally big bite, his taste buds exploding with flaky, salty pastry, ooey gooey chocolate, and crispy edges along the corner.

He likewise moaned, and Cass giggled while she picked out another pastry.

An hour later, Harrison had his two dozen beignets for the boys at work, and Cass had their leftovers from breakfast sitting on her lap.

Back at her house, Harrison said, "Wait for me, okay?" and jumped down from the truck. He jogged around to open the door for her, then took the boxes so she could get down. He put his doughnuts back in the cab and carried her pastries toward the front door. They went up the steps together, and Harrison's throat clogged with the things he wanted to say.

"That was the best breakfast I've had in a long time," Cass said, smiling. "Thank you, Harrison."

"I don't think you eat breakfast," he teased. "So of course that was the best one you've had in a while."

"It was more than that." She took the pale blue pastry box from him, and it matched her clothes. She set it on the bench outside the front door and looked at him. Something edged her eyes, but Harrison couldn't read it very well.

He wanted to hug her, so he drew her body against his and held her there. "I miss you already," he whispered. "When can we go out again?"

Cass breathed in deeply and held him close, so Harrison didn't let go. "It's Saturday tomorrow," she whispered. "Are you working?"

"I'll have to go in at least a little." He stepped back, his hands sliding down to her hands. He held them both and looked at her. "Are you guys hitting the beach again?"

"We're doing a tour in the morning," she said. "Then, yes. A lazy afternoon on the beach, and Grant promised us a big feast, because I guess one of his clients is having a huge summer bash and there will be lots of leftovers."

"It's the Sandcomber Beach Bash," Harrison said. "I'll come sit on the beach with you. Hang out with everyone."

"It's a date." Cass smiled at him. "I'll text you where we are tomorrow afternoon."

"Sounds good." He should leave, but he couldn't force himself to do it. Cass didn't move either. Harrison slid his hands up her arms and took her face in his hands. "I hope I don't crash and burn on this."

He leaned forward, catching sight of Cass's eyes drifting closed just before his did.

He touched his lips to Cass's, hoping he'd remember what to do.

Turned out, he did. Fire licked down his throat, igniting every cell in his body. His hormones raged at him, and he stepped closer and pulled Cass flush against him with one hand. He kept that hand on her back as he kissed her harder, faster, deeper.

And since he couldn't stop, and she wasn't pulling away, he kept kissing her and kissing her.

Chapter Sixteen

Cass kissed Harrison back with as much fervor as he gave her. His kiss started out like an explosion, and she definitely felt that heat driving through her veins. He settled the stroke into something powerful and beautiful, and Cass felt cherished and sexy and valued with every touch and breath they took together.

She finally pulled herself together and remembered she stood on her front porch, with her son and two of her friends just behind the door to her right. She ducked her head and broke the kiss, Harrison's ragged breathing now in her ear.

She had no idea what to say, because it felt like that kiss had said it all. It had voiced all the passion and teasing and flirtatiousness between them. It had screamed about her desire for him and his pure male attraction to her. It had broadcast to both of them that this wasn't casual, or something for only the summer, or that didn't have the potential to be long-lasting and fiery hot at the same time.

She finally looked up at him, those deep green eyes looking for some confirmation. "You're not a bad kisser," she said, her voice caught somewhere in her throat.

Harrison laughed in that sexy, low voice of his that made her female cells vibrate and hum. "You don't have to say that."

"One of the best kissers I've ever kissed," she said. "And I'm not saying anything I don't have to say."

Harrison ducked his head, his breath flowing over her shoulder. She wished she'd worn something sleeveless so she could feel it, be skin to skin. "Kissing definitely makes you my girlfriend," he whispered.

"Okay," she whispered back. Then she guided his head up so she could kiss him again. As she sank into the touch and let him hold her up while he explored her lips—oh, yes, he was a good kisser—Cass let herself fall for him a little.

Just a little, so it wouldn't hurt too badly when she had to let him go to work and face her reality for the day.

"I'm just going to get some more sunscreen," she said later that day. Joy and Lauren watched her, and Cass simply needed to get away from them. Harrison had been right. They were driving her crazy, and it was only three p.m. Shopping with six women was always a bit of a mess, especially with strong personalities like Bea's, Lauren's, and Cass's.

Yes, she could admit she had a strong personality. She liked things her way, and she ducked into an awful souvenir shop she'd normally never enter. Maybe this way, no one would follow her.

She'd told Bessie and Sage she didn't need a babysitter. She didn't need a care companion. She was fine, and she could take care of herself here on Hilton Head. Having everyone here almost felt suffocating, and she wiped her hand along the back of her neck and took a long breath.

The woman behind the counter barely looked at her, and Cass ducked between two aisles to further conceal herself. If she stayed in here too long, she'd get bombarded with texts. And she better come out with whatever she'd said she needed.

The problem was, she couldn't remember what that was right now. A tiny chair, one made for a child, sat at the end of the aisle, and Cass sank into it. She pulled out her phone and texted Conrad about their mother-son dinner date that night.

He responded with, *Yep, I'm planning on it. I think I got a job today.*

Confusion ran through Cass. *A job?*

Right here on the island. They needed someone to lead bike tours, and I guess I impressed them on a mountain bike. He sent some laughing emojis, but Cass didn't know how to respond. He was going to stay for the summer? Or for...how long?

Cass tapped to call him, and Conrad answered laughing. "Hey, Mama. Yeah, it's my mom." Someone on the other end of the line said something she couldn't decipher, and then their voice faded away.

"You got a job here?"

"Yeah," Conrad said. "It's with this guy, Ryan Royce.

He owns an outdoor tour company, and I ran into him at the gym."

"He just recruited you for a job?" Cass asked. She didn't think so. Conrad had to be doing something, and he often did stand out in a crowd.

"He saw me using the weights," Conrad said. Cass read between the lines. *Everyone* had seen him using the weights. Conrad worked out constantly, and he had West's tall, lean body, so his muscles really stood out.

Cass reached up and rubbed her forehead. "You made *a scene* at the gym." She wasn't asking.

"It was a heavy lift," Conrad said. He laughed. "Mama, I got a job."

"That's great," she said. "Really. I'm glad." She didn't ask him how long he'd be in Hilton Head. School started at Baylor just after Labor Day, so it could only last for two months. "You'll need to go get some more clothes."

"I'm gonna have Ben mail me some things," Conrad said. Of course. Why fly back to your dorm in Waco when your roommate can box up a few things and put them in the mail?

"Sounds good," she said, because Conrad didn't need advice. He just needed support. "When do you start?"

"Tomorrow morning," he said. "I'm gonna be here for a few more hours to do some training, and then I'll be doing a tour in the morning with another guide."

"Great," Cass said. "I'm shopping right now, and we can move dinner or cancel it if you're busy." She didn't want him to be busy and miss their dinner, but if he did, she could see Harrison again... Cass pulled in a slow breath and held it.

"I'll talk to Ryan and let you know."

"Okay, talk soon." Cass ended the call and looked at her phone. Surprisingly, none of her friends had texted her. Yet.

She got to her feet and wandered down the aisle. In a kitschy shop like this, the sunscreen would be at the counter, and she asked for some. The woman sold her an overpriced spray bottle of the stuff, and Cass went to rejoin her friends.

Lauren and Joy waited on the bench where Cass had left them, and she held up the bottle as she approached. "They're still not out?"

"Bessie can get lost and die in a kitchen store," Lauren said dryly. Cass sank onto the bench beside her. She smiled and agreed. Lauren went right back to her phone, as she usually did in down times. Her job kept her running, to be sure, but Cass glanced over to find her texting with someone, not checking and answering email.

She also didn't wear her normal frown or look of consternation while she dealt with clients or coworkers. Now, she wore a smile, her eyes filled with delight.

"Who are you texting?" Cass asked, because she'd seen a woman in this situation before. Most recently, her daughter who'd gotten married last fall.

Lauren looked up, her joy washing right out of her eyes. "No one." She tucked her phone under her leg, the conversation over just like that.

"Oh, come on," she said. "You don't have to stop texting him."

"How do you know it's a man?"

"You should see your face," Cass teased.

Lauren gave her a dry look, her eyes filled with knowledge. "I didn't ask you anything about your face when you came in from your date this morning." She kept her voice low, but Joy sat on her other side, not that far away.

Cass didn't need to keep secrets. She just didn't want to be hounded to death. "Yeah, and what did you see?"

"Your lip gloss was all smeared." Lauren took her phone out from under her leg.

"You floated all over the house," Joy added, her smile nearly blinding. "You obviously kissed Harrison with coffee breath."

Cass laughed, which made the other two do the same. "I did," she said. She grinned at her friends. "And he was *delicious*." She giggled again, and Lauren linked her arm through Cass's and leaned into her.

They all sighed together, which caused them to dissolve into another round of laughter. When they quieted again, Lauren said, "So this is nothing yet. Really, it's not." She flipped her phone over and over in her free hand. "Since I'm going to be here for a few months, when this guy asked for my number, I gave it to him. We've been texting."

"'This guy'?" Cass asked. "Who? You've been glued to my hip for days."

Joy said nothing, but she and Cass exchanged a glance. "I know who it is."

Cass could admit she'd been wrapped up in her own life lately. Since West had died, really. Between moving here, dealing with Conrad's ire, calling her twins all the time, having her friends come into town, and starting a new relationship, and Cass hadn't noticed as much as she otherwise might have. "Who?" she asked. "Wait. You don't have to tell us. If you want to keep it to yourself right now, that's fine." Cass squeezed Lauren's arm against her ribs.

"Really. I know you like to keep things private for a while."

"I do," Lauren said. "But he wants to go out tonight, and I'd like to go..." She looked at Cass with wide eyes, then turned and looked at Joy, clearly seeking permission.

"Then go," Cass said. "I'm going to dinner with Conrad." She switched her gaze to Joy. "I don't know what everyone else is doing."

"Bea and Grant have something with his sister," she said. "Bessie is making dinner for me and Sage at your house."

"See?" Cass said. "You could go."

Lauren kept her eyes on Joy. "You think so?" She and Joy had a special relationship, and if Joy didn't think Lauren should go, she'd tell her.

"I think you should go if you'd like," Joy said. "It's going to be finger foods, Bessie said. She won't mind."

Lauren nodded and extracted her arm from Cass's. She looked down at her phone, swiped it on, and started texting again. Cass leaned over in a really obvious way to see who she was talking to, and the name *Beach Body Blake* sat at the top of the screen.

Oh, and those texts... Flirty. *Very* flirty.

Cass grinned past Lauren's bent head to Joy, who likewise raised her eyes to Cass's. *Blake*, she mouthed.

Joy grinned and giggled. "Not just Blake," she said right out loud. "*Beach Body* Blake."

Lauren looked up then, but Cass didn't believe for a moment that she hadn't realized she'd been spied on. Cass raised her eyebrows, her smile so wide it hurt her cheeks. "What?" Lauren asked. "He's super-hot. How is that my fault?" Her phone dinged, and her attention flew back to it.

She grinned and leaned back against the bench. "And we're going out tonight." She sighed like she'd just conquered a great enemy. For all Cass knew, she had.

Joy squealed on her behalf, and Cass held up her hand for Lauren to give her a high-five. Once that excitement died down, she looked around again for the other half of their group. "Where *are* they?" she asked. "I'm ready to get out of the sun." This shopping center wasn't her favorite either, and Cass would rather be in the air conditioning, with some of her peach iced tea and boiled peanuts, browsing online.

"There they are," Joy said. She stood and picked up the two bags of things she'd bought. Cass hadn't found anything yet, and she got to her feet too as Bea wove past a slower-moving elderly couple. She wore anxiety on her face, and Cass started toward her.

Her phone chimed too, but she chose Bea over it. "You okay?" she asked.

"Bessie bought an entire set of stoneware," Bea said with some acid in her tone. "There's no way she's getting that back to Texas."

Cass knew instantly that she'd be storing Bessie's cookware at her house until she could get it back to Sweet Water Falls one piece at a time. She looked past Bea to find the others, but Bessie and Sage weren't there.

"We're ready to go," she said. "Does she need us to bring the van around?"

"Yes," Bea said tiredly. "I'll tell you where." They started to walk toward the parking lot, and Cass checked her phone.

Conrad: *I'm going to have to miss dinner, Mama. They want me to go out on an evening boat cruise. Is that okay?*

Her heart leapt right up behind her tongue. Normally,

she'd be disappointed—and she was. She absolutely was. She wanted Conrad to know how very important he was to her—but she was also excited.

No problem, baby, she texted him. *I'll be fine.*

She slowed her step and let Joy, Lauren, and Bea go ahead, Bea still ranting about the "mess of kitchen items" both Sage and Bessie had purchased. "As if we don't have kitchen stores in Texas!" Bea practically yelled.

Cass tapped and stalled beside a big truck, as if it would somehow muffle her voice. Harrison's line rang once, then twice, and she thought he might not answer. At the tail end of the third ring, he said, "Cass. What's goin' on, sweetheart?"

"Listen," she said. "Conrad had to cancel our dinner tonight, and I was hoping you weren't busy... If you're not, we could go out tonight."

"Oh, someone wants to see me again." He laughed, and Cass felt the giddiness prancing through her as she joined in. "Two dates in one day, Cass?"

She turned her back on her friends as Bea twisted to see where she was. She held her head high. "Yeah, two dates in one day. Unless you'd rather spend a few hours with someone else."

"I would not," he said, his voice almost a growl. "I won't have much time to plan something, but I think I can put a decent date together with such late notice all the same."

Cass grinned at the ground. "I can plan something."

"Oh-ho, I don't think so," he said. "Don't worry, Cass. It'll be amazing."

"What will we do?"

"Why do you need to know?" he challenged, his voice full of teasing.

"A woman has to wear certain clothes for certain things," she said, infusing a slight British accent into her words.

He laughed and said, "Normal clothes, Cass."

"So I can't know what you have up your sleeve?"

"Nope," he said. "I'll pick you up at six-thirty."

"Cass," Bea called, and she turned back to her friends.

"I'll come to you," she said. "The girls are having dinner at my house."

"Hm, I don't like that," he said. "But I suppose this one time, it'll be okay."

"Thank you, Mister Southern Gentleman," Cass said dryly. "I'll see you tonight."

"Can't wait," Harrison said, and as she ended the call and prepared to pretend like she'd just talked to anyone but Harrison, she honestly felt like he couldn't wait to see her.

Warm, fuzzy things filled her whole body, and she practically skipped over to Bea. "Sorry. Let's go get Bessie and all of her stuff."

"It isn't even going to fit in here," Bea said.

"Really?" Cass looked at her, shocked. "She bought that much?"

"She bought a *lot*," Bea said, rattling the keys. "Now, get in. We have to get everyone and everything dropped off, and I need to get ready to go to dinner."

Me too, Cass thought, but she kept the words to herself.

Chapter Seventeen

Lauren blew out her hair, brushing it until it lay shiny and straight over her shoulders and down her back. She put in her blue and white earrings that mirrored Chinese pottery. They didn't match her khaki-colored T-shirt dress at all, but once she looped the bright blue belt around her waist, the outfit would come together.

She swept a hint of blue onto her eyelids and applied a deep, dark red lipstick to her lips. It was almost burgundy, and she pressed the creamy stuff between her lips and stepped back from the mirror in the guest bathroom.

Cass's house was *incredible*, and Lauren appreciated the finer things in life. Cass had said she could put a desk in another of the bedrooms for an office, but Lauren didn't want to impose. She'd put the desk in the same bedroom where she slept, because it was certainly large enough.

Satisfied with her appearance, she stepped out of the bathroom and went across the hall to that bedroom. Her suitcase sat open on the stand, but when she moved in next weekend, she'd actually unpack and hang her things in the closet or fold them neatly and put them in the dresser. Lauren loved clean lines and color-coding everything from her novels to office supplies to the pens she used to sign documents.

She unplugged her phone, though it hadn't had a chance to fully charge yet, and headed downstairs. Laughter filled the kitchen, and part of her wanted to stay here with Joy, Bessie, and Sage. She loved all of them, and she wasn't sure why she felt so...hollow without a man in her life.

Even with the boyfriends she'd had and broken up with over the years, she simply knew a friendship wasn't as close or as intimate as a romantic relationship. At least for her.

Sage whistled as Lauren strutted into the kitchen. She did a model walk in her blue heels, paused, cocked a hip, and then spun so violently she almost fell down. She laughed along with everyone else, and Joy began a slow-clap and a chant.

"Hot-tie, hot-tie, hot-tie," she said, her face beaming with light. Lauren's face filled with heat, and she waved off the chant before it could grow real legs. Thankfully.

"You look *amazing*," Joy said. "You had this in your suitcase for this weekend?"

"I had a meeting this morning," Lauren said. "So I packed the dress. The heels are Cass's." She looked down at her shoes. They fit decently well. "And the belt and earrings."

"No wonder they look so good together." Joy scanned her from head to toe. "They probably cost more than my house. Each."

Lauren grinned and shook her head, though Cass didn't

skimp on anything, least of all her jewelry and accessories. She took a deep breath, the moment between her and Joy sobering. She stepped into her and hugged her, feeling the fierceness in Joy's return grip. "I'm sorry," she whispered.

"Don't you dare," Joy whispered back, plenty of hardness in the tone too. She stepped back and held onto Lauren's slight shoulders. "I am okay. I'm jealous, yes, but very happy for you. Blake is handsome and employed, and he doesn't work for you." She smiled. "So go have fun, and I'll be right here on this couch to hear all about it when you get home."

Lauren nodded, her emotions spiraling up to the top of her head and back down to her toes. She hadn't experienced this level of excitement about a first date in a while. Usually, a sense of dread accompanied her getting-ready ritual, as she hadn't met the man in person before, or the conversation via the dating app had been fast and she felt ill-prepared for how the chatter might go.

This was neither of those, and she slicked her hands down the front of her dress and exhaled. "All right," she said. "I'm off."

"He's not picking you up?" Sage asked from her perch on the barstool several feet away.

She shook her head. "We're meeting this first time. He's on his way back to the island from...somewhere. So coming all the way to this side of the island—we decided to meet somewhere so we could eat before midnight." She smiled, because she didn't mind meeting for a first date.

She headed out amidst good cheers from her friends to have fun, not to kiss him, and to be ready to tell them how it had gone, and she settled behind the wheel of her car, glad to be out of the fray. She understood Cass on a whole new level now, and she should've left when Cass did twenty minutes ago. She'd gone to meet Harrison too, so meeting a man for a date wasn't all that abnormal.

Lauren drove to the appointed restaurant and parked. She'd arrived a few minutes early, nervous as she was, and she told herself, "You're okay. You've already talked to this guy lots of times." And she liked him. She knew his favorite color —blue—and how he took his coffee—cream and sugar, nothing more.

She knew his middle name—Harvey—and she knew he had two brothers and a sister. She knew their names, and she knew he'd been living on Hilton Head Island for about two decades. He owned a financial planning firm, and he dressed like he had money. A lot of money.

She was suddenly so glad she had access to Cass's wardrobe to help her dress up her plain clothes. She ran her fingers through her hair and got out of the minivan. Inside the steakhouse, a wall of noise and the scent of salty steak sauce hit her full force in the face. She wanted to walk right back out, but Blake had said this was the best restaurant on the island—and the crowd would probably testify of the same thing.

She waded through the crowd to the hostess station. The woman there looked one breath away from committing homicide, and Lauren had never been happier to have a non-food-service job in her life. "Do you have a reservation?" she asked.

"Yes," Lauren yelled. "Blake Williams? Should be at seven-fifteen."

The woman found the reservation, marked it, and looked at Lauren. "We'll buzz you when the table is ready."

Lauren took the buzzer and smiled as she moved out of the way. All of the seats and benches had been taken, and Lauren didn't have a date to cuddle into. She didn't have a family to laugh with or play a game with as the time passed. She inched her way into a corner where she could see the front entrance, and she waited.

Parties went back, but her buzzer didn't go off. When it finally did, the clock read seven-forty, and Blake was twenty-five minutes late. He hadn't texted yet, and Lauren didn't want to take a table from someone if she wasn't going to use it.

Her stomach grumbled for food, then flipped and swooped at the thought of sitting down at a table alone. She couldn't do it.

She moved over to the hostess station and held out the buzzer. "I'm sorry," she said. "My date isn't here, so I'm not sure if I should..." She let the words hang there, and the near-homicidal woman now wore sympathy in her eyes.

Lauren's jaw hardened. She didn't need that sympathy or empathy. "I'll let you know when he's here," she said, and she dropped the buzzer on the podium.

She turned on her gorgeous heel and left the restaurant, imagining the people to part the way the Red Sea had for the Israelites. They didn't, not really, but in her mind, they did.

Outside, the air had started to cool a little, and the breeze grabbed at her hair the way it always did here. She looked right and left, as if Blake would come rushing up to her. He didn't.

He hadn't texted or called, and Lauren minced her way

back to the horrendous minivan. Perhaps she should've had him pick her up, then she wouldn't be getting stood up at the best restaurant in town.

Safe in the van, she dialed him, her mind racing as fast as her pulse. The phone rang and rang...and rang.

Lauren couldn't go back to Cass's now. Everyone would know that the date hadn't happened or hadn't gone well. "What are you going to do instead?" she asked. "Go get a smoothie and waste a few hours on the beach? Then what? Make up a story about how *amazing* tonight was?"

She shook her head. It would be better to get out of these imposter shoes and the heavy makeup on her face. Then she could cry that everything had been going decently well with Blake via text over the past two days, but that he hadn't been able to force himself to come meet her for dinner.

"Maybe he got back together with his girlfriend," she said. "Or he feels bad that they literally broke up two days ago and he's already going out with you."

She didn't know, but she waited fifteen more minutes, called him again, got no answer, and left the steakhouse parking lot. Back at Cass's house, she texted him that she'd left, and she really hoped he had a good reason for not showing up and not answering his phone.

Then, gathering all of her strength and all of her courage, she got out of the van and went inside the house.

"Who's that?" Bessie asked.

"Just me," Lauren called, immediately kicking off the blue heels. The right one hit the wall too hard and left a mark, but she'd scrub it off later. She went through the foyer and into the living room.

Joy, Bessie, and Sage had come out of the kitchen and stood in a wall, facing her. They all wore wide-eyed surprise on their faces, and Lauren sighed.

"He didn't show up," she said. "He's not answering his phone."

"No." Joy came toward her, and Lauren slumped into her arms after a few steps. "Honey, I'm sorry."

"Maybe he has a good reason," Bessie said.

"It better be a *really* good reason," Sage said, bitterness high in her voice. "Men." She scoffed and went back into the kitchen. "But Lauren, you're in luck. We haven't eaten all of the bacon-wrapped smokies yet." She came into the living room with two little sausages on sticks, a glossy, sticky glaze on them. "Come on, now. Anything can be fixed with meat candy."

Lauren smiled and stepped out of Joy's arms. "Thanks, Sage." She took the meat candy and ate one in a single bite. The salty, the sweet, the crispy bacon, and sticky glaze—all of it made a party in her mouth. "Mm. Whose recipe is this?" She looked between Bessie and Sage.

"That's my sister's," Sage said, grinning.

"You two should put together a cookbook," Lauren said. She continued into the kitchen and sat on a barstool too. An array of food sat on the counter, and it was obvious they'd just been snacking and talking and enjoying one another's company.

They welcomed her back without another question, for which she was grateful. She did keep her phone with her, and it was on, but Blake didn't text or call.

Chapter Eighteen

Blake startled awake as the door to his son's hospital room opened. A nurse entered, and he sat up straight as if the man cared if Blake had fallen asleep. "How's he doing?" he asked, not bothering to keep his voice down. They had turned down the lights on the floor a couple of hours ago. Maybe. Blake wasn't sure when.

"He's sleeping," he said, looking over to Tommy. "The doctor said he'd look at his arm in the morning and see if it needed surgery." They'd put a semi-permanent cast on it anyway, and Blake had spent most of the night trying to get Tommy to calm down, then on the phone with Jacinda, explaining what had happened.

He wasn't supposed to have Tommy until Sunday night, but his ex had wanted to go on a last-minute weekend trip with her boyfriend. He wasn't doing anything, and he'd gone to Carter's Cove to pick up his boy. He was planning to take him to his mother's, then meet Lauren for dinner.

Lauren.

His heart wailed at the thought of her. She'd called a couple of times, and each time he'd been too busy to answer. First, he'd been laying over his son as Tommy thrashed against the doctors and nurses trying to give him a shot. By the time he'd calmed from that, and Blake thought he might have five minutes to send a text, Jacinda had called in a sheer panic. She'd wanted to board the first plane back to South Carolina, and Blake had had to take and send no less than thirty-seven pictures of their son so she'd know he was okay.

I'm handling it, Blake had told her. *Stay in Cayman.*

He wished he had a significant other he was friendly enough to take a trip with, and as the nurse took Tommy's vitals and started to leave the room, Blake once again thought of Lauren. It was the middle of the night—seriously twelve-thirty-two—and he wasn't going to call or text her now. He'd stop by in the morning. She had one more day here on the island, or rather on Hilton Head, as he and Tommy had never made it off Carter's Cove, and Blake could maybe salvage the situation.

He started calculating how much time he'd need to drive from here to the bigger island next door, and if Tommy didn't have to have surgery tomorrow, they'd probably send him home. His momma would fillet him alive if he left the now-injured minor home alone to go talk to Lauren...

Blake sighed. No matter how he sliced and diced the numbers—something he was very good at and did for a living—he couldn't find a spare half-hour to get over to that pristine waterfront community and talk to her. She wouldn't just be sitting around her friend's house, waiting for him to show up.

So you'll call in the morning, he told himself as he yawned. Yeah, he'd call in the morning...

MORNING CAME, AND WITH IT, TOMMY'S PAIN AND extreme fear of needles. Blake was so going to use this incident the next time his son wanted to skateboard, do "stunts" on his bike, or anything besides walking. His feet had grown too big for his body, which was lanky and all out of proportion as it was. He stood nearly six feet tall as a twelve-year-old, and his hands barely seemed attached to his body.

Awkward was not a strong enough word to describe Tommy. Blake stood at the side of his bed, blocking the work the nurses were doing with the needles, and said, "Good news, bud. No surgery."

His son looked at him with those dark blue eyes that mirrored Blake's. "So we can go home?"

"Yes, sir," he drawled. "And we'll get breakfast on the way, and I'll get you set up in the living room, and you'll be fine."

"I won't be able to do my swimming lessons," he said, already pouting.

Blake's impatience swam forward, and he pulled on it hard. "We'll sign you up another time," he said.

"What about the campout next weekend?"

Blake glanced over to the door as a herd of doctors walked in. "Herd" probably wasn't the right term, but did they seriously have to travel in packs? This was a teaching hospital, so there were always three times as many staff around—including doctors.

"We'll ask," he said. He didn't want to miss the campout either, but he didn't want his son's shoulder and arm to be hurt for any longer than necessary. That was practically a death sentence in the summertime. Blake already struggled to keep his son busy during the day, and now he couldn't even play video games.

His friends were split between here and Carter's Cove, with his closer ones on this island instead of where Blake lived, as he went to school here on Carter's Cove.

He greeted the doctors while Tommy sulked, and Blake once again called on his patience. His son hadn't thought once about his accident had upset Blake's life. And why should he? Blake had no life that Tommy knew of.

"Good morning," he said to the doctors. "Can we take him home today?" He hated himself for using the royal "we" as if he had someone to help him stashed away in his pocket.

Doctor Midas, who'd been on-call in the ER last night, smiled and beamed at Tommy. "Yep. We do need to keep you in the sling for at least a week. Then I want another x-ray so I can see what's happening in that shoulder."

"Okay," Blake and Tommy said together.

"But you don't have any broken bones." He turned to a colleague and pulled out some films. He stuck them to a lightbox on the wall and started showing Tommy and Blake the inner workings of Tommy's arm and shoulder. "So since you're growing, that's why the bones were able to slip instead of break. So it's good news. You'll be bruised and sore, probably." He switched off the light and faced them again.

"No more tricks on your bike, young man," he said with that blinding smile still in place. How he did that after working all night, Blake would never understand. He felt like he'd rubbed sand in his eyes, needed a toothbrush with a lot of minty toothpaste, and a fresh set of clothing.

"No, sir," Tommy said.

"The ligaments and tendons are stretched and sore." Doctor Midas addressed Blake now. "That's why he's in pain. We've got a prescription sent downstairs for you for that. And once his discharge paperwork is printed, you'll be good to go." He clapped Blake on the shoulder like this would happen soon.

Blake had been in the hospital with his mother for her hip replacement surgery, and an hour in this place was like a lightning strike everywhere else. So he settled back into his chair, ignored his son when he ordered breakfast from the cafeteria, and tapped out text after text to Lauren.

He erased every single one of them, nothing quite right. He sighed and looked over to his son. Tommy looked up from his tablet. "What?" he asked.

"I couldn't meet someone last night," he said. "And I don't know what to say to them."

"Camille?" Tommy asked. "Is she mad at you?"

"Not Camille," Blake said quietly. "We broke up a few days ago." He looked at his phone again. The truth. He needed to tell Lauren the truth, but the truth was, Blake didn't tell women about his son until things were going fairly well. He saw no need to add the complication to the first few dates, before he even knew if he liked the woman well enough to get more serious with her.

Tommy knew it, and Blake liked to think he was protecting his child. Really, he was protecting himself too, and he knew it.

He tapped out, *Listen, I have a really great reason I couldn't meet you last night. Can I drop by and see you for just a few minutes? Will you be at Cass's house?*

He didn't hesitate or second-guess, though he'd typed up at least a dozen versions of that same message now. He sent it, and then he leaned back in his chair and sighed. His phone buzzed almost instantly, and he swiped it up in front of his face.

I can't, Lauren said. *We're already gone and I'm not sure when we'll be back. Even then, we're only staying for as long as it takes to get ready for the Beach Bash.*

"The Beach Bash," Blake repeated, an idea forming in his mind. He hadn't specifically been invited to the Sandcomber Beach Bash, but it happened on a public beach. And he was allowed out on public beaches.

Sandcomber? he asked.

I have no idea, Lauren said. She was clearly brushing him back into the corner where she'd kept him for the past two summers. He didn't know what had been different between them this year, but he'd definitely felt some flirty energy from her at the fireworks a few nights ago. Then he'd deliberately stayed late at Harrison's the other night, only to take a walk on the beach. Three houses down, he'd found Lauren lingering out on the patio alone. It had felt serendipitous, like he was meant to run into her simply so they could connect again more easily. He'd talked to her for a few minutes, asked for her number, and they'd been texting since.

If only he'd have been able to meet her for dinner last night.

Blake hated living in "if-only" land, so he shelved the

thought and tucked his phone in his pocket as a pair of nurses entered the room. One of them held up a handful of paperwork and both of them smiled. "It's your lucky day," the one with the papers said. "Your daddy signs all of these, and we get you both out of here."

Blake had never signed his name so fast.

THAT EVENING, THE SUN HAD FULLY SET BEFORE HE found Ty Parker and learned that no, Grant had not brought his friends to that night's Beach Bash. He'd come a couple of hours ago and taken the leftover food for a party of his own. No, Ty didn't know where they'd gone.

Blake had a good idea, and he practically jogged back to his truck, in complete disbelief that he'd wasted thirty minutes at the wrong party, talking to the wrong people, and basically doing all the wrong things.

In truth, this thing with Lauren was starting to feel cursed. "Whatever this thing is," he muttered. He got himself to the north side of the island, and he had to text Harrison to get the blasted code to get through the gate.

Are you guys at your house or Cass's? he asked.

Mine, Harrison sent back, and with any luck at all, he wouldn't say anything to anyone about why Blake didn't know that. Or that Blake was almost there.

Since Harrison didn't live too far into the community, Blake pulled up to his house only a minute later. He'd gotten out of his SUV and taken a few steps toward the expansive front porch when the door opened, and a woman walked out.

His heartbeat fired through his body, but it only took him a moment to realize it wasn't Lauren.

Her friend Joy came down the steps, pulling her sweater tighter around her body. She looked left and right like she didn't want any witnesses for what was about to happen. Then she zeroed in on him.

Joy Bartlett was not about to let Blake Williams into the house. Oh, no. He could get himself right back in his car and get off this property. "She doesn't want to see you," she said, hugging herself tighter against the wind.

"I just need to talk to her for five minutes," Blake said. At least he'd stopped coming toward her.

Joy held her position at the bottom of the steps. "She sat in that restaurant for almost an hour."

Blake let his head droop toward the ground. "I feel terrible about that." He sounded like he might be speaking the truth.

"Tell me the reason you couldn't make it," Joy said. "And couldn't answer the phone. And couldn't text her until this morning. If I think it's a good enough reason, I'll tell her. Then she can decide if she wants to talk to you again or not."

Blake looked at Joy, and she may only stand an inch or two above five feet, but she drew herself to her full height and gave him all the attitude she'd given her sons when they'd come home in the middle of the night without calling her. He considered her for several long seconds, and then he said, "Okay, but I have to tell it fast. I have to get back to my kid."

Joy's eyes widened. "You have a child." She deliberately didn't phrase it as a question. She wanted him to think Lauren told her everything. Out of everyone, Joy suspected Lauren did confide in her the most, and that was a delusion she was willing to keep even if it wasn't true.

"Yes." Blake ran a hand through his hair, and Joy could see why Lauren liked him. He was tall, tan, and trim. He probably ran in the mornings before work. He could probably cook, and throw a football for his son. Or if he had a daughter, he could braid her hair and take her to dance lessons.

"I don't usually tell women until a few dates in," he said. "So I hadn't told Lauren about Tommy yet. I wasn't supposed to have him this weekend, but my ex-wife wanted to go on a last-minute trip. So I went to Carter's Cove to pick him up. We went to the skate park so he could show me some of his new tricks, and he fell. Hurt his arm."

Joy's maternal instincts started to kick in, but she held her ground. She said nothing as she nodded a single time. Men like Blake needed to know they couldn't just smile and apologize and everything would magically be okay. In Joy's world, that wasn't how things worked.

She told herself he wasn't her ex-husband, and just the thought that her husband, whom she'd loved, was no longer hers sent a spike of pain into her heart. She'd told the other ladies she wanted a hot summer boyfriend, but that wasn't true. She wasn't really ready for another romance. A fling, maybe, but Joy had never been into short-term relationships.

"He's deathly afraid of needles. Like, *deathly* afraid.

Like nothing you've ever seen before. The first time Lauren called, I was actually laying on top of Tommy, holding him down so he didn't punch and kick the nurses. The kid is wiry, but strong. And six feet tall." He put a smile on his face. "The second time she called, I was on the phone with Jacinda, who was in full panic mode and telling me she was going to fly home from Grand Cayman."

It sounded like he had some high-stress people in his life, and last night had been extremely difficult for him. Lauren would surely understand that. Joy knew she liked this man; Joy had seen her face while she'd been texting him yesterday afternoon to set up their date.

"After that," Blake said. "It was too late. I was too tired. My son had gotten some meds and he was finally sleeping." He sighed like he'd like to be sleeping right now too. "I fell asleep in the chair, and when the nurse came in again, it was twelve-thirty. I did text her this morning to try to talk to her."

"I saw the texts," Joy told him. Lauren had shown her, and they'd brainstormed about what to do. Lauren wasn't a very forgiving person in general, but Joy didn't tell Blake that. He'd find out soon enough. Or maybe he wouldn't. "Is your son okay? He's home?"

"Yes," Blake said. "No broken bones. Some sprained or stretched ligaments or whatever. He's in a sling. Can't do his swimming lessons next week, but the doctor did say we could still do the campout if he doesn't have to strain his shoulder." He flashed a smile, and Joy returned it.

For her personally, a single dad would be a turn-on. For Lauren...she wasn't sure. She knew Lauren wanted children, but Tommy sounded a lot older than a baby or a toddler. "How old is your son?" she asked.

"Twelve," Blake said. He glanced at his wrist. "I'm afraid I can't stay much longer. I wandered all over the blasted beach looking for her already, and I've been gone too long as it is." He looked up. "You'll tell her?"

"Yes," Joy said. "I'll tell her."

Blake rushed at her and gathered her into a hug. "Thank you, Joy." He stepped back and cleared his throat. "Will you tell her I'm really sorry? That if she'll give me another chance, I'll make it up to her ten-fold?"

Joy looked up into his face. "You really like her, don't you?"

"I'm intrigued by her," he said. "I'm *very* interested in getting to know her better. It's hard to say if I 'really like' her, because we haven't spent a lot of time together." He backed up a step and added, "I love talking to her via text, but I'd love to see her in person before she leaves. If at all possible."

Joy nodded, because he clearly didn't know Lauren was coming back next weekend, and to stay for longer than a few days too. Joy had seriously considered coming with her, but it felt like such a tagalong thing to do, and Joy didn't want to be that friend.

She'd miss Lauren terribly, because while she could cook, she wasn't anywhere near the caliber of Sage and Bessie, and their talk of canning, recipes, and substitutions bored her sometimes.

"Thanks, Joy." Blake retreated to his SUV, got in, and drove away. Joy turned around and went back inside Harrison's house. She very nearly collided with Oliver Blackhurst.

She planted both hands against his chest to steady herself, and Oliver grabbed onto her wrist.

"Sorry," he said to her, obviously barely seeing her. He had his phone pressed to his ear, and he said, "No, not you. I just ran into someone." He went outside, his voice growing frustrated, and Joy watched him go.

"Someone," she said out loud. Oliver knew her name. They'd talked several times tonight. She found him good-looking and charming, even if he had a loud voice and could out-boom anyone with his laughter.

He'd barely seen her, and Joy hated feeling invisible. She'd felt like this a lot lately, and she turned toward the back of the house as the door there opened and the noise level of music, chatter, and laughter increased.

Lauren entered the house, looking like she was ready to try again with Blake right now. "So?" she asked, hurrying toward Joy. "What did he say?"

Joy's chest stung, but she loved Lauren, and she didn't think Blake had been cruel or mean on purpose. "Okay, so I think you're going to want to text or call him," she said. "Let's sit down and I'll tell you everything."

She'd barely started the story when Bessie and Sage joined them, and that brought in Cass and Bea too. Soon, Joy finished the story, and they all looked at Lauren, as it was clearly her turn to smack the ball back to Joy.

"You should call him," Bea said. "Blake's a nice guy."

"He didn't tell her about his son," Bessie said.

"But for a good reason," Cass said. "He probably feels protective of him."

"Or women break up with him once they find out,"

Lauren said. She looked at Joy. "He didn't say anything else about his son? Is he a lot of trouble or something?"

Joy thought for a moment. "He just said he's deathly afraid of needles. Wiry but strong. Over six feet tall." He hadn't sounded like he had special needs or caused trouble on purpose to her.

Lauren nodded. "Okay, I think I'll call him in the morning." She smiled around at everyone. "Does that sound good?"

No one argued, and Bea and Cass went into the kitchen to brew coffee. Bessie met Joy's eyes, and she raised her eyebrows. Bessie wouldn't say anything though.

"If you're going to call him anyway," Joy said, and Lauren looked up from her phone. She'd perched on the arm of the recliner during the story, but her phone was never far from her. "Why not put him out of his misery tonight?" Joy shrugged like she didn't care one way or the other. "He seemed really sincere, Lauren. He said he'd make it up to you *ten*-fold."

"And he was already going to take you to the best steakhouse on the island the first time," Bessie said, grinning.

She looked between Bessie and Joy. Then over to Sage, who'd said nothing. "Fine." She got to her feet. "I'll go call him right now."

Joy watched her go, and she leaned back into the couch. She looked over to Bessie. "At least she has someone to call."

Bessie scooted over and laid her head against Joy's shoulder. "You can always call me, Joy."

"I know," she whispered. Her mind wandered along dangerous paths where she was completely invisible to everyone around her. "Thanks, Bessie."

"Are you going to come back here with Lauren?"

"No," Joy said. "It doesn't feel right."

"Maybe you'll meet a hot cowboy once we're back in Texas."

Joy rolled her eyes, and then she and Bessie both started laughing—for that idea was truly laughable.

Chapter Nineteen

Harrison started getting up thirty minutes earlier than usual every morning. He used the time to drive to Gourmet Goods and get sweet tea and a pastry for Cass. The first several mornings, he'd simply left them on her front porch. She had no reason to be up and waiting for him by seven-thirty, and she'd told him via a late-night text that she was more of a night owl than an early bird.

He was the opposite, due to his work schedule, but they managed to see one another every day. Sometimes he simply stopped by her back patio on his therapy walk after work, and sometimes they had scheduled, planned dates.

One morning, a little over halfway through July, he pulled into her driveway with her cinnamon bun—no walnuts—and found her sitting on the front steps. He grinned at her as she did the same for him, and she opened the passenger door before he'd truly brought the truck to a stop. "I knew you were the one bringing me breakfast every day." She climbed right on inside the cab and slammed the door.

"Yes, ma'am," he said. "I didn't realize you didn't know it was me."

"I think Conrad found the stuff a couple of times."

He handed her the light blue pastry bag, and she beamed like a star straight from heaven as she looked at him and then it. She unfolded the top and peered inside. "Oh, a cinnamon roll." She sighed. "This is just what I need today."

"Yeah? Something big going on?"

"I'm meeting with my first client here in South Carolina," she said.

"Oh, right, yeah, you said that last night." He'd had another boring zoning meeting, but he'd survived it in style by texting with Cass. "Lady Brunner."

"I wish people would call me *Lady Haslam*." She spoke the last couple of words in a lower-pitched voice, adding in some unknown accent.

"I'll call you that if you want." He kicked a grin at her as she pulled her sticky cinnamon bun out of the bag. She took a big bite, which got the white frosting all over her face, and they both laughed.

He reached across her and opened the glove box to get out a napkin for her. "Are we still on for tonight?" He'd sniffed around and found the only dance happening within a hundred miles for people their age. They'd have to drive to Charleston to attend, but he'd bought the tickets a week ago.

"I'm good," she said. "You're the one who sometimes gets hung up at work."

True. He had canceled on her a couple of times now, and she'd shown up at his house with boxes of pizza and cases of his favorite soda. She hadn't said so out loud, but Harrison had gotten the impression that she didn't care much what they did, as long as she got to see him and do it with him.

He wasn't sure how to handle that. It felt like a lot of pressure, like he wasn't the man she thought he was. Like he had to be better than he was, or that eventually, Cass would figure out that he was just...simple. He was a simple man, living a simple life.

"Not tonight," he said. "And you need to wear something nice. We're goin' to Charleston. I'll be here at five, not a minute later."

"Charleston?" Her eyebrows went up. "Why are we going there?"

"It's a surprise," he said, smiling. "You're always trying to ruin the surprises."

"I am not."

"I said to dress nice."

"There are levels of nice, Harrison."

He leaned his head back against the rest and closed his eyes. "Tell me about them, and I'll tell you which one."

"I'm assuming a dress or skirt."

"Yes, ma'am," he murmured.

"So we're to a three already," she said. "Should it be a dress...or a skirt?"

"Either."

"So not formal."

"Nope."

"So a three or a four, depending on the person," she said.

He had no idea what a three entailed, or a four, but he knew he'd get the high end of level four from Cass. Heck, what she wore to sit on her front steps on a summer morning was nicer than what most women wore—at least the ones Harrison knew.

"What are you wearing?" she asked.

"The pair of slacks I wear to fancy meetings," he said. "My light blue shirt. This great tie my momma gave me for my birthday last year in the hopes that I'd start goin' to church with her." He chuckled. "I didn't, by the way." He opened his eyes and turned his head to look at Cass. She'd eaten about half of her cinnamon bun, and she placed the rest back in the bag.

"I noticed you don't go to church," she said. She dusted her hands off and used the napkin. "Is there a reason why?"

"I'm tired on Sunday," he said with a sigh. "Getting up and all dressed to go to church... It feels like a lot of work."

"Fair enough." She gave him a smile. "Do you believe in God?"

"Yeah," he said. "I just don't really get organized religion."

"Does it bother you that I go?" she asked.

"Not at all."

She nodded, and Harrison hadn't realized this was something she'd noticed or needed to talk about. "Five o'clock tonight. Level three or four." She smiled at him. "I'll be ready."

"Good," he said. "Now kiss me, and then I have to go. I can't be late for work."

She laughed as she leaned toward him, and Harrison met her halfway to kiss her. She tasted like sugar and cinnamon, and that was downright sinful. He kissed her and kissed her, and the next thing he knew, she'd climbed right into his lap.

He felt like they were teenagers who simply couldn't get

enough of one another, and he finally came to his senses and said, "I should go."

She opened her eyes, seemed to realize where she was, and scrambled back to the passenger seat. "Yeah." She ran her hand through her hair, and Harrison jumped from the truck as she reached for the door handle.

He met her as she slid to the ground, and he took her effortlessly into his arms. "I'd kiss you like that every day," he whispered.

"I'm so embarrassed." She buried her head in his chest. "Sorry, Harrison. Really."

"For what?"

"For climbing on your lap like a lovesick puppy." She stepped back and ran both hands through her hair now. Her face flamed bright red.

"You think a man doesn't want to know you want to kiss him?" He was partly teasing and partly not.

She looked up at him. "Kissing is one thing."

Sex was another. Harrison nodded at the unspoken words. He swallowed. "Well, don't be sorry. I like kissing you."

She nodded and said, "I'll be ready at five, okay?"

"Can't wait." He turned as she went past him and watched her enter the house. Part of him wanted to follow her and another part of him knew he wouldn't be sleeping with her any time soon. Not only because of her religious beliefs, but because a woman like Cass had to be all the way in love with a man before she'd welcome him into her bedroom, and while she might like kissing him too, they still had a long way to go to be in love.

Harrison felt himself falling in that direction though,

and he didn't fight against it at all. His relationship with Cass might be new, but that also meant it was exciting and invigorating, and he needed all of that in his life right now.

He needed *her* in his life right now, and he did thank the Lord above that he'd found her. Now, he just had to figure out how to keep her.

HARRISON WAS RUNNING LATE, BUT IF HE HADN'T hit every red light between work and home, he'd have made it to Cass's right on time. Instead, he pulled in five minutes late, after texting her to stay in the house until he rang the doorbell. He didn't want to find her sitting on her steps, waiting for him again.

He didn't want her walking down to his place. He didn't want to meet her somewhere.

He jumped from the truck for the second time that day, adjusted his tie, and ran up the steps to her big, wide, front door. He wanted to pick her up Southern-gentleman style, with flowers and fresh cologne on. He wanted to be wowed by her as she answered the door or came walking out of the kitchen after Lauren had let him in.

He couldn't wait to see what she wore tonight, but he forced himself to take an extra breath before he reached for the doorbell. He'd not had time for the flowers, but at least he'd spritzed on the cologne.

The doorbell gonged through the house, loud enough for him to hear outside. He couldn't tug on his shirt-sleeves, because they were short, and he settled for pulling at his tie one more time. Then he let his hands fall to his sides as he heard someone approaching on the other side of the door.

He'd bet his life it wasn't Cass, but her son. Sure enough, Conrad opened the door, and Harrison gave him the brightest smile he had. "Hey, Conrad." He'd not spent a lot of time with the teen—young adult—since the night of their manly grilling party, when he'd come back with a bottle of Miracle Whip and angry questions about Harrison dating his mother.

The whole can of worms had been blown open then, and they'd never really been addressed.

"Hey, Harrison," the other man said. "Come on in. I guess she's having an earring crisis, and she said she'll be out in a minute." He stepped back from the big door, and Harrison entered the foyer.

"You guys painted in here." He looked at the walls, which were no longer gray, but a light, robin's egg blue.

"Did we?" Conrad looked at the walls for what they were: walls. He obviously wasn't impressed. "My mother is never happy with what we have. She's always changing something." He didn't say it in a mean or judgmental voice, but it certainly sounded that way in Harrison's ears.

Conrad turned and walked further into the house, and Harrison wasn't sure if he should go with him. Cass's bedroom sat to his right as he entered the living room, the back wall of windows overlooking her patio straight ahead. The stairs leading to the second floor sat to his left, and the living room opened up ahead of him, with the kitchen and dining room around a corner.

Her son went that way, and Harrison decided he'd already entered the beast. He might as well go all the way into the belly. He followed Conrad into the kitchen, where he'd sat at the bar, a bowl of noodles and broth in front of him. He still wore his tour company uniform, which was a pair of forest green shorts, and a bright yellow shirt with navy blue and dark green writing on it. He'd propped his phone up against a gallon of milk, and he tapped the screen to start the show again.

So he clearly wasn't interested in talking to Harrison. Still, Harrison asked, "How's the job?"

Conrad nodded and finished chewing his food. "Good. Great. I really like it."

"Do you?"

"Yeah." Conrad looked at him, his eyes a step or two darker than Cass's. She'd told Harrison he looked just like West, and Harrison felt like he was being judged by both the father and the son as the nineteen-year-old sized him up. "Don't tell my mom, but I'm thinking of taking my gap year this year."

Harrison's eyebrows lifted like a shot. "Oh, yeah? And staying here?"

"Yeah." He went back for another forkful of noodles. "I don't know. I liked Baylor, but—"

"She's almost ready," Lauren said, interrupting them. Her shoes slapped the floor as she passed from carpet to tile. "She says you can drive fast on the way to Charleston." She smiled and gave Harrison a light hug.

He kissed both of her cheeks, smiling all the while. "I can," he said. "We have a little buffer."

"Charleston?" Conrad asked. He turned fully toward Harrison. "What are you two doing in Charleston?"

"It's a secret," Harrison said.

"Sounds scandalous," Lauren teased. She moved into the kitchen and clicked on a burner. She lifted the teakettle from it and moved to the sink.

"You're not going to sleep with her, are you?" Conrad asked.

Harrison drew his attention from Lauren filling the kettle to Conrad, shock moving through him. "I, uh—" he stammered. "No."

"Good." Conrad narrowed his eyes at him. "I'm surprised she's dating at all, to be honest."

"Conrad," Cass said, catching all of them unaware. She moved to Harrison's side before he could truly look at her. The scent of her expensive perfume arrived a moment later, and she slipped her arm through his. She wore a black and white dress, fitted on the top and flaring at the waist. It fell in a wide skirt to her knees, and then the shapely, sexiness of her legs captured his full attention.

She wore a pair of black heels on her feet, with a buckle around the ankle that looked like it had been studded with diamonds. For all Harrison knew, they were real and not cubic zirconium or cheap gems. Nothing Cass owned was cheap, he knew that from the scent of the perfume still enticing his pheromones.

"You have no right to tell him that," she lectured her son. "I know what I'm ready to do, young man."

Lauren said nothing, and in fact, she turned her back on the whole conversation as if that would make her invisible.

"Whatever," Conrad said, turning back to his dinner.

Cass looked at Harrison, and he looked at her. He could feel her weight on his lap from that morning, and when she smiled at him with those ruby-red lips, he could only smile back. "Ready?" he asked.

"Yes, sir," she drawled. "What else were you and Conrad talking about?" She looked over to her son, and Harrison did too.

Conrad's eyes widened and filled with apprehension, and that was Harrison's clue to keep what he'd said about his gap year to himself. "School," he said vaguely. "Work."

"Sounds innocent," Cass said. She stepped over to her son and cupped one hand around the back of his neck as she leaned down to say something to him. She held there for a few seconds, then backed up. He nodded; she did too; then she faced Harrison.

He got the full view now, and she lifted one arm as if brandishing an umbrella, and said, "How do I look? This is a new dress."

"It's phenomenal," he said, drinking in her curves and swells. His throat turned to sand. "I really like it. You look fantastic."

She'd painted her face, but he'd seen her in makeup before. Maybe not this much, but enough. She wore a pair of black teardrop earrings, and they matched the shape of the gem sitting right in the center of her collarbone. It was held up by a thick, silver chain, and once again, Harrison got the impression that everything she owned cost a lot of money.

It made him wonder why she liked him. He didn't dress the same as her. He didn't drive a vehicle like hers. He only had the house he did because he'd gotten a deal on it. Feeling very self-conscious, he reached for her hand. "Ready?"

"Ready." She squeezed his fingers, her eyebrows going

up. She didn't say anything as they left the house, and as he helped her into the truck and she smoothed down her skirt. He wasn't sure what she'd seen on his face, but when he got behind the wheel, she looked at him. "What's wrong?" she asked.

He wanted to say, "Nothing," but they were both too old to play games. So he didn't say that, but the words he wanted to say tangled and knotted, and he couldn't get them out.

Chapter Twenty

Cass had seen something, she'd thought, on Harrison's face. Inside, when he'd been looking at her and complimenting her. He'd cleared it quickly, but the way his throat worked now, she knew there was something.

Her pulse vibrated before it settled back into a regular beat, but he still hadn't said anything. She fought the urge to fill the silence with the sound of her own voice. She did that sometimes with Conrad, but she'd learned not to do it with West. He'd eventually say what was on his mind. Jane did the same thing, and Cass casually looked out her window as Harrison left her driveway.

"What do you like about me?" he finally asked, his voice barely loud enough to reach her ears.

Her phone rang, startling her from such a strange question. She had no idea how to answer that question, and a bit of regret tugged through her as she pulled her phone from her clutch. "It's my mother," she said.

Instant fear drove through her. "Shoot." She looked over to Harrison. "It's *my mother*."

"Okay," he said.

"I haven't told her anything."

"What do you mean?"

Cass didn't want to have to call her back. She swiped on the call, shaking her head. "Hey, Momma," she said as cheerfully as she could. She hadn't even told Conrad some of the things she'd done. The people she'd called.

Or Harrison...

"Cassandra," her mother drawled.

Cass pressed her eyes closed. She was in real trouble here, and her pulse beat out double-time. "You found out about the house," she said.

"I ran into Miles Pince, yes," she said. "He said he can't *wait* to get your house on the market. I was *sure* he was wrong."

"Momma," she started, but her mother had just been gearing up.

"I made a complete fool of myself in front of everyone," she said. "Then I get home, and Daddy says he knew you'd list it the moment summer was over. That you've already decided to make Hilton Head your permanent home."

"Momma," she tried again.

"Then I find out from social media. *Social media*, Cassandra, that you have purchased a house there. I thought you were renting for the summer."

"That is not true," she said. "I told you I'd bought a place when Conrad decided to come with me." Maybe she'd made it *sound* like she'd done so *because* Conrad had wanted to come stay on the island for the summer. Either way, she'd told her mother.

"And all of your friends have been there," Momma continued as if Cass hadn't spoken. "And that you're dating someone new." Her voice quivered then, and Cass looked over to Harrison.

"I meant to tell you about Harrison," she said. "Really, Momma. There's just been a lot going on."

"I'll bet there has," she said. "New floors. Some fancy butcher block. Your son's new job. And a boyfriend. A *boyfriend*, Cassandra. Imagine my humiliation with Miss Barbara asked me how long you've been seein' each other, and I had no idea."

"Oh, boy," Cass said. "Miss Barbara. Why are you still going out to lunch with her anyway?"

"Don't turn this on me," Momma barked. "Start talking about your boyfriend."

Cass looked at Harrison, who'd turned the radio completely off for this conversation. "He's sitting right here with me, Momma. We're goin' to Charleston for a date tonight."

"Put him on."

Cass shook her head, but she knew she would. When Momma got in a mood like this, there was no turning back the tide. "I just want to remind you that you didn't like West for at least a year before you came around."

Momma scoffed, but she didn't try to deny it.

Cass looked over to Harrison as she lowered the phone. "I'm sorry for whatever's about to happen." She tapped the speaker button and said, "He's here, Momma. Harrison, my momma just found out we're dating."

"Pleased to meet you, ma'am," he drawled, really laying on the Southern accent thick.

"Oh, he sounds proper," Momma said. "I can't figure why you'd be hidin' him from me."

"I wasn't," Cass said. "Like I said, things have been busy here. I'm setting up my company, which has been a ton of filings and paperwork. Things with the house, the patio, Conrad..." She let the words die there, because they'd started to sound like excuses.

"I'm sure you've seen this young man plenty," Momma said.

"Yes," Cass said as a sigh. "Momma, this is supposed to be special night for us. We're going to *Charleston*."

"I'm taking her dancing," Harrison said. He smiled at her, a hint of trepidation in his expression. "If I'm not too terrible, we might still be together after tonight." He chuckled. "I'm not much of a dancer, you see."

Cass couldn't speak at all. He was taking her dancing? Her heart melted into a puddle as she looked at him, trying to find the right words to say.

"Cass'll help you," Momma said. "She's a very good dancer." She'd clearly softened too, and Cass wasn't sure what Harrison had said or how he'd said it that had worked that magic. "Cass, I'll let you go on one condition: You call me in the morning and plan to have a nice, long chat with your mother."

"Yes, ma'am," she said. She ducked her head as if in trouble. "I will."

"I won't say anything to Liz either. I'm assuming she doesn't know."

"No, I'll call her too," Cass said.

"The girls?"

"They know," Cass said.

Momma exhaled, her way of saying, *So I'm the last one. Great. Thanks, Cass.*

"Momma, it wasn't purposeful. I didn't mean to leave you out. I just..."

Several seconds of silence passed, and Momma finally said, "You're moving on. It's okay, Cass."

"I'll call you tomorrow." She imagined her Momma nodding, both of them emotional now, and she ended the call. She tucked her phone back into her clutch and stared out the windshield.

"I needed my parents a great deal after West's death," she finally said.

Harrison reached over and took her hand. Everything she needed to say to him gelled, and she wiped at her eyes with her free hand. She'd warned him about the tears, and she'd actually done very little crying in front of him. "I've always been very independent. Strong. Momma didn't understand me for a while, but then when I needed her, she was there. She liked that I couldn't do everything alone."

"It's okay to be like that sometimes."

"Yes." Cass switched her gaze out her passenger window. "I should've told her. I meant to. She's just not as...immediate as she once was. And she's right. I'm moving on. Moving on from Texas. Moving on from West. Moving into a new life that's not there. Moving back to my strong, independent self."

Harrison gave her a few moments of quiet before he said, "She seems to really love you."

Cass sobbed, just once. "Yes," she said. "Both she and

Daddy love me." She looked over to him, her grip on his hand tightening. "I like you, Harrison, because you're so even when I'm this big roller coaster going up and down. You steady me. You make me feel anchored, and I really like that." Not only that, but she needed it. "I feel safe with you. I think you're handsome and hardworking. I love how you take care of me. You bring me my favorites in the morning. You take me to restaurants with food I'll like. You literally doctored me up once, and I really think it's because of you that my heart has been healing so fast."

Her mouth felt like she'd been sucking on cotton she'd talked so fast and said so much. "And now you're taking me dancing?" She shook her head, another splash of tears hitting her cheeks. "You plan perfect dates. You show up looking amazing. You think I'm amazing... what's not to like? Everything you do, you do for me. It's like I'm the queen, and you're living to make sure I'm happy."

She sniffled and wiped her nose. She reached into the glove box for another napkin. Thankfully, he had another one after this morning's cinnamon roll mess. "I'm not trying to be the queen," she said. "I swear. You don't need to worship me. But it feels like you are, and I...like that. West treated me like that, and I loved feeling like my opinion mattered to him. Like he thought about me when we weren't together. You do that. You're smart, and talented, and I don't care if you can dance or not."

"Okay," he said. "You don't have to keep going." He released her hand, and Cass took the opportunity to mop up her face. She did, the silence in the cab reverberating with all she'd said.

Too much. She'd said far too much. And she wasn't done yet. "Why did you have to ask?" she whispered.

"I don't know." He sighed. "Every time I see you, I'm reminded of how...different we are."

"Different in what way?" She wadded up the napkin, which had far too much dark makeup on it, and stuffed it into the cupholder beside her.

"You're glamorous," he said. "Sophisticated. Classy. Wealthy."

She jerked her attention to him, not caring that she might have raccoon eyes and was going to check in the mirror on the back of the sunshade. "Wealthy?"

"Everything you own is top-of-the-line," he whispered. "That dress is new, and it probably cost hundreds of dollars. I've had these slacks for over a year. The tie is old too, I've just never worn it. I'm shabby, and you're chic, and I don't know. I felt self-conscious. I wondered why someone like you would possibly like someone like me."

Cass didn't know what to say. She wasn't sure if she needed to defend herself or not. "Well." She pulled down the sun visor to check her makeup. "Shabby-chic is huge right now, so I can't imagine why we can't be together."

Harrison chuckled as he shook his head. "You know what I mean."

"No, I don't," she said. "I'm not *wealthy*, Harrison. My husband died, and I got a life insurance policy. Our house in Texas was almost paid for, so I used the money to buy the house here. Almost all of my clothes are old too. I've only worn them a few times each, so they look brand new. Yes, Lauren and I went to the mall and managed to find this today, and believe it or not, but it was on the clearance rack. I guess people in Hilton Head don't wear black in the summer." She sniffed like such a thing was terrible and brushed something invisible from her skirt.

"Praise the heavens we're going to Charleston tonight then," he quipped.

Cass blinked and then burst out laughing. "And you're funny, Mister Tate. You know when to take a serious conversation into something lighter." She took his hand in hers again. "I really like that about you too."

She wanted to address what Conrad had said about the two of them sleeping together, but Cass decided a phone call from her momma, and then a cry-fest, and *then* a confessional about why she liked him was probably enough for one night.

And they hadn't even reached the city yet.

"Are we eating dinner first?" she asked.

"Dinner is part of the dancing, sweetheart."

She smiled over to him. "Really, Harrison, you're one of the sweetest men I know."

He shook his head and looked out his window, clearly uncomfortable with the compliments. "Just tryin' to win you over," he said. "My flaws will come out soon enough."

She kept smiling. "Oh, yeah? And what might some of those be?"

"I have mud on my boots constantly," he said. "So my house is a mess. Doing laundry at my place? It's like a crime scene. I need to bring in the National Guard just to get in my laundry room."

Cass laughed and gestured for him to keep going.

"I want a dog, but I have no way to take care of it. I drink way too much coffee. That bill is astronomical, and since you'll have to be my sugar mama, I think it's only fair to warn you about it up front."

She giggled and held up her hand. "I'm *not* wealthy, Harrison."

"All of my money is tied up in my business," he said.

"And yet, you have an astronomical coffee bill," she teased.

"Seems that way." They laughed together, and the sound of it chased away some of the lingering melancholy.

They arrived in the city, and Harrison took her toward the sea. Cass's excitement grew and grew, until he parked behind a row of historic houses. "We're going in there?" she asked.

"The Arboretum," he said. "Dinner and dancing once a month. I was lucky to get these tickets. They usually sell out months in advance." He unbuckled and looked over to her.

"How did you get them then?"

"I called a friend," he said. "Pulled some strings."

He was definitely pulling on her heartstrings, and she waited in her seat for him to come around and get her door. She let him lift her down, his hand strong and sure on her waist. They faced the building together, and then Harrison led her inside.

Cass paused just across the threshold, sure what stood before her eyes wasn't real. For it was a tree. A live, growing tree with a trunk so thick she'd never be able to wrap her arms around it. Heck, even if she and Harrison tried to span it with their four arms combined, they couldn't.

"Harrison," she breathed. "Look at this." She gazed at the tree, which went right up through the floor, and which had various handprints stamped on its trunk in bright colors of paint. She wanted to do that and leave her mark here, on this magical place in Charleston.

"Hello," a woman chirped. "Here for the Summer Swing?"

"Yes, ma'am," Harrison said, and he had to tug on Cass's hand to get her to move past the tree growing right there in the lobby. She couldn't wait for what she might see next.

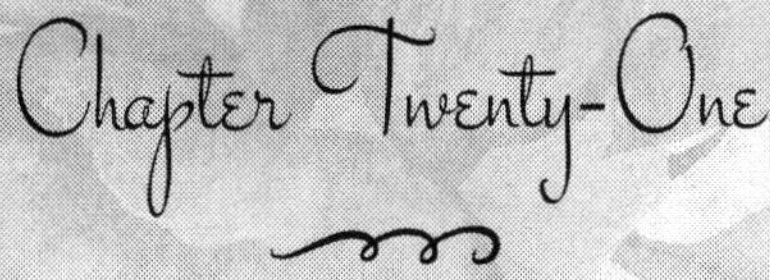

Chapter Twenty-One

Harrison swayed with Cass in his arms, wondering what he'd been so worried about. Everything with Cass was easy, even "meeting" her mother for the first time, and talking to her about their differences—his inadequacies.

Dinner had been wonderful, served to each person in a series of five courses. The dancing had started about a half-hour ago, and Harrison had kept up with every number. Cass couldn't stop talking about all the plants, shrubs, and trees—yes, live trees—growing in the building, and Harrison had to admit they were all pretty cool.

He moved her closer to the moss wall, as she liked to reach out with her hand and trail her fingers through it. She'd done so a couple of times tonight, and he figured one more would be enough.

She'd said her mother loved to garden, but he suspected she felt some connection to Mother Earth too. Otherwise, she wouldn't have reacted to the big tree downstairs the way she had.

Dinner had been on the second floor, and there had been a few more branches to contend with. The dance floor was on the third story, and someone had weaved lights and ornaments among the leaves and branches near the top of the tree. Cass had already touched several of those too, exclaiming over each one.

"I'm going to Sweet Water Falls at the end of August," she said.

"Yes," he murmured, having nearly forgotten he wasn't in a dream. "To take Conrad back to Waco." He wouldn't tell her what the boy had told him, not unless she asked.

"And for Supper Club," she said. "Joy's hosting the last week of August, so Bea and I can be there."

He nodded. "I think I even put it on my calendar."

"I was thinking..." She didn't finish the thought, and Harrison would never pretend to know what was in her head.

"Yeah?" he prompted, but she shook her head, her lips pressed together.

When their eyes met several seconds later, she wore apprehension in her gaze. "Nothing," she said. "Really."

"Okay," he said, kneading her closer and closer to him. Much closer, and he'd likely end up stepping on one of her feet. Or both of them. "But you can tell me what you're thinking." He spoke in a low, husky voice, and pure satisfaction poured into him when she shivered.

"I was thinking," she said again. "Maybe you could come with me. Meet my folks." She shook her head. "But then I realized it won't work with your schedule, and Bea and I already have our tickets, and she's staying with me, and yeah. I decided it didn't feel right."

He nodded, because he couldn't argue with that. "Another time," he said. "I would like to meet your family."

"Yours lives here," she hinted. "Your mother, at least. A brother is closeby, isn't he?"

"Yes," Harrison said slowly. "My mother for sure. And my brother is right here in Charleston, actually." He'd almost moved here last year after Claudia had left him.

"Yes," she said. "I'd like to meet them all."

Harrison pulled back slightly. "We've only been dating for a few weeks."

"Eventually," she said. "I don't mean tonight."

He nodded, but he had a feeling Cass would like to go faster than they currently were. He wasn't sure why he was the one dragging his feet. "Well, Spence is probably down for anything. Momma too. Heaven knows I'm over there all the time for her, and she'd probably die and go to heaven if I asked her to make a meal for the two of us." He sighed like putting up with his momma was a real pain, but it wasn't.

"She knows about us?"

He nodded, swallowing. "They all know about you. I've told them I'm dating."

She nodded, her nerves like a scent on the air now. "Well, that's good. Any time would work."

"Sure," he said, not really committing to anything. He could call his mother in the morning and set something up. He wasn't trying to hide Cass from them. Or them from her. He'd simply been giving them...time.

The song wrapped up, and they announced dessert would take place on the roof. Cass gave a little squeal of delight, and Harrison thanked his lucky stars that Spencer had been able to get him these tickets. His brother worked in publicity, and he could often get last-minute seats for shows and events like this. They weren't always good, but since there was no stage tonight, Harrison and Cass hadn't had any obstructed views.

Dessert was an assortment of items on a buffet which bordered the wall. He could see clear across the city from here, and the sight of the lights in the dark sky took his breath away. Cass curled into his chest, and the moment became tender and perfect for him. "This is spectacular," she whispered. "Thank you so much for bringing me to this."

She tilted her head up to see him, and he looked down at her. He moved a few inches, and she rose up to meet him, and this rooftop kiss in Charleston sent his whole world askew.

He fell, and fell, and fell, and it sure seemed like he was taking Cass with him.

He remembered he was in public, so he didn't kiss her for too terribly long or go too deep—he could do that later—and he pulled away gently. They both sighed and looked out over the city again, and Harrison sure did enjoy holding her within the circle of his arms, breathing with her, and experiencing this night with her.

Memories, he thought. That was what he wanted to create with a person. Real, true, tender memories he could reflect on time and again. Experiences he could think about and *feel* things for someone. This night had definitely done that for him and Cass. It had brought them closer together, and as she gushed over the cheesecake and then the chocolate mousse, Harrison could only smile—and add her excited face to his memory bank.

"Come on, Spence," he said to his brother a couple of weeks later. "Get the paddle board, and let's go."

Spencer looked up from his phone as if he didn't realize they were going to the beach that day. "Right." He didn't get up though, and Harrison rolled his eyes. He wasn't in the mood for tonight's beach picnic for some reason.

"I'm headed outside," he said. "Come out and down to the beach when you're ready. You'll see us." He left his brother inside the house and went out onto his back patio. His nerves fluttered at him, because he'd finally organized a meeting for Cass and Spencer.

Baby steps, he told himself. She hadn't met his mother yet, and Harrison hadn't wanted to bombard her with new people. He trusted his brother, and he wanted his opinion first.

They both knew this afternoon on the beach was for the two of them to meet, and Harrison felt like a hinge that had been put in the wrong place. He carried a small cooler with drinks in it, a big denim blanket his momma had made for him years ago, and a plastic grocery bag with sunscreen and his bucket hat in it.

August was only days away, and Harrison couldn't believe how quickly the summer had passed. He'd gone to the Everglades with Cass, Bea, and Grant exactly two months ago, and while he hadn't started dating Cass for another couple of weeks after that, it still felt like longer than that.

Cass was bringing Lauren and Conrad to the beach with her, though her son could only stay for about an hour before his tour tonight. Harrison didn't mind. He wanted more people there so things wouldn't be awkward for Spencer. Frankly, his brother was awkward in family situations, making his job in publicity all the more baffling.

He said he could handle strangers, because they didn't know anything about him. Harrison had told him Cass would be a stranger to him, but his brother would probably still say something awkward. He was a good judge of character, though, and Harrison figured he would be safer than unleashing his mother on Cass.

Harrison looked north when he reached the sand, but he saw nothing from Cass's back patio. It still sat a distance away, and he walked toward it. His back had been healing steadily since he'd been doing the therapy his doctor had told him to do, and he'd determined to keep doing it though he was better now.

His first indication that Cass had opened her back door was the sound of Beryl's voice. The golden retriever loved the beach, and Harrison grinned as the golden-brown bullet came flying down her steps. He whistled through his teeth, and Beryl changed his course to come toward Harrison.

He laughed as the dog came wagging up to him, his whole body snaking back and forth in greeting. "Howdy, buddy," he said to the dog. "Did she finally let you out, huh?" He looked up to Cass's house, but it was Lauren coming down the steps. Conrad came behind her, with no sign of Cass yet.

They met on the sand, and Lauren started telling him about something at work. Harrison loved her stories, because she worked with some real bigwigs—or people who thought they were bigwigs—and they did some stupid things sometimes.

"Oh my goodness, Harrison," she said. "You'll never believe what happened."

"What?" he said.

"Well, you know how a lot of us work remotely?" she asked. She spread out a blanket and put her beach bag down on it. She flipped her sunglasses back so he could see her eyes. "Myself included?"

"Yes." He glanced back to his house, but he didn't see Spence.

"Well, we're in a meeting, and the Senior VP says, 'I need everyone to be in the office next week. Like, back to full-time, in your local office.' He looks at me and says, 'We can talk about your local office, Lauren. I know you're in South Carolina, working for the Miami office, but have a house in Texas...'" She trailed off, because her situation was unique. "Anyway, it goes silent. He's looking around. I'm looking around. Everyone's looking around, and we're all online, right? This weird array of screens with everyone just hoping they don't have to be the first one to speak."

"This is gonna be good," Harrison said. He spread his own blanket next to hers, noting that Conrad had set up chairs. Three chairs.

"Finally, the Marketing Manager—the *Marketing Manager*, Harrison." She thumped his chest. "Says, 'Uh, I can't be in my local office next week. I don't live in Houston anymore.'" She trilled out a laugh. "It was dead silent, Harrison. Like, graveyard silent."

"He doesn't live in Houston anymore?"

"He'd been working remotely for so long, he moved. To

Saint Louis!" She laughed again, though Harrison was sure it hadn't been funny to anyone else in the meeting. "I guess his wife's parents are there, and he figured...I work remotely now. He hadn't told *any*one. Sold his house. Moved to a completely different state—and not that close either—and said nothing." She shook her head, and Harrison said nothing, a bit shocked.

"He'd moved?"

"Took his family and moved." Lauren grinned like the Cheshire Cat. "And the best part? He wasn't the only one! Our lead analyst, who worked out of the parent company office in Manhattan goes, 'I moved to Arkansas. What's the closest local office to that?' It became an uproar!" She turned back to the house. "About half of them had moved without saying anything. Mark was *so* mad." She smiled like this was great news for her, but Harrison wasn't sure how. "I wonder what Cass needs help with. I better go see."

"I'll go get my brother," Harrison said. "I don't know what's taking him so long."

"I'll keep an eye on Beryl," Conrad said, but he'd really buried himself in his phone.

Harrison started back toward his house, and it was definitely the longer of the walks. Lauren and Conrad had come straight down from Cass's, but he had to walk back down the beach and around the curve of the island. He'd just gone over a swell in the sand, which housed a long line of grasses that swayed in the breeze when he heard someone laughing.

A voice he knew well.

Cass's voice.

She and Spence came into view in the next couple of seconds, and they walked along like they were old pals. He paused to watch them, and he shouldn't have been surprised. Cass was personable and kind. Spence was good with strangers. She'd never expressed any anxiety over meeting his brother or his mother.

All of that came from within Harrison. Even now, his first instinct was to jog toward them and make sure Spence didn't say anything foolish. A flash of irritation shot to the top of his head that Cass had walked over here and met him by herself. Harrison didn't want that.

"Hey," he called, lifting one arm as if waving in a greeting. He tamped down the frustration that this meeting hadn't gone the way he planned. As he neared the pair of them, he asked, "What are you doing over here?"

Cass wore a pair of sunglasses, but as he got closer, he could see her eyes. "I saw him looking for us when I came outside," she said. She grinned at Spence, who honestly looked a little star-struck. "He said he gets lost easily."

Gets lost? Harrison shook his head. "I said to go out to the beach and you'd see us," he said to his brother.

"I did," Spence said.

"You're up in the grasses." Harrison brushed some as he walked by. "This isn't the beach."

"We found him," Cass said, which he also didn't appreciate.

He suppressed his sigh and said, "Lauren went back to your place to see what you needed."

Cass looked that way, obviously able to take a hint. "I'll text her," she said. "I got everything. I just ran into Spencer here." She met Harrison's eyes again. "I introduced myself."

"I can see that." He turned back to the swatch of sand he

and Lauren and Conrad had claimed. "Did you introduce yourself to her, Spencer?"

"Sort of," his brother said. "She already knew who I was."

Harrison worked hard not to roll his eyes. "Okay." He walked a little too fast, and he got ahead of Cass and Spence before he forced himself to slow down. No one said anything, his mood having poisoned the laughter and easy conversation they'd been engaged in previously.

He didn't care. He hadn't wanted them to meet that way, and the situation was annoying. They reached the blankets, and Cass sighed as she sank into her chair. "Can you put up the umbrella, baby?" she asked her son.

"Conrad," Harrison said, and the young man looked at him. "This is my brother, Spencer. Spencer, this is Conrad, Cass's son."

"Hey, man." Conrad got to his feet, his smile wide. He shook hands with Spencer, who said, "Hey," back. "Do you work at Royce Tours?"

Conrad started setting up the umbrella for his mother. "Sure do. It's great."

"We've done some publicity for them," Spencer said.

Harrison said nothing as the conversation continued around him. Instead, he pulled out the can of sunscreen. He sprayed down his neck, ears, and arms, and pulled his bucket hat on to further ward off the sun.

"Conrad's always loved the outdoors," Cass said, now fully shaded. "Thank you, baby. This is great."

Lauren returned, but she didn't take the third chair. While Spencer and Conrad started throwing a football, Cass nodded to the chair beside her.

"This is for me?" he asked.

"That's right," she said. "I told you I can't get up and down off the ground."

He grinned as he took the seat. She put her hand in his, and he wasn't going to complain about that either. He nodded over to Lauren. "She's on the ground."

"She's younger than me," Cass said.

"And my tailbone already hurts," Lauren said, getting up. She took the other chair on Cass's other side. With the umbrella and cooler between them, there was a five-foot buffer.

"I'm sorry I ran into your brother," Cass murmured.

Harrison waved her apology away. He didn't say it was fine, because he couldn't change it. What was the point of being upset about it?

"Harrison."

"What?"

"You're mad."

"I'm not mad," he said. "I'm frustrated." He watched Spence and Conrad throwing the ball. It was only a matter of time before Spencer tried to recruit the younger man to his crew, and Harrison didn't want to have to step in between that.

"It took a lot for me to even arrange this meeting, and it didn't go the way I wanted." He looked over to her. "It's frustrating, that's all."

"I'm sorry," she said.

"It's not your fault."

She tugged her hand free, and things stayed tense between them. Harrison wasn't sure why, but when Conrad had to get to work, he suddenly wanted to leave too.

Spencer had finally relaxed, and he carried the conversation with Cass and Lauren. Harrison just listened, their voices finally ebbing into the sound of the waves.

When it was time for Spencer to hit the road, Harrison didn't kiss Cass before they left. He did say, "I'll text you later, okay?" and she'd nodded.

He stewed over the afternoon that evening. Into the next day. For a week. He wasn't sure what had gone wrong, only that he hadn't felt like himself.

Spencer had said, *Cass is great, Harrison. I liked her a lot.*

He generally was a good judge of character, but Harrison had been so off that day, and he still didn't know why.

One morning, while he shaved and thought about what pastry he'd get for Cass that morning, a lightbulb went off in his head. "You weren't yourself," he said to his reflection. "You weren't Harrison the man. The sexy boyfriend who plans fun dates and takes the perfect pastry to your girlfriend every morning. You were *Spencer's overprotective, anxious brother.*"

They weren't the same person—they were versions of the same man—and Harrison hadn't liked being with Cass when he wasn't himself.

I figured it out, he sent to her. He swiped his keys from the counter and added, *I'll tell you when I drop off breakfast.*

Oh, I'm not home, she said. *Sorry, I meant to text you. Sariah and Robbie texted me late last night and said they were almost on the ground in Atlanta. I drove down to pick them up.*

Harrison paused in his garage to read and then re-read

her texts. “She’s not home,” he said aloud. “Her daughter and son-in-law are here.”

Sorry, Harrison, she sent. *But you’ll get to meet them.*

It’s fine, he said, because it was. *I can’t wait to meet them, and I guess I’ll eat all the peach-mango tarts.*

She sent a laughing emoji and then a piece of pie, and Harrison got himself out the door and over to Gourmet Goods. He could leave a bunch of pastries in her house—Lauren was still there—for when she returned with Sariah and Robbie.

He did just that, his throat closing as he left her house and headed to work. He wanted to meet her daughter and son-in-law. He did. He just wondered if things between them would change yet again, and how her kids would react to him in person.

After all, the idea of your widowed mother dating was one thing. Actually seeing her boyfriend was quite another. Harrison went to work with snakes in his stomach, all of them hissing about how *thingssss* with *Cassss* were about to get more complicated.

Chapter Twenty-Two

"And you two can stay here." Cass pushed open the door for the bedroom at the end of the hallway, the one furthest from the steps she'd climbed with Sariah and Robbie in tow. She beamed at her oldest daughter as she entered the room.

"Wow, Mom," she said. She didn't go far. "This is incredible."

"It's meant to be a second-level master suite," Cass said.

Sariah looked at her, pure interest in her eyes. "And you have the bed made and everything."

"I figured you and Robbie would come visit eventually."

Sariah had more questions, but she didn't vocalize them right now. She turned and started wandering toward the bed. Yes, Cass had bought furniture for the bedroom. Conrad had a queen-sized bed in his room too, and Lauren did as well. They each had their own bathroom, and Cass had saved this second suite for Sariah and Robbie. Even if they only came every so often, it would be a nice sanctuary for them.

"I wanted it to be easy for everyone to come," she said. Maybe then they would.

"Conrad said you didn't sell the house in Sweet Water Falls," Sariah said. She jumped on the bed, laughing. Robbie joined her, and Cass couldn't help giggling with them. They'd had a long flight, and they both looked absolutely bushed.

"I didn't," Cass said. "I'm going in a week or two for Supper Club. I'll decide what to do then."

Sariah sat up, and Cass was reminded that just because she was married now, and recently finished with college, didn't mean she was a peer for Cass. She was still Sariah's mother, and she still needed a mother. Cass couldn't ask her what to do.

"You haven't decided?" Sariah asked.

"Sort of." Cass turned away from her. She didn't have to explain anything to Sariah, something she'd been telling herself about Conrad for several weeks. She grasped the smaller of their bags and tugged it across the thick carpet and into the room. "I'll let you get settled."

"Let me, Miss Haslam," Robbie drawled. He was born-and-bred Texan, and Cass would be shocked if her daughter and her husband ever lived anywhere else. Of course, she'd thought that about herself once too.

He hurried across the expansive room and dragged the suitcase further into the room. Then he came to retrieve the others. Cass stood out of the way and hugged Sariah when she came over. "If you want to meet Harrison, we can go to dinner tonight."

"Okay," Sariah said. She yawned, and Cass let them go into the room and close the door. She sighed too, a yawn of her own not far behind. She'd gotten up really early to make the drive to the airport, and she wished her daughter had not tried to make it a surprise. Sariah was practical, but she had some of West in her, in that she loved showing up where she wasn't expected to be.

I hate surprises, Cass thought as she went past Lauren's bedroom and downstairs. She supposed she'd had too many unpleasant ones in her life, and she'd rather be prepared than wake up at three a.m. and then make an hour-long drive in the dark. She was thrilled Sariah and Robbie were here, though, and she hoped they'd stay as long as they wanted.

Lauren was likely in a meeting, and she'd come to the kitchen when she finished. She had the best stories out of anyone Cass knew, and she flipped open her paper calendar. She kept one online too, so she could access it from her phone, but she loved the scent of paper. Of ink. Of seeing her handwriting and drawing sketches of rooms, furniture, and textiles.

"Let's see." She couldn't just go back to bed. She had a meeting today with Chelsea Bergstrom, and then she had to get down to the carpet store to pick out samples for Mrs. McDonald.

Cass thanked her lucky stars—and the Lord above—that she'd been able to find clients on Hilton Head so quickly. She'd given out her portfolio and references, and her first two clients had both taken less than four hours to decide to hire her after their initial meeting.

If she could get Chelsea on-board, she'd have three clients, and Cass rarely worked with many more than that. It might not seem like a lot, but she'd learned that people who hired someone like her had...demands. And she had to be available to listen to them—and then meet them—at the drop of a hat.

Her phone rang, and she picked it up. She didn't know the number, so she employed her professional interior designer voice as she said, "This is Cassandra Haslam."

"Yes," a cool female voice said. "Please hold for AnnaMae Hank."

"I—" Cass cut off as frilly music filled her line. They'd called her, and she had to wait on hold? "AnnaMae what?" she muttered.

She flipped through her designs, her mind moving through Mrs. McDonald's kitchen and how Cass could get more usage out of the strange layout. She'd starred one wall, and she needed to get out there with a general contractor and see if it was load-bearing or not. If that wall could come down...

She'd ask Harrison to go with her. He'd know, and while she sat on hold, she smiled at the vision spreading before her. Her and Harrison should work together. He could build the properties; she'd design them. Inside and out.

He probably had an architect, but Cass could consult with them. She'd often asked for West's opinion on her designs, but the man had been hopeless other than saying, "It looks amazing, hon. They're gonna love it."

Her clients had not always loved her designs, but she did have a lot of happy customers. Enough to move her company and get started without too much trouble.

"Cassandra Haslam," another woman said, her voice deep and rich and gravelly.

"Yes, ma'am," Cass said. "You must be AnnaMae Hanks."

"It's just Hank," she said. "No S on the end."

"Ah, I see," Cass said. "Well, what can I do for you?"

"I was at lunch the other day with someone," she said, and she spoke in the slow, Southern way Cass had heard a lot of here in Carolina. "And she showed me some of your work. I went online and looked some more, and I'm interested in you."

"Okay," Cass said. "Are we talking a kitchen redesign? A house? New build?" She needed more direction than "I'm interested in you." She flipped the page in her calendar, looking at next week. She flew back to Texas on Saturday, and honestly, she couldn't wait.

"This is for my country club, dear."

"Your...country club." Cass blinked and looked up from her calendar. Beryl stood at the back door, and she moved to slide it open for him. He'd bound down to the beach, barking and biting at the waves as they came ashore. But he always came back.

Off he went as AnnaMae said, "Yes, dear. I own the Highmarshall Country Club out near the Sea Pines."

"Oh, yes," Cass said, though she could barely navigate to the grocery store and back. "Lovely area over there." She had been to the Sea Pines area of the island, because they had good shopping. And a lot of wealth in that part of town, including apparently, a country club.

"Yes," AnnaMae said. "The club is in dire need of a refresh. Dining hall. Kitchen. Lobby. Guest rooms. Conference rooms. Locker rooms. All of it."

Cass moved out onto her patio. "A refresh? Like new

paint and carpet? Or a redesign? Like a new layout, with new paint and new carpet?"

"All of the above," AnnaMae drawled, taking forever to deliver the line.

"I'd need to see the scope of the project," she said. "I have a free consultation, but it has to be scheduled, and I have to be on-site where the design will take place." She'd learned that long ago. She would not just "pop by" to go over the layout, take measurements, or get a potential client's wishlist without an appointment. At least an hour.

And for AnnaMae Hank-with-no-S? Probably two hours.

"What's your schedule like?" she asked.

Cass returned to the house and flipped the pages in her calendar. "I could get you in this week on..." She paused, as if she was so busy she couldn't make it work. And she was. Her friend was here. Her kids. Harrison. Her other clients—potentially three by this afternoon. "Thursday morning," she said. "Or next week before noon on Monday and Tuesday, and afternoon on Wednesday and Thursday."

"Lisa?" AnnaMae asked.

"We could make Monday morning work, ma'am," she said. "If Miss Haslam can meet at ten-thirty."

"Ten-thirty next Monday is great," Cass said, wondering how AnnaMae had gotten her assistant on the line too. "I'll put you down then. I'll see you at the country club."

"I'll make sure you have a code and a pass to get through the gate," Lisa said, her voice polite and professional. One did not get as close to Southern royalty as she did without those qualities.

"Great," Cass said. "Thanks." The call ended, and she

turned back to outdoors, as Beryl was still out there. She whistled for him, and the dog came sprinting through the loose sand. Then the harder packed stuff with grasses, and then up her steps in a single bound.

She laughed at him, scrubbed his head, and let him in the house before she slid the door closed and sealed the heat out.

Her phone chimed again, and Cass almost wanted to throw it into the ocean so she could ignore it easier. This was a message from Harrison, though, so she looked at it with different expectations than a business call.

Did you get the treat I left for you? he asked.

She hadn't seen anything on the front porch. *No*, she said, heading in that direction. *Where did you leave it?*

Conrad had gone to work while she'd been at the airport, and she wouldn't put it past him to have taken something from the porch.

On your kitchen counter.

She turned back around. He'd been in her house? She wasn't sure why that surprised her, only that it did. She couldn't smell his cologne, and if he'd stopped by earlier that morning, he'd have been wearing it.

She looked up from her phone, her eyes sweeping the island countertop. How she'd missed the two stacked blue pastry boxes, she'd never know. "Wow," she said with a smile. Of course Harrison would take care of her and her friends and family. That was what Harrison did best.

She tapped to call him instead of using her slow thumbs to text. He answered with a chuckle and then, "I don't tease you about your wife. Leave me be." A pause, and then he said, "Hey, sweetheart."

"You brought two boxes," she said. She reached for the first one, wondering who on his construction crew was teasing him. She pulled in a breath at the rows of beautiful pastries. "Of peach-mango tarts."

Her mouth watered, and she'd definitely be able to make it through the day with these. She wanted to hoard them all and not tell anyone else he'd brought them. She could eat a few each day.

"Only one box of those," he said. "The other box is an assortment. I thought your daughter might want to sample, the way we did."

"She'll love this," she said. "Thank you, baby." The endearment tripped out of her mouth, because she'd never called him anything but Harrison. She called her children "baby," and she'd often called West that same thing.

But not Harrison.

He said nothing, and the silence stretched into something awkward. She closed her eyes and wondered why that had come out of her mouth. She liked Harrison. A lot. A whole lot. That was why, and she shouldn't be embarrassed about it.

"What's your schedule like tonight?" she asked. "Sariah and Robbie are sleeping today, but I said we might be able to go out together tonight. So they can meet you." She hadn't thought much of it when Sariah had finally brought Robbie home for her and West to meet. Her daughter had talked about him for months before she'd let Cass and West into their relationship, and Cass *had* told her kids about Harrison.

Maybe not the same things Sariah had shared with her, but enough.

"I'm sure I can make it," Harrison said, and Cass thought his voice sounded a touch cool. "Will Conrad be there?"

"I doubt it," Cass said. "He charms the evening crowds too well." He did, and he made more in tips with the afternoon and evening groups than any during the day. He actually preferred to work later in the day, and Cass rarely saw him in the evenings. "But I can invite Lauren."

"Sure," he said.

"So a real family affair," Cass said with a smile. Her stomach clenched and trembled, but no one would know unless she told them.

"Seven?" he suggested. "I'll call Burke's and get a table for five."

"Oh, Sariah will like Burke's."

"Great, see you then."

"Harrison," Cass said quickly, before he could hang up. "Thank you for the pastries. They...look great." What she really wanted to say was that they meant a lot to her. They told her each and every day how much he thought about her. And she needed that right now.

"You're welcome, sweetheart. See you tonight."

The call did end, and Cass pressed her phone to her pulse as she moved the full box of her favorite fruit tarts to see what was in the one beneath. The assortment included croissants and eclairs, and she plucked her favorite—the chocolate croissant—from the bunch and headed into the kitchen to make fresh coffee.

Now that she had a date with her prince to look forward to, Cass could survive anything that came her way today—including only a couple of hours of sleep.

THE DOORBELL RANG A FEW MINUTES AFTER SEVEN, and everyone in the beach house turned toward the front door. "I'll get it," Sariah said.

"He's *my* boyfriend," Cass shot back. They both moved at the same time, but Sariah was faster, especially in her flats where Cass wore heels.

"You answered the door when Robbie came over," she said.

"No," Cass argued. "You guys arrived together." She followed her daughter, because she wanted to introduce her to Harrison, not just have them meet. She suddenly understood on a deep level why he'd been upset with how Cass had met Spencer.

She took the last few strides across the lobby after Sariah had the door open, and Harrison stood there with a huge bouquet of flowers in his hands. He looked up from the blooms, and he was absolutely adorable.

"Wow," Sariah said.

"Hello, Harrison," Cass said smoothly. "Don't you look amazing tonight?" She laughed and took several quick, running steps into Harrison's arms. He grinned and received her, and Cass only stood in his arms for a moment though she'd like to stay there for longer.

She faced Sariah now too. "Sariah, this is Harrison Tate and my favorite flowers on the planet." She took the assortment of daisies from him, only mildly surprised at his thoughtfulness. "Harrison, this is my daughter, Sariah." Robbie approached, with Lauren bringing up the rear. "And her husband, Robbie. They've been living in Taiwan this summer."

"Hullo." Harrison charmed everyone with his Southern drawl and his firm handshakes. Cass kept one eye on her daughter's reaction, but Sariah gave nothing away. In fact, she'd walled everything up and off, and Cass didn't like that.

She'd done the same thing after West's death, and that was how Cass had known she'd been hurting. Could she be in pain right now too? Watching Cass date someone else?

Guilt gutted her, and her smile slipped. "Should we go?" she asked. "We do have a reservation."

"Yes, let's go," Harrison said. "I brought the nice truck if Lauren wants to ride up front with us?" He looked at her.

"I'm fine with whatever," she said. She brought up the rear and pulled the front door closed behind her. She wore a ravishing red dress tonight, and honestly, Cass would be shocked if she didn't leave with someone else. Who'd be eating at Burke's alone, Cass didn't know. But Lauren deserved to get picked up in that dress, which ruched over her stomach and hips, but lay flat everywhere else.

She worked out a lot, and Lauren had glorious, long, dark hair. She knew how to wear makeup and she knew how to talk to men, and Cass had grown to love and appreciate her more since West had died. And particularly, this summer where she'd been staying with Cass on the island.

She'd run into a bit of trouble with Blake Williams, but Cass thought if he'd just try a little harder, she'd go out with him. She'd talked about him a lot, but it was always, "He'll have to work some sort of special spell to get me to say yes to another date with him."

In Cass's opinion, that was just a defense mechanism

Lauren had created so she didn't have to be hurt. Cass understood that, as she'd compartmentalized as much as possible in the past eighteen months since West's death.

Cass caught up to Sariah and leaned closer to her. "So. What do you think?" she whispered.

Sariah looked up at her, her eyes full of wariness. Cass's heart beat erratically for a moment. "I think Conrad is right," Sariah said. She slowed to a stop, and everyone went ahead of them.

Cass wasn't sure what Sariah and Conrad had talked about. She folded her arms and waited.

"He's...not Daddy," Sariah said. She got moving again, and Cass could only look after her.

Of course Harrison wasn't West. Why did her children think she was trying to replace their father? That wasn't what this was about at all. Not even a little bit.

"It's great that you have Robbie and get to spend time with him every day," she called after her daughter. Her stomach stormed, and words boiled and bubbled beneath her tongue. "You have your own life, Sariah. I don't even know where Jane is, as she didn't check-in with me this morning. She's out doing whatever she wants, without regard to how I'm feeling."

Sariah faced her—everyone did. Lauren started toward her, but Cass didn't want to be silenced. She shook her head, but Lauren kept coming. "Cass," she said.

"No," Cass said. "Conrad left right after graduation. With you. You two had each other. Who did I have?"

"You had us," Lauren said.

Cass looked at her wildly, her chest vibrating in such a strange way. "I don't understand why my children don't want me to be happy. Why they think I have to be alone forever now. How they can't see how very lonely I was in Sweet Water Falls." Tears fell down her face, and Cass hated this kind of crying.

Sariah stood next to Robbie, who had his arm around her shoulders. He stood in a protective, comforting stance, a look of worry and concern on his face. Couldn't Cass have that? And if not, why not?

"Cass," Lauren said again. She touched Cass's arm. "Let's go inside for a minute, okay?"

"You guys go without me," Cass said, and she'd probably be horrified if Harrison had said he wasn't going to go to dinner with his friends and family but she should. "I don't feel like going out. I mean, I'm just supposed to stay home by myself from now until forever, right?"

"Mom," Sariah said. "That's not what I said."

"I heard you," Cass said. "You said he's not Daddy. Of course he's not! And why should he be? Your father has been gone for a year and a half! What's the proper mourning period, Sariah?"

Her daughter shook her head, tears leaking out of her eyes too.

"I deserve to be happy too," Cass said. She spun on her heel and went back inside, practically wrenching the door off the hinges as she did. Lauren went with her, and she closed the door in a much quieter way than Cass would've.

"I'm going to bed," Cass said, her head held high. She'd had a great time getting ready that evening. Lauren had sat first with her, and then she'd gone upstairs with her friend while she got ready. She'd helped Sariah with her hair, and they'd talked, and now...

Now everything felt bruised and broken. It felt wrong and warped, and Cass could only remember feeling like this —just like this—one other time in her life.

The night West had died.

She marched around the corner and down the hall, Lauren's heels making noise as she came too. "I don't want to talk about it," Cass said. She turned back to face her friend. "My kids think I should lock myself in a tower and never *see* another male. I don't understand." She began to cry again, but she wiped angrily at her face. "I'm not talking about it. I'm not going. I just want to take a bath and forget I thought this might be a nice dinner among adults."

Lauren nodded. "For the record," she said quietly. "I think you're right. Sariah shouldn't have said anything but the positive. She met him for five seconds."

Cass wasn't sure what that had to do with anything. "Does he take some getting used to?"

"Not at all," Lauren said. "Oh, honey." She drew Cass into a hug. "You *do* deserve to be happy, and you deserve to feel good about Harrison. He's a great man. Don't listen to your children."

"They're so loud," Cass whispered. "They're in my head all the time." *All* the time. Every second. Questioning her. Making her feel stupid for moving to South Carolina. For moving her business. For going out with someone new.

What they didn't understand was that if she didn't do any of those things, she'd have been swallowed whole by that house in Texas by now. She wouldn't be herself anymore, and she'd just started to feel normal again.

She stepped back and drew in a breath. "You should go

without me. Someone needs to see you in that dress." She smiled at Lauren. "Maybe call Blake and see if he's available."

Lauren smiled, and Cass caught the spark of hope in her eyes before it withered and died. "No, but I am hungry."

"I'll take you to dinner," Harrison said from the end of the hall. "Sariah and Robbie decided to just go grab something from the street trucks on the beach tonight." He met Cass's eye, pure concern in his.

"I'm sorry," she whispered. "I didn't mean to cause a scene and make the evening a mess."

"I'd love to go to dinner," Lauren said with grace and elegance. She joined Harrison at the end of the hall and linked her arm through his. She smiled at Cass and said, "We'll bring Cass back her favorite, and then you two can have a little picnic in the living room." She smiled, tugged on Harrison's arm, and they left.

Cass continued into her bedroom and closed the door about the same time the front door snicked shut. Then she crumpled to the floor, her knees to her chest, and sobbed.

Why didn't she deserve to be happy too?

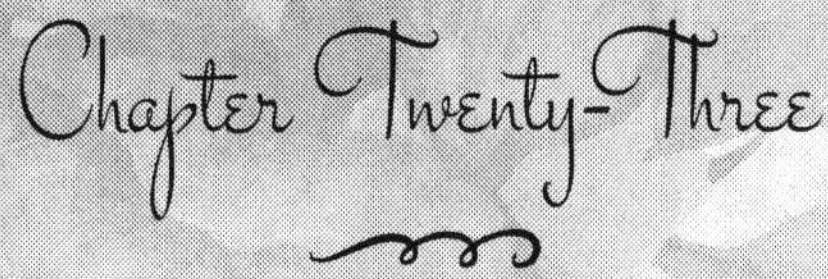

Chapter Twenty-Three

Lauren really liked Harrison Tate, and she could see why Cass did too. The man was kind, and spirited, and he knew everyone on the island. They all knew him too, and they liked him. They shook hands with him, and laughed with him, and asked him how the build was going.

When they finally got to a table, Lauren took a deep breath and blew it out. She met Harrison's eyes briefly, and then picked up her menu. "So." She flipped past the appetizers. She had no room for more than a few bites in this dress. "What would be Cass's favorite here?"

"The chicken pot pie," he drawled out without a moment's hesitation. "She loves it."

Lauren caught the tail end of a smile on the Southern gentleman's face before he dipped his chin toward the menu too. She'd told Cass the truth—Harrison was a good man. He didn't take "getting used to."

She could also see why her children were a little surprised at Cass's choice for a boyfriend. He didn't scream refinement, nor did he seem like the type of man to draw any attention to himself at all. Cass liked being taken care of, which wasn't a bad thing. Lauren wanted the same.

But West...West had been refined. He never wore anything but slacks and polos, or a suit and tie for work. The man's most exciting activity was bird-watching, for crying out loud.

Harrison was his complete opposite, in so many ways.

Lauren wondered if Cass had been happy with West, and she could see why her children didn't like the idea of Harrison. Because it made them wonder the same thing, and while they weren't great at showing it, they did want their mother to be happy.

"What are you going to get?" Harrison asked, and Lauren looked up from her thoughts.

"I don't know." She closed the menu again. "Why don't you order for me?"

His eyes widened as his eyebrows went up. "You want me to order for you?"

"You know me," she said. "I've been living here almost as long as Cass." She glanced up as a man approached the table. He filled their water glasses and asked for drink orders.

"I'll take some Prosecco," she said, giving him a smile.

"I've got one right here for you." Another man took two more steps and arrived at the waiter's side.

Blake Williams.

And he held two glasses of champagne, not just one.

Lauren's throat went dry at the sight of the drink—oh, how thirsty she was—and then turned into a desert at the sight of the man.

Blake wore deep, dark blue slacks that almost had a sheen

to them. His dress shirt was light blue, open at the throat, and pulling across his chest like it might be a tad too small.

She swallowed and strengthened her resolve. "No, thank you," she said.

"You don't want this Prosecco?" Blake lifted one of the glasses and took a sip from the other. His dark blue eyes sparkled like gems. "It's good."

"You probably poisoned it," she said.

He burst out laughing, and that only drew more attention to their table. The waiter backed up and said, "I'll give you a minute."

Harrison stared at her from across the table, and she looked at him for help. He leaned forward and said, "If you want to go sit with him, it's fine. I'll order my and Cass's food to go."

Had he not heard her? Did Cass tell him nothing about what Blake had done to her? Yes, yes, his son had been hurt. Lauren knew. She didn't hold a grudge, but she also wasn't going to make it really easy for the man to walk into her heart, stomp on it, and then leave her bleeding.

She'd texted him to forgive him, but he hadn't asked her out since. Did he think waltzing up with champagne erased that? Or was romantic?

"No," she hissed to Harrison. "I don't want to go out with him."

"He didn't say go out with me." Blake actually slid onto the bench beside her. She scooted over, giving him a glare. "He said you could come sit with me." He placed the second flute of champagne on the table in front of her, and Lauren almost lunged for it.

Almost.

"I'm fine here." She folded her arms and glared at Harrison now. "We're having a great time."

Blake took another sip of his drink and looked over to Harrison too. "Yes, how's your girlfriend, Harry?"

"She's feeling under the weather tonight," Harrison answered smoothly. "How's Tommy?"

"Good." Blake gave a light laugh. "We've been to the hospital twice this summer, and I told him if there's a third time..." He trailed off, and Lauren found herself wanting to hear the end of that sentence.

She looked at him, which was a huge mistake. His eyes locked onto hers, urgency in them now. "You look amazing," he said earnestly. "That dress is just...you pull it off like no other woman would be able to."

A bit of discomfort moved through her despite the compliment. Harrison cleared his throat as if to remind Blake he and Lauren weren't alone, and she suddenly wished they were.

"Listen, I need a new marketing manager," Blake said.

Lauren leaned away from him, shocked she'd started to move in. But she had. "Excuse me?" she asked.

"Blake," Harrison said in a voice laced with warning.

"No, I do," Blake said. "Lauren, you'd be perfect for the job."

She blinked at him, sure this wasn't why he'd brought her a glass of Prosecco. Was it? She shook her head, trying to get her thoughts to align. "Thank you," she said diplomatically. "But I have a job I really like, and I doubt you could afford me."

She picked up the glass of champagne and took a delicate sip. "But thank you, really."

"Name your price."

"Okay," Harrison said. He scooted to the end of the bench and stood up. "Come on, Blake. You should get back to your party."

In her peripheral vision, she saw him wave to someone. She couldn't look away from Blake, however. She saw desire in his eyes, and she felt it swimming through her veins too. She'd always been attracted to him, stemming back two summers ago to the Fourth of July when she'd come to visit Bea that first time.

"Oh, you're here with your firm." Harrison tugged Blake to his feet. "Look. John's here for you, Blake. Go on now. Get on back to them."

Blake went, thankfully, because Lauren wasn't sure what might've happened if he hadn't. Harrison exhaled as he sat back down, and their eyes met across the table.

"He's a great guy," Harrison said. "Who's been drinking with his colleagues."

Lauren nodded, because she'd been out with plenty of businessmen and women who drank too much. He'd regret everything in the morning.

With shaking fingers, she lifted her drink again. *Hopefully not this*, she thought, but then she wondered if Blake would even remember this encounter. She almost didn't want him to, and she found her eyes drifting in the direction he'd gone.

He wasn't there anymore, and Lauren's sadness bumped up a notch.

Harrison didn't bring him up again, and he kept the conversation alive during dinner. They took home a meal for Cass, and Lauren immediately retreated upstairs to her bedroom while Harrison went down the hall to Cass's. She didn't care if they stayed in there or came out to the living room.

Cass was a grown woman and could make her own choices. As she passed the bedroom where Robbie and Sariah were staying, her step slowed. She had half a Texas-mind to go in there and berate the girl for adding to Cass's burden.

In the end, that wasn't Lauren's role, and she went by the closed door, the scent of oily Chinese food floating on the air.

In her own room, she changed out of the amazing dress she'd worn that evening and into something far more comfortable. She wondered if she'd have caught Blake's eye in her sweatpants and oversized T-shirt.

"Probably not," she muttered to herself. Besides, *catching* someone's eye wasn't the problem for Lauren.

It was *keeping* their attention for longer than a few months she couldn't seem to do.

Chapter Twenty-Four

Joy picked up the crock of pulled pork and hurried with it over to the table. It went right in the center, and she stepped back to assess. Buns, cut and ready in the cutest little basket she'd ever seen.

Cole slaw, chilled and waiting on the table.

Pulled pork, check.

Her daddy's famous, award-winning barbecue sauce? Standing at the ready for anyone who wanted to sauce up their sandwich.

Potato chips—ridged potato chips—had been poured into a huge bowl and sat ready at the end of the table. She'd set that with her best dishware, her sterling silver utensils, and her grandmama's hand-stitched napkins.

Maybe she'd gone a little overboard. But Bea and Cass would be here for Supper Club tonight, all the way from the East Coast, and she'd invited Cherry Forrester. The woman had said she'd come too, and Joy's nerves bounced around like a ping-pong ball getting smacked from one side of the table to the other.

The doorbell rang, and she spun toward it. Bessie opened the door before Joy could take a single step, and she called, "It's just me."

"Come in." Joy moved in that direction now. "You don't need to take off your shoes."

Bessie did anyway, saying, "I like not wearing them."

"Then everyone thinks they need to." Joy bent and picked up Bessie's shoes. She deposited them in the laundry room while Bessie went into the kitchen.

"This looks amazing, Joy."

She hugged her, holding extra-tight for a few moments. "Thanks." She sighed as she stepped back. "Cherry's coming."

"So your text said." Bessie smiled. "It might be nice to have an extra person on the months Bea and Cass don't come."

"That's what I was thinking," Joy said. "Plus, I'm never leaving Sweet Water Falls, so we need more members in the Supper Club."

Bessie nodded, and the doorbell rang again.

"It's us," Lauren trilled out, and laughing and squealing commenced. She'd been in Hilton Head for almost two months now, and Joy missed her more than she could admit. She hugged Lauren so tightly, the two of them just stuck together without saying anything.

When she finally stepped back to embrace Cass and then Bea, she noticed that Lauren had tears in her eyes. "When are you coming home?" she asked.

"Soon," Lauren said. "Before the next Supper Club."

"Good," Bessie said. "Because you're the hostess next month." She grinned and hugged Lauren while Joy turned her attention to Bea.

"Wow," she said. "Look at your hair." She reached out to touch it, and Bea simply smiled and let her. "You didn't cut the top this time."

"It's a little wispy," Bea said, running her fingers through it. "But I like how different it is."

Different was a good way to describe it. It was almost pure white now, and Joy knew that came from a bottle, because Bea was definitely brassier than that. The sides and back of her head had very nearly been shaved, but the top was still long. She'd styled it up and around, and it swooped in a beautiful style.

Cass looked the same as she usually did. Decked out in clothes that said so much with so little. She wore no makeup and no jewelry tonight, which was a bit odd. But because she was so classically beautiful, it didn't matter.

Her hair had been pulled all the way back, which she also didn't do very often, but they had flown in from Carolina today. Maybe it had been a tough night or a rough flight.

Joy hugged her hard too, and said, "Come see what I made for Harrison."

"You made something for Harrison?" Cass went with her, and Joy nearly burst with excitement.

"Yes," she said. She opened the fridge and got out the jar. "And fine. I went to a truffle-making class at Sweet Water Taffy, and Gretchen was selling these." She handed the jar of jelly to Cass. "But look. Harrison said he loves jalapeño jelly, and it's hard to find. Now he'll have some." She beamed like this was wonderful, because it had made her feel wonderful to buy it for him.

Cass grinned at the jar. "Joy," she said. "He'll love this. Thank you." She hugged her again, snapped a picture of the jelly, and sent it presumably to Harrison.

"Was Gretchen doing the class?" she asked.

"Yes," Joy said.

"I'm surprised by that," Bessie said. "She's due any day now with that baby."

"She was *huge*," Joy said. "But right up front, showing us how to dip the truffles." Gretchen was also married to a Cooper brother—Cherry's middle brother.

The doorbell rang again, and it could've been Sage or Cherry. Since the door didn't open and no one walked in, Joy knew it was Cherry. "All right, ladies," she said. She smoothed down her blouse. "This is her, and we don't need to be scaring her off from the very first minute."

"You act like she hasn't met us before," Lauren said.

"You haven't met her," Joy said. She and Bessie had, but Bea and Cass? Joy wasn't sure if they had. They knew of Cherry, because she belonged to an old family here in Sweet Water Falls. Everyone knew the Coopers, and even if Cherry had left town for a while, she was still small-town royalty.

And only a couple of years older than Joy.

She opened the door to find the dark-haired beauty standing on the porch. She held no less than three loaves of bread in her arms, with a plastic bag swinging from her wrist.

"Cherry." Joy lunged at her as one of the dark brown loaves toppled. She caught it and added, "I told you not to bring anything."

"I couldn't do it," Cherry said with a nervous laugh. "My momma taught me to show up with food, and I work at a bread store."

Bessie crowded out onto Joy's small front porch too, taking the rest of the bread from Cherry. "Howdy, Cherry."

"Hey, Bessie."

"If that's your momma's jam, I'm going to make a run for it." Bessie grinned, and Cherry handed her the bag.

"I wasn't supposed to bring it anyway." She smiled back and looked at Joy. She nodded to the bread. "And that's day-old, so don't be thinkin' I did anything great."

"Day-old from The Bread Boy still equates to delicious," Joy said. She stepped back and let Cherry into the house. They faced the trio of women on the fringes of the kitchen, and Joy nodded to Lauren on the end. "This is Lauren Keller. Next to her is Cassandra Haslam. And then Beatrice Callahan."

"Turner," Bea said. "I got remarried a couple of years ago."

Foolishness wove through Joy. "I knew that, of course." She shook her head. "Sorry, Bea."

"It's fine." She waved her hand at Joy.

"I still introduce myself as Cherry Cooper," Cherry said. "And I've been married for three years now." She grinned at Bea. "I think you and I were in the same math class in high school." She raised her eyebrows. "No?"

"I honestly have no idea," Bea said, laughing. "My life has been through so many iterations since high school."

"Oh, girl, mine too," Cherry said. She fit in well with the group, and Joy smiled to herself. Sage walked in a moment later, and Joy clapped her hands together.

"All right, everyone," she said, giving the ladies a chance to settle down. "It's barbecue night, and we don't normally make speeches, but it's my house. So." She surveyed all of them, noting how Cherry didn't stand apart from the group, but right next to Lauren as if they were also old friends.

"Bea, Cass, and Lauren have been on Hilton Head all summer, so we need a Real Update from them."

"A capped Real Update?" Bea asked.

"That's right," Joy said. "No holding back." She held up one finger and shook it at them. "And I'll know if you do." She switched her stern gaze to Cherry, where it softened. "Cherry Forrester is here with us tonight, so I want her to introduce herself."

She looked at Bessie and Sage. "And then the rest of us can do our Good News Minute, okay? That way, everyone gets a quick update." She swept her hands toward the dining room, which sat behind the four women still standing and beside the kitchen. "Let's sit and get the wine flowing though."

They did that, small conversations breaking out again. Joy let them, because she knew she could rope this crew back to a single conversation easily. In fact, she met Lauren's eyes, and said, "You start, Lauren."

"Well." She exhaled. "Joy knows this, because I called her and talked her ear off about it." She gave Joy a shy smile and tucked her hair behind her ear. "Blake Williams...he's going to be the death of me. I think I'm going to give up on him."

"No," Bessie said, the word almost a moan. "Why?"

"He offered me a job." Lauren rolled her eyes. She sighed. "And in my best red dress too."

"That's a killer red dress," Cass said. "It addled his brains, that's all."

Lauren waved her wine glass and then took a sip. "That's all. I'm done. My job is great. I'll be back in Sweet Water Falls to host the next Supper Club. Blah blah blah. Cass?" She looked at the brunette next to her.

Cass drew a big breath. "I'm here to go through the house again. I'm taking Conrad to college in a couple of weeks. Then..." She looked over to Bea, the two of them exchanging a glance. Joy hated being on the outskirts of things, but she supposed she had her own close relationships inside the Supper Club too. "Then I don't know," Cass finished.

"What do you mean you don't know?" Joy asked.

"I mean, I'm not sure I can sell the house here," Cass said. "I'm not sure I want to go back to Hilton Head."

Silence descended on the group, and Joy looked at Bea. She looked as shell-shocked as Joy felt, so perhaps she hadn't heard this before.

"Why wouldn't you go back?" Sage asked. "You have a beautiful home there."

"I have a beautiful home here," Cass said. "I don't want to talk about it. That's my Real Update. Bea?" She hadn't poured herself any wine, and she didn't try to hide behind the glass. Cass had never tried to hide behind anything.

Bea blinked at her, then shook her head. "I'm still trying to catch up. Uh..." She looked around the table. "Grant hired me as his full-time secretary. So far, we haven't killed each other." She smiled and brushed something from her plate. "Shelby is going back to her mom's soon. I'm going to miss her. My kids are all alive and well still." She cut a look at Cass. "So I'm good."

She looked at Bessie, who sat beside her. "Uh, yes." Bessie cleared her throat. "Good News Minute for me is that Cherry." She nodded to the woman beside her. Joy hadn't assigned any seats, but they'd all found a comfortable place for them. "Has given me two weeks off to take my Norwegian cruise."

"Wow," Joy said, and she started the applause. The others joined in, all congratulating Bessie for finally taking a vacation.

"Is this the one you're doing with your sister?" Lauren asked from the head of the table.

"Yep." Bessie nodded to Cherry. "You're up."

She smiled around at everyone, but the edges of the gesture shook. "Y'all make this sound so easy, but I can't think of a goldarn thing to say."

"You're just introducing yourself," Joy said.

"Oh. Uh, I'm Cherry." She lifted one hand. "I run The Dough Boy for Shane West, because the man is brilliant with dough, but not so much with anything else." She relaxed. "I'm married to Jed Forrester, and we own Cowboy Ranch. It's always in a state of constant repair and fixing up, but my husband says we are too. As people. We love it, and he lets me have as many goats and dogs as I want, so I can't really complain." She laughed, and everyone joined in with her. "That's about all." She looked at Sage, who covered her hand and patted it.

"I'm not sure if this is good news or bad news," she said. "But I think it won't be a surprise to anyone. I certainly wasn't surprised by it." She smiled, and once again, Joy sensed something scared behind the action. She loved Sage, but the woman kept to herself a lot. She did a lot of things herself, including all the trips they'd gone on.

"Jerry and I are separating," she said. "I'm going to file for divorce once he's moved out." No tears escaped, and in fact, her smile returned. "We just...he's like a roommate, and I think we both want more."

After another few beats of silence, Cass said, "I understand that, Sage. I'm still sorry."

"Thank you," Sage said. She drew a deep breath. "It's fine, ladies. I think it'll be good in the long run." She looked at Joy, as they'd made it all the way around. "Your turn, Joy."

She startled, because she'd heard a few surprising things at the table tonight. "My Good News Minute is that I've been offered a permanent classroom aide position at my elementary school." She accepted the congrats and applause on her behalf. "And...I joined a dating app."

That caused an uproar, but Joy waved both arms above her head. "Nope. I'm pulling my Cass-card, and I don't want to talk about it." There wasn't much to say anyway. She hadn't actually gone out with anyone yet. "Dinner is ready, so let's eat."

She grinned as everyone did what she said, and she caught Cherry Forrester's eye a few minutes later. She lifted her eyebrows, and Cherry nodded. She exuded warmth and confidence, and she laughed and talked with the others there.

Yes, she'd fit in great with this Supper Club, because Joy really felt like they needed to replenish if they wanted to keep going. She watched Cass, and the other woman might not know exactly what she wanted, but Joy had the very real feeling that she'd be back in Hilton Head before long.

Bea lived there already. Lauren would figure out something with Blake—or someone else on the island.

And that would leave Joy, Sage, and Bessie with only a trio. So they needed more people, and while others hadn't fit, Cherry certainly did.

Chapter Twenty-Five

Harrison flipped the burgers on the grill, the noise around him grating on his nerves. Spencer had come for Labor Day, along with his wife and family, and Harrison had invited Bea and Grant. He'd invited his sister and her family, and the vibe on the beach this holiday felt...familial.

If only Cass were here.

She was currently in Waco, helping Conrad get settled into his new apartment. He'd decided to return to Baylor, and Harrison would never tell a single soul about the relief he'd felt when Cass had told him that.

She'd been in Texas for the past couple of weeks, and Harrison really missed her. He got to sleep for an extra twenty minutes, because he didn't have to run over to Gourmet Goods and get her coffee and pastries.

He actually found himself wishing he did. It hadn't been a chore or a burden to him; he loved seeing the beautiful brunette in the morning before work. The sight of her glorious smile, and the taste of her lips, helped him through the long, hot days on the job.

He enjoyed laying in the hammock with her, or walking along the beach for his physical therapy with his hand tucked around hers. He loved talking to her, and he'd go to any restaurant or movie just to be with her and inhale the scent of her fruity, flowery perfume.

The fire beneath the burgers sizzled, and Harrison frowned. He'd gotten lost inside his thoughts again, and he wondered if he'd fallen in love with Cass.

You have, he told himself, and instantly he tried to deny it. An argument ensued within himself, and he still hadn't declared a winner before Grant came up beside him. "Those done?"

"Ready." Harrison turned toward him, slid the spatula under a burger, and put it on the plate his best friend held. He piled them up, and he followed Grant onto the patio. He'd opened the shade, so the sun wouldn't bake them, and he stayed silent while Grant put the food on the table.

"We're ready," he said. "Bea's got all the salads, and Harrison's got all the trimmings for the burgers." He smiled at his wife, who curled into his side and wrapped her arms around him.

Harrison swallowed and looked away, once again thinking he'd fallen for the woman who lived a few houses down. Spencer bumped him, and Harrison came back to the present. "Hey."

His brother held an empty plate, and he handed it to Harrison. "No cheese?"

"You're lactose-intolerant," Harrison said.

"That's why I made the Greek salad," Bea said. She

smiled at Spencer and Harrison. "Spence, your wife is amazing."

"Yeah?" Spencer's attention diverted to Bea, and he certainly didn't need to be told how awesome Jenn was. He loved her deeply, and they had a great relationship. "Why's that?"

"She said she'd give me the recipe for this dessert salad." She carried a plate with only the cookie monster salad on it, which included whipped cream, green apples, and yes, cookies. Bea lifted a bite of the fluffy stuff to her lips, smiling as they closed around the fork.

Spencer chuckled, and Harrison started down the table and filled his plate with potato salad, dessert salad, and then he stacked cheese, lettuce, tomatoes, grilled onions, and then a couple of small slices of pickled jalapeño. He squeezed mayo, mustard, and ketchup on his top bun, and then he pressed it all together.

He turned away from the food table, the big, oval table where others had started taking their seats in front of him. Bea sat beside Grant, with Julie on her other side. Julie's husband was behind him in line, but a free seat sat beside her.

Harrison wouldn't take that one. Jenn had sat down at the end, and Spence would take the seat beside her. A second table had been set up for the teens and kids there, and Harrison didn't want to sit there either. There was room at the adult table, but Harrison was the only one there without a date.

You have a girlfriend, he told himself, and then he forced himself to go sit down in an empty seat beside Grant.

"When's Cass gonna be back?" Grant asked just before

taking a big bite of his burger. He bent over and tilted his head to the side, opening his mouth wide to get everything in. He'd made a double-quarter-pounder, and Harrison honestly didn't know how he'd eat all of that.

"Uh, this week sometime," Harrison said. "Thursday, I think. She's listing her house in Texas, I believe, and then she's got to meet with that country club she signed."

Grant nodded. Bea threw a glance to Harrison, but she said nothing. Still, Harrison caught something in her eyes he wasn't sure of, and he didn't like it. He watched her for another few moments, but she didn't look his way again.

Later that afternoon, while his brother's kids ran through the shallow water and the sun beat down on them even through the umbrellas he and Spence had pounded into the sand, Harrison's fingers flew over his phone.

Everything's okay with Conrad?

Yeah, Cass said. *I think I cried more dropping him off this time than last year.*

Harrison frowned, and instead of continuing to text, he tapped the button to call her. The line rang, and she picked up quickly.

"Hey there," she said. "How was the barbecue?"

"Good," he said, relaxing into his camp chair at the sweet sound of her voice. "Why more crying this year?"

"I just think...I think last year, I was still a little numb from everything." She exhaled mightily enough for it to echo through the line. "This year, it reminds me that I'm going to be all alone again."

Harrison swallowed and looked right, hoping a few more inches would mask his voice from his brother, who sat next to him. "You're not alone, sweetheart," he said. "You'll be back here on Thursday, and I'll be waiting at your place with whatever you tell me you want for dinner."

He watched a man walk his dog, and a mother hand her child a square of a sandwich. Cass said nothing, and Harrison wasn't sure why. He wished he could see her face, and he could easily turn this call into a video chat to do so.

"Harrison," she finally said. "I'm not sure I'll be able to come back this weekend."

His heartbeat started to race, and he swallowed before he asked, "Why not?"

"Sariah wants to go through the house, and I need more time here with her."

"Sure," Harrison said, though he hated the thought of Cass in her old house in Texas, going through things with her daughter. At the same time, Cass had never held back from talking about her husband. "And you're okay? With that?"

"Yes," Cass said. She sighed again. "She's changed her tune. Now she's saying she doesn't want me to sell the house."

"Conrad didn't either," Harrison whispered. "Could you just keep it until...?" He didn't know what came after that. Until what? More time had passed? Her kids were okay with letting go of it?

"I don't want it," she said. "I'm...I'm just trying to manage a lot here, Harrison."

"I know, Cass." He reached up and wiped his forehead. "What do you need me to do? I can come help with the house, or..." He once again trailed off, not sure what to say next. He swallowed, his throat narrowing to the width of a coffee-stirring straw.

"No," she said. "You're so busy there. Building four is a week behind, and I'm fine."

"Cass." The tension and uncertainty radiated through the line, but Harrison didn't know what to say to ease it.

"I'm okay," Cass said, her voice turning bright again. "I am. It's just a lot."

"Conrad's place is okay?" He could maybe get her talking about something else. Something to take her mind somewhere else.

"It's great," she said. "He knows his roommates, and he'll be happy there."

"He almost didn't go back," Harrison said.

"He told me," Cass said. "I think I would've lost my mind with him in South Carolina with me for much longer." She gave a light laugh, and Harrison joined her.

"He's a good kid," Harrison said.

"Yes, he is."

Harrison looked at his brother, who gazed back at him. "Heard from Jane?"

"She's in Michigan," Cass said. "She said she'll probably be here by Saturday, which is the other reason I have to stay in Sweet Water Falls for a little longer than planned."

"Wow." Harrison's eyebrows went up. "How long has it been since you've seen her?"

"Almost nine months," Cass said. "I am excited to see her."

"I bet." He smiled then. "I want some pictures of you and your girls, okay?"

She laughed again, and Harrison could finally smile. "All right," she said, and when she said that, she sounded Texan. Harrison had to believe that she'd at least come back to

Hilton Head to deal with her house here. She'd taken Beryl with her, and he told himself that houses could be sold from thousands of miles away.

And yet, she'd gone back to Texas to sell the one there which she'd shared with West and her children for so long.

He couldn't help wondering if she'd come back to the island—to him. He certainly didn't have the same pull as everything else in Cass's life, and though the call ended on a happy note, Harrison felt worse than ever as he slumped in his chair.

"Everything okay?" Spence asked.

"Yes." Harrison flashed him a smile. "Everything's great."

Chapter Twenty-Six

Cass smelled the coffee as she woke up, glad she had a place to stay here in Texas. She could just as easily rent somewhere when she wanted to visit her friends and have Supper Club. Right now, Sariah and Robbie were staying in one of the bedrooms, and it was convenient and easy for everyone to have the space to stay.

Beryl curled up next to her knees, and Cass reached down to pat him. It would be harder to rent somewhere with Beryl, and she told herself she wouldn't be traveling back and forth that often. When she did, she'd leave her dog on Hilton Head.

As she came closer and closer to consciousness, she remembered what day it was. Saturday.

Jane should be here by noon, though Cass didn't really think she would be. Jane arrived precisely when she wanted to, and not a moment sooner. She ran late all the time, and Cass thought it would likely be suppertime before her younger daughter showed up.

That gave her and Sariah all day to finish going through the house. Though she'd just woken up, exhaustion pulled through her. Her daughter was being extremely picky and somewhat standoffish about the things Cass had left behind.

How can you just walk away from this place? Sariah had asked last night. Cass hadn't answered her, and they'd separated and gone to bed without speaking. Honestly, the tension pouring through Cass all came from her children, as Conrad echoed Sariah's feelings about the house.

He'd asked her now that the summer was over whether she'd be selling the house. She'd told him yes, and they'd fought as they carried his boxes into his new apartment. She'd cried so much after driving away, because yes, she'd miss her son, but mostly because she now felt an insane amount of turmoil over what she'd thought she'd already decided.

Sariah didn't approve of Cass's relationship with Harrison. Conrad had only tolerated him all summer. Neither of them wanted her to sell the house in Texas. Jane would likely have an opinion too, and Cass didn't have to guess at what it would be.

Cass and West had faced their trio of children plenty of times, and Jane wasn't a swing vote. The kids always ganged up on their parents, and Cass wasn't sure she'd be able to stand strong against both of her daughters.

She felt so emotionally fragile, though she'd spoken to Harrison every day this week. Though he'd told her he'd be happy with whatever decision she made, that he was waiting for her back on Hilton Head, and he couldn't wait to see her again.

She'd been gone for too long already, and Cass rolled out of bed and walked into the shower. She and Beryl then went down the hall to the kitchen, where Sariah nursed a cup of coffee, her phone in front of her. Her daughter looked up from the device, her smile coming quickly. "Mom."

Cass had paused at the corner leading from the master suite, and she lifted her chin. "Good morning, Sariah," she said as diplomatically as she could.

Sariah tilted her head. "You're not still upset, are you?"

Cass deflated on the spot. "No." She went into the kitchen and poured herself a cup of coffee. "But Sariah, this is *my* house. I can do whatever I want with it."

Sariah said nothing, and when Cass faced her, her daughter's face had turned hard again. "Mom, none of us want you to sell this house."

"Once again." Cass pulled open the drawer and took out a spoon. "It's my house. You haven't lived here for five years. You're married and on your own. Conrad's at college." She stirred her coffee deliberately, trying to cage the wild storm raging inside her. "Jane moves from place to place every single day."

She looked up, her stomach squeezing. She'd done so much for her children; they had no idea. When West had traveled for work, Cass had held everything together. When they got teachers they didn't get along with, Cass pulled strings and got them transferred. When Sariah had gone over her wedding budget by five thousand dollars, Cass had written the check, no questions asked.

She didn't want them to experience disappointment if she could prevent it. She knew life was cruel and difficult, and if she could shield them from that as much as possible, Cass had done it.

Sariah stared back at her now, and Cass told herself to be brave. She'd voiced her opinions plenty of times in other situations. At Supper Club. In discussions with West. With her assistants within her interior design business.

Somehow, standing up to Sariah was ten times harder. "I don't want to live here," she said as evenly as possible. She sighed as she looked around. The painting above the fireplace reminded her of West. The dark red leather recliner was where he sat in the evenings. He'd fixed the stones in the hearth when they'd cracked.

Everywhere she looked, she saw West.

"I miss your dad," she said.

"That's why you have to stay here," Sariah said.

"Why?" Cass challenged. "So I can be engulfed in grief and sadness every single day of my life?" She brought her eyes back to her daughter's. "I miss him. I love him. But Sariah, I deserve to be happy too."

"You're still grieving," Sariah said.

"No," Cass said. "I'm not. I'm ready to move on, and you're holding me back. I've reached a level of healing and I'm trying to find a fresh start so I can be happy, and you don't want me to." Her chest lifted as she gasped for air. She couldn't believe she'd just said those things, but as the words rang through the silent kitchen, she felt their truthfulness.

"Mama." Sariah got to her feet, but Cass stayed very still. "Of course I want you to be happy."

"I'm happy in South Carolina," Cass said.

"I just don't want you to rush into anything."

"It's been eighteen months," Cass said. "How can that possibly be considered rushing?"

"Harrison's...well, he's not really your type, Mom."

"How would you even know?" Cass asked. Her frustration grew and grew, and she honestly didn't have the energy for this conversation. "We have to finish today. I'm not changing my flight again." She'd rebooked for Tuesday, hoping Jane would be tired of Sweet Water Falls after three days. To Cass's knowledge, her daughter hadn't stayed in one place for that long yet this year.

She left the kitchen and headed for the hallway. She'd stacked all of the things she still needed to figure out what to do with before she listed the house in Conrad's old bedroom, and she and Sariah had gone through almost everything. For Cass, it was the second time through, and she'd selected nothing from the boxes.

Sariah had two she would be taking with her, once she and Robbie found an apartment in San Antonio. Her husband had gone north to the city to look for something this weekend, and Cass had prayed mightily that he'd find the perfect place.

"Jane says she's staying for a couple of weeks." Sariah's footsteps scrambled behind Cass. "You can't leave on Tuesday."

Cass said nothing as she faced the obstacles in the bedroom. That was what these boxes represented for her. Obstacles. Other than this room, and a few hours of cleaning and straightening now that she and Sariah had been staying in the house for a couple of weeks, the house was ready to list.

She'd paid a landscaping company to keep the yard in tip-top shape all summer. She'd wiped away the dust and cobwebs when she'd first arrived. She really was ready to walk out of this house, give the lock one final turn, and face her future.

"Mama," Sariah said.

Cass lifted her coffee to her lips and said nothing.

"Robbie and I could take the house."

Cass's eyebrows went up as surprise moved through her. "You have a job in the city that starts in two weeks."

"I can commute."

Cass smiled and shook her head. "It's two hours one-way, Sariah. That isn't going to work."

Her daughter looked around, clear frustration in her expression. "I—sell it to us anyway. We'll figure out what to do with it." She met Cass's gaze with defiance and challenge in hers.

Cass didn't want to deny her, though she knew Sariah and Robbie couldn't afford this house. Not what Cass could get for it on the open market, at least. Her heart tore again, battling within itself as to what she should do.

She didn't want to cut ties with Sweet Water Falls. She had friends here. Family. She'd love to come visit. She simply didn't want to live here anymore. She really was ready to move on. She thought of the beach house on Hilton Head, and how free she'd felt there. She might still run into a friend who she'd known, or who had worked with West, but the entire sky wasn't painted with sadness.

She didn't have to choose which road she took so carefully, just so she wouldn't go by the strip mall where West had died.

She didn't have to feel his very essence in the walls, or imagine she could still smell his cologne in the sheets and bath towels.

She really was ready to take the steps she'd taken, and she didn't want to go backward.

"I don't know," she said. She put her coffee on the windowsill and faced Sariah again. "Honestly? I think we all need a fresh start. You have Robbie, this new job in the city, and he's only got a year of college left." She smiled at her daughter, but Sariah's eyes shot flames at her.

They then welled with tears, and she spun away from Cass. "You're going to erase him." She stomped out of the room, leaving Cass with the whiplashed words moving through her mind.

"No," she said quietly. "I'm not. He lives in all of us." She looked around the bedroom. "A house is just a house. Why can't they see that?"

A home was created by those that lived there, breathed there, loved there. Cass felt nothing in this house anymore, and for her, that was only another sign that she didn't belong here.

She left her son's old bedroom and went into the kitchen. Sariah wasn't there, and Cass turned in a full circle as she scanned the living room, dining room, out to the deck, and then toward the front door to find her.

A sigh fell from her lips, and she went to look outside. Sariah's husband had taken their car to San Antonio that day, and she found her daughter sitting on the front steps, her knees curled to her chest. She sobbed, and Cass's heart broke all over again.

She hesitated, which made her feel even guiltier, and

then she hurried to her oldest daughter's side. "Hey." She sat next to her, and Sariah didn't resist as Cass drew her into her chest. She cried there, and while Jane had usually been the one to break down and have temper tantrums growing up, Cass had spent plenty of her time consoling Sariah too.

She didn't know what else to say. They'd said enough for now, and Cass could only pray that when Jane showed up, she'd finally find an ally among her children.

Jane didn't arrive by lunch, as Cass predicted she wouldn't. She and Sariah had gone through the last of the boxes, and Sariah had put the three she wanted to keep in the bedroom where she and Robbie were staying.

Her husband had kept her up-to-date on all the apartments he'd looked at that day, and he was currently making the drive back from the city.

In the kitchen, Sariah browned ground beef for their shepherd's pie, and Cass cleaned up the potato peels from the sink. The pot bubbled on the stove, softening the potatoes so she could mash them and put them over the filling.

The front door opened, already drawing Cass's attention before Jane yelled, "All right, folks! I'm here!"

Sariah squealed and abandoned her post at the stove. She ran for the front door and engulfed her twin in a hug. The two of them laughed, and the beauty of that moment touched Cass's heart.

At the same time, she hardly recognized the person standing in the doorway. Jane's hair wasn't its normal color, but a deep blue-black that obviously came from a bottle.

And it had been shaved on one side. The other side bore three braids that connected into one ponytail below her ear, and she sure looked like she could use a hot shower and a square meal.

She separated from Sariah and held up a white plastic bag. "I stopped and got brisket." She beamed like this was fabulous news. Cass actually looked at the sizzling ground beef in the pan, hoping Sariah would say something about it.

She didn't, but she towed Jane into the kitchen by the hand, her face alight too. "Mom, look who's back."

"Hello, dear." Cass took Jane into a big hug too, feeling her younger daughter melt into the embrace. Cass did the same, because she hadn't seen Jane in such a long time, and she did love her daughter with her whole heart.

"Mama." Jane's voice broke, the only sign Cass would get that she missed having a permanent place to call home. That she missed Cass at all. She sniffled and pulled away only a few seconds later. "Sorry I'm a little late. It was hard getting a ride out here."

"You should've called," Cass said, refusing to think about her petite, slight daughter getting into a truck with someone she didn't know. If Cass didn't think about it, and she didn't see it, then it didn't happen. She peered at Jane, whose light brown eyes sat halfway between milk chocolate and copper. The perfect mix of Cass and West.

She reached out and touched Jane's ponytail. "When did you get your hair done like this?" It couldn't be more than an eighth of an inch on the right side, so it had been shaved recently.

"Last week," she boasted. "I met this guy in this tiny little town in Canada. You wouldn't believe how small." She laughed, and she did radiate life to those around her. Cass marveled that she and Sariah were the same age and had been born within minutes of each other.

Of course, they weren't identical twins, but fraternal. In essence, they'd shared the womb, but nothing else about them was the same. Sariah wore her hair straight and shiny, without a stitch of color in it. All the same, she beamed at Jane like the best friends they were.

"Tad asked about you," Sariah said, to which Jane burst out laughing.

"Did you tell him I'm not interested?"

"Of course not." Sariah stirred the beef around and shook her head. "I said you'd be here this weekend, and I'd give you his number." She left the stove again and opened the drawer beside it. After plucking out a bright pink piece of paper, she gave it to Jane.

Jane looked at it with wide eyes, then looked at Cass. "What am I supposed to do with this?"

"You settle down and stop traveling the world," Sariah said with a bit of bite in her tone.

Cass swung her gaze to her. She'd never said anything about Jane's choices or lifestyle.

"Mama's going to sell the house," Sariah continued. She picked up the nearby cutting board with chopped carrots and onions on it. They went into the pan with the meat, and she got stirring that all together too. "We have to do something, and I can't do it while you're off in Peanutsville, Canada."

Jane burst out laughing, and Cass had the smallest glimmer of hope that she'd be on Cass's side. But the moment the laughter started to die, she zeroed in on Cass. "You're going to sell the house?"

Cass lifted her chin, because she had to face the girls alone now. Just like she did everything now. Alone.

"Yes," she said. "I'm going to list the house for sale on Monday morning."

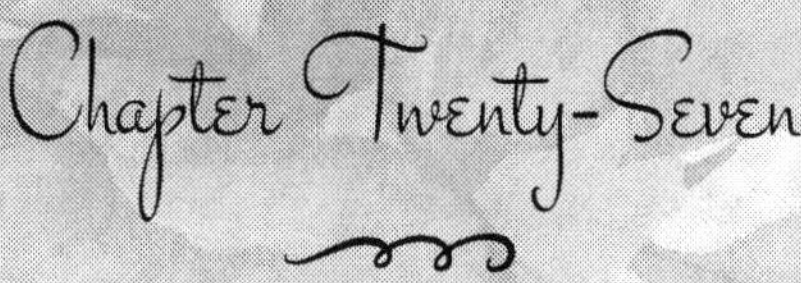

Chapter Twenty-Seven

Harrison smiled at his device, the glow of it making a halo around his head and face. *You'll be home tomorrow, right?*

He didn't want to pressure Cass, but she'd extended her trip twice now. She was supposed to return to Hilton Head last Thursday, and then she'd moved it to Tuesday. Then her younger daughter had come back to Sweet Water Falls, and Cass had expected her to be in and out of town in a day or two.

Apparently, that was what Jane had done for West's funeral, as well as for her brother's graduation. She'd been backpacking and traveling across six continents for the past year and a half—after dropping out of college mid-semester—and Cass funded it all.

Harrison had spoken to her several times since she'd left Hilton Head three weeks ago. Every conversation they had where he could hear her voice, he heard the indecision. The regret. The guilt. The helplessness, and the unhappiness.

He simply didn't know how to erase it for her. He'd gladly shoulder it...if he knew how.

How? he asked himself as Cass didn't respond.

He knew what that meant. She wasn't going to return to Hilton Head tomorrow. She'd pushed off her return another week last Tuesday, and Harrison had a long week in front of him too. He'd made it through Monday, but anyone who worked in construction knew every day was long and tiring, not just the first one back after a weekend.

His bedroom was too quiet. Just like his whole house. Like his life since Cass had left the island. He honestly didn't know what would happen next. He really liked her, and he really wanted her to come back, but...

He wasn't sure she would.

The longer she stayed in Sweet Water Falls, the more likely she was to never return to Hilton Head. Not only that, but she'd been threatening to list her house for sale, and she hadn't done that either. And if she had a nice place to live there...why would she come back here?

He hated thinking like that, but it felt absolutely true down in his soul.

I'm sorry, Harrison. I won't be coming back tomorrow.

He read her text a couple of times, hearing his name in her low, sexy voice. The one that told him she liked him and wanted him to kiss her once they were alone. He also noted she didn't say she'd be coming "home" tomorrow the way he'd asked. She just wouldn't be coming *back*.

I figured, he typed out. *What can I do to help you?*

His phone rang, despite the late hour. He didn't bother to silence it or sit up as if he'd been caught doing something he shouldn't. Cass's name sat there, and he almost didn't answer the line. "You've just been texting with her."

He swiped on the call and said, "Hey."

"Sorry, I just remembered that you're an hour ahead of me."

"Yeah, it's after midnight," he said, smiling up to the ceiling. Just the sound of her voice soothed him.

She sighed, and he once again wished he lay at her side to hold her against his heartbeat and tell her everything would work out. He wasn't, so he said nothing. She'd called him, after all.

"I think I'm going to stay for Supper Club next week," she finally said.

"That's ten more days," he said.

"Yes."

Harrison swallowed, as he hadn't anticipated that. Why he hadn't, he wasn't sure. It definitely seemed like all signs were pointing to her staying in Texas...permanently. "Cass." He cleared the worry and roughness from his voice. "Just be level with me. Are you coming back to Hilton Head or not?"

"Of course I am," she said, her voice strong and vibrant. Cass tended to put on a show, though, and Harrison knew it. He'd seen this act, and by the end of it, she'd dissolve into tears and admit she didn't know what to do next.

He certainly didn't either.

"Okay," he said anyway. "How about this, then? I have a credit card and a car. How about I fly into Sweet Water Falls this weekend? I'm dying to see you."

"Would you?" she asked.

He couldn't quite believe the hope in her voice. "Yeah, sure," he said easily, as if taking the time off to fly to Texas would be easy for him. He could already think of a half-dozen reasons it wouldn't be smart, one of which was that both of her daughters were at the house with her.

And not just her house. The house she'd shared with West. Where she'd raised her children.

He swallowed. "You'd come pick me up at the airport?"

"Yes," she said with a giggle. "Thank you, Harrison. It'll be so fun, you'll see."

"Yeah?" He closed his eyes now. "What will we do? Walk on the beach?"

"Sure," she said.

"I'll have to meet Jane."

"She says she wants to meet you." Cass had told him all about her daughters and their resistance to her selling their childhood home. He thought it was more than that, but he hadn't pressed her on the issue. She'd said nothing about him, though he knew Conrad and Sariah hadn't taken to him easily for whatever reason.

"And we can go get one of those caramel apples you're always bragging about?"

She trilled out a light, quiet giggle. "Yes."

"Go out to dinner at your favorite place?"

She didn't answer, and Harrison opened his eyes. "I'm sorry, Cass."

"I need some new favorites," she said, and it sounded like an admission. "But we can go to this great place in Corpus Christi. That's where you fly in."

"Corpus Christi," he repeated. "Okay."

Neither of them said anything else, but it sure was nice just breathing with her and imagining she was in the room with him. "Cass," he whispered, about to blow things wide open. Maybe. He wasn't sure about that, actually, and he had to be sure.

"Yeah?" she whispered back.

"I'm lying in bed," he said. "And listening to you breathe with me, and it's so nice. It's like you're here with me, and I can just reach over and touch you." He did that, but the other side of the bed sat empty and cold. "I wish you...I want you..." He didn't know how to finish, and maybe that was the end of what he needed to say.

I want you.

She didn't respond, but Harrison could still hear her breathing. It came in spurts, actually, which made her pinched, nasally voice which said, "I miss you, Harrison," make so much more sense.

"I didn't mean to make you cry."

"It was a nice vision," she said. "I haven't had someone breathing in the room next to me in a long time, and I'd forgotten how comforting that is."

He remained silent this time, and they breathed in and out together again. His eyes drifted closed, and she was right. What a comfort it was to have another human being who cared about him—who cared if he kept breathing—in the same room as him.

He woke sometime later, his arm aching from how he held it up near his head. He wasn't clutching his phone anymore, and he sat straight up when he realized he'd fallen asleep while on the phone with Cass.

A groan pulled through his chest and throat, because his arm had fallen asleep. He searched for his phone while shaking out his hand, and he found it beneath his extra pillow.

The call had ended, and the clock read just after two. So he'd been asleep for a couple of hours, and Cass had likely hung up on him before she'd fallen asleep. He could hope, at least.

He got up and plugged in his phone, padded into the bathroom, and then stripped off his shirt as he went back to bed. He fell asleep again with thoughts of Cass in his head, and that was exactly how he wanted to end every single day.

HARRISON SHOULDERED HIS BACKPACK AND waited for the flight attendant to open the door. He wasn't sitting in the first row, but close enough to the front to see the two women up front still getting things ready. Of course, the moment the seatbelt sign had gone off, everyone had jumped to their feet like they'd plow through the narrow aisle to the door first.

He didn't understand that, other than his back hadn't liked the length of the flight. He'd gotten up for that, then took a few moments to fold up his headphones and make sure he had everything stowed in his pack. He hadn't checked a bag—or even brought a carryon.

He'd be in Texas for less than forty-eight hours, and all he needed was a single change of clothing, a pair of swimming trunks, and some pajamas. Along with his few toiletries, everything had fit in his backpack—and that was with the fancy-pants headphones that came in a case the size of Harrison's head.

Spence had given them to him for his birthday, and he did love traveling with them. They blocked out so much noise from the plane, and Harrison hadn't had a headache after a flight since he'd gotten them.

The doors opened, and Harrison's heart jumped. Because of the long taxi along the tarmac, he knew Cass was here with both of her daughters. He told himself he didn't need to act any different than normal. He wouldn't be able to maintain such a façade anyway, and they'd either like him or they wouldn't.

It's not that Sariah doesn't like you, he thought.

Cass had told him that exact thing after the disastrous evening that was supposed to be fancy and fun. He'd ended up going out with Lauren, who'd had a run-in with Blake, and the whole night had been a disaster.

Except for the part where he sat on Cass's bed with her while she ate her chicken pot pie. She'd been in joggers and a tank top that kept slipping off one shoulder, and Harrison held onto that sexy image of her as he went down the aisle and off the plane.

He kept putting one foot in front of the other, and he eventually went past security and out into the main part of the airport.

Everything in his life grew brighter, then shone like diamonds, as he saw Cass rushing toward him. He smiled too, jogged the remaining distance between them, and swept her right up off her feet.

She laughed, but all Harrison could do was hold on. His emotions stormed through him, and he knew then that he *had* to be with her. He set her on her feet, leaned down, and kissed her right there with everyone in the airport flowing around them.

"Mm," he said, finally minding his manners. "I missed

you so much." He leaned his forehead against hers, glad when she didn't try to put any distance between them at all.

He opened his eyes to find her looking at him. She grinned and said, "I'm so glad you're here." She sure looked happy, and Harrison tucked his hand in hers and faced the baggage claim area of the airport.

"I don't have a bag," he said.

"My girls are right over there." She nodded to her right, and Harrison easily found Sariah. She was almost a mini-Cass, though she didn't have the height. She stood next to her husband who did, also sandwiched by a black-haired girl wearing what appeared to be every shade of blue in her shorts and T-shirt—the latter of which looked like it had been made out of a fishing net.

Surprise filled him, because he hadn't expected Jane to be so different. He'd seen pictures of her, of course, and she looked normal wearing hiking shorts and tank tops, boots and a backpack.

With her electric blue eye makeup, this young woman looked like she wanted to become part of the ocean the moment they made it to the beach.

"Hey, Harrison," Robbie said, stepping forward to shake hands. Harrison smiled at him and said hello as they shook.

He grinned at Sariah, and said, "I heard you guys got the apartment."

That cracked her icy exterior, and she melted right in front of him. "We did."

"I'm so glad." He stepped into her and kissed both of her cheeks lightly. "All moved in, or when is that happening?"

She exchanged a glance with Robbie and then her

mother, and Harrison looked at Cass too. "Uh, tomorrow," she said with a bright smile. "We'll talk about it later." She indicated Jane and said, "This is my other daughter, Jane."

"Mama." She rolled her eyes. "You said you wouldn't say it like that."

"Oops." Cass pressed one palm to her forehead. "I'm sorry."

Harrison grinned at Jane. "It's great to meet you." He moved into her and gave her a light hug, quickly stepping back to Cass's side.

"Jane, this is my boyfriend, Harrison Tate." Cass smiled at him, and he couldn't help but return it. It was just so amazing to see her. To touch her. To stand beside her.

Pure tension filled the bubble surrounding them, and he cleared his throat. "Did you guys park, or...?"

"Yes." Sariah turned and started toward one of the many doors leading into and out of the airport. "We're in short-term parking, and we've been here forever. Let's go before we get a ticket."

With that, she marched away from Harrison, taking her twin with her. Robbie looked at Harrison with a quick smile and then scampered after his wife.

Harrison sighed, glad the initial introductions were over. But Jane hadn't said anything to him at all. Not even a *hello* or a *nice to meet you too*.

Just...nothing.

"So they're not giving in," he murmured as he placed a kiss against Cass's temple.

"If anything," she said. "They're doubling down."

"But you're listing the house."

"Monday morning," she said. "The photography team came to take pictures yesterday."

And it had caused World War Haslam, as far as Harrison knew. Cass had called yesterday afternoon before he'd gotten off work, and she'd been weepy and angry at the same time as she told the story.

He watched her daughters go through the sliding doors, and then he said, "Well, we better hurry up. I wouldn't put it past Sariah to leave us here without a ride."

Cass narrowed her eyes in the direction her children had gone. "You're probably right." Her expression cleared quickly, and she darted in front of him as he started to walk. "What if we just...run away?" She put both hands flat against his chest. "I can rent a car. And we'll just drive...south. Go to the beach. Find a cute bed and breakfast that serves the best food in Texas." She smiled at him, though her dark eyes only harbored anxiety and pain. "Just me and you."

He wanted to do all of that. Right now.

They couldn't, though, and he took Cass's hands in both of his. "Cass, honey," he said real slow, real Southern-like. "I'm a big boy, and I can handle your daughters."

"I can't," she whispered.

"Yes, you can," he said, giving her an encouraging smile. "Because I'm here now, and you're not doing it alone."

New fire lit her eyes, and she tipped up and kissed him again. Harrison could honestly do that for a good long while, but Cass broke the kiss after only a few strokes. "Okay." She tugged her white-as-driven-snow blouse down and faced the exit. "Okay, we can do this."

Harrison went with her, not quite sure what "this" was, but willing to do anything Cass needed him to do.

Chapter Twenty-Eight

Cass let Robbie drive her SUV, and she sat in the middle of the backseat, a place she hadn't occupied in quite some time. Sariah rode in the front passenger seat, which left Jane to ride on Cass's right side.

She'd squeezed as close to Harrison as she could get, practically sitting in his lap, both of her hands covering one of his. They'd been talking about his build, his crew, and his family for the past half-hour, and it still felt like Sweet Water Falls sat a good distance down the road.

"So you own a construction firm?" Jane leaned forward and looked at Harrison. Cass watched her, not sure what she was looking for. No matter what, she wouldn't let her twins bully Harrison this weekend, or make him feel unwelcome here. They'd made it impossible for her to return to Hilton Head, and she really wanted to be with Harrison.

For several days there, she'd questioned that. Perhaps her twins saw something she couldn't. But the moment she'd laid eyes on him, all of those doubts and fears had disintegrated. Her feelings had grown deeper and stronger, not weaker, and she squeezed his hand as he said, "Yep, that's right."

"How long have you been doing that?" Sariah asked from the front seat. Her voice was crisp yet pleasant, and she reminded Cass so much of herself.

"Oh, 'bout twenty years now," Harrison said with a sigh. "Most days, I don't regret it." He chuckled.

"Why would you?" Sariah twisted to look at him. She really looked at Cass, and then dropped her gaze to her and Harrison's hands. Her lips pursed slightly, but she held her tongue.

"It's hot in Carolina," Harrison drawled. "Like Texas here. And the tourism business doesn't care about cement supply chain, and sometimes there's some...difficult people to deal with." He glanced at Cass, who gave him a bright smile. "Your mother understands. She's working with some of the fussier women on the island right now."

"You are, Mama?" Jane asked.

"Yes, dear," Cass murmured. "I have several clients on Hilton Head, one of whom is a country club remodel." And it hadn't been easy doing everything from Texas when her clients were in South Carolina. She'd kept all of that to herself, of course. Her daughters had never really understood how much Cass did behind the scenes to make sure everything looked and ran smoothly on the surface.

The conversation switched to what Sariah had graduated in—English and education, thus her months in Taiwan this summer—and then to what Robbie was studying—computer science. No one asked Jane what she was doing, and Cass wondered if she felt bad about that.

She reached over to her daughter and gave her a smile too. "What about you, Janey? Are you going to head back out into the world soon? Go to school?"

Jane didn't seem to mind the question, and she'd definitely become more relaxed since she'd been on the road. Cass had spent a couple of weeks with her now, and yes, there was definitely something different about her. She couldn't put her finger on exactly what, because Jane had always been the more laid-back of the twins.

Maybe not this laid-back, but much looser than the tightly laced Sariah.

"I don't know, Mama." She leaned her head against Cass's shoulder. "I'm sleepy."

Sariah muttered something from the front seat that sounded like, "You took too many of those things," and she looked from the side-back of one daughter's head to the top of the other.

"What things?" she asked.

No one said anything, and new apprehension filled the SUV. Her house sat on the outskirts of Sweet Water Falls, and they passed the first road that led to the furthest ranch on the west side of town.

"Sariah?"

"Nothing, Mom," she said, her tone somewhat exasperated.

"What things, Jane?" she asked, not about to let this go.

"It's nothing, Mama." Jane giggled and looked up at her. "Just a tiny CBD gummy."

Cass blinked, her eyes growing wider and wider. "You take those? Jane, how many did you take?"

Her smile seemed stretched now, and it wasn't diminishing. Cass looked over to Harrison, who wore a stoic expression on his face. Neutral. He wasn't going to get involved.

"Sariah," Cass barked.

"She takes too many," Sariah said. She twisted back again. "Where's the bottle, Jane?"

Jane seemed to be floating, and she certainly wasn't going to assist. Sariah let out a terribly exasperated sigh and grabbed Jane's purse from the floor. It wouldn't have mattered if Jane didn't want her to; her reflexes were nothing compared to Sariah's.

She pulled out the bottle—which looked like a vitamin bottle. In fact, Cass had thought Jane was taking gummy vitamins for the past few weeks—and uncapped it. "This is empty."

She looked at Jane with fear in her eyes too. "Jane, you must've had five or six of these."

"Five or six," she said, still grinning strangely like the Cheshire Cat. "I'm fine. I've taken more before." Her head lulled against Cass's arm again, and she wanted to hold her up, keep her together, until the drugs wore off.

Her heartbeat pounded, and she wasn't sure why. She wasn't responsible for Jane's actions. Not when the girl was twenty-two years old.

"Jane," she said, but she didn't know how to continue.

"We're back," Robbie said. "Harrison and I can get her in the house, and she'll sleep it off this afternoon." He met Cass's eyes in the rearview mirror. "Okay?"

She nodded at him, because he'd been the one sane spot in her life these past couple of weeks. Jane and Sariah even ganged up on him, and Cass didn't even think they realized it.

Her jaw tightened as they rounded the last corner and her house came into view. Well, at least the trees in the front yard. As Robbie approached, Cass also saw another car, and her pulse picked up speed again.

"Conrad's here," she said at the same time Sariah did. Her tone carried surprise; Sariah's did not. She'd likely called him and told him about this weekend's plans, as Conrad hadn't mentioned anything to Cass about coming home for a weekend visit.

This isn't your home besides, she reminded herself.

Robbie parked alongside Conrad's white sedan, meeting Harrison's eyes once more. Sariah and Robbie piled out of the car, and with Jane out of it, she leaned closer to her boyfriend and said, "I didn't know he was coming. I have a bad feeling about this."

"It'll be okay," Harrison said just before opening his door. He got out and turned back to help Cass. "Will you get my backpack so I can help with Jane?"

"Yes, sir," she said. She went to the back of the SUV to do that, and she brought up the rear as they all paraded up the front steps and into the house. It was an extremely familiar position for her, bringing up the rear, carrying the most stuff. The buck always fell to Cass, and she took care of everything for every family trip, every picnic, every afternoon at the beach.

She packed lunches. She brought sunscreen. She made sure everyone had what they needed to be happy, and anytime someone forgot something in the car, Cass was the one to go get it.

She carried so much for her family, and she'd always done so happily. Now, though, the teensiest pocket of resentment had crowded into her heart. Inside, she closed the door quickly behind her, hoping to shut out the negative emotion as if it could be done physically.

She dropped Harrison's bag over the back of the couch and then bent down to give Beryl an *I'm-back* scrub. He wagged his tail and smiled his golden retriever smile at her, and when she lifted her eyes, she looked right into a pair that had once belonged to West.

These were Conrad's eyes, though, and while her pulse pinched, Cass smiled. "Hello, son." She drew him into a hug. "What are you doing here?"

"Sariah said your boyfriend was coming." At least he hadn't lied about it. "Sounded like a real family affair, so I thought I better make the trip." He did smile as he stepped back, and Cass returned it.

"Nothing exciting," she said. "I haven't been back to Hilton Head since I dropped you at school, and we miss each other. That's all." In fact, she wanted to take him outside and around to the walk-out lower level. He had a hammock on his back deck, and she loved lying in it with him. They'd sink together, curled into one embrace, and just enjoy the come and go of the hammock as it swung.

This house had a hammock hanging from the underside of the deck too, and she'd found Jane there a couple of times in the afternoon, napping. She knew now that her daughter had probably eaten too many CBD gummies and then had to nap in the hammock, and Cass didn't know what to do about that.

Robbie and Harrison returned to the kitchen, and Cass tucked her hands in her back pockets. "You want the tour?" she asked, glancing around at everyone. She couldn't believe she'd suggested such a thing, as if Harrison would want to see where she and West had raised their family.

"You know what?" She looked around at everyone. "I'm going to order lunch. We can eat it on the deck." She pulled out her phone and started tapping. "Who wants what?"

No one said anything, and Cass knew this would be up to her and Sariah. Her daughter had promised to be on her best behavior this weekend, as Harrison was only going to be here for twenty-nine hours, several of which Cass still had to rope him into helping to move Sariah and Robbie to San Antonio.

"Harrison, let's go for a walk." She shoved her phone in her back pocket and reached for him.

"It's burning hot outside," Sariah said, but Cass ignored her. She'd make a fine mother of teenagers, and she found herself hoping her daughter had a dozen girls who would throw their attitude right back at her.

"We'll survive." She turned and left the house, Harrison coming with her. His footsteps didn't land the same way West's had, because he wasn't wearing cowboy boots. When she turned at the bottom of the steps so she could hold his hand, Harrison had put on a cowboy hat.

She froze, every cell in her body suddenly vibrating. "Wow," she said.

"Ma'am." He tipped the hat, his smile gorgeous and growing wider by the second.

She laughed and hung onto him. He wrapped her in his arms and laughed with her. "Where did you get that?" she asked between the giggles.

"You went still at the sight of it," he teased. "You have a thing for cowboys I don't know about?"

"I'm from Texas," she said, as if that summed up her feelings for cowboys.

"I'm gonna take that as a yes." He reached up with one hand and pushed his cowboy hat lower. His smile faded, and they didn't walk anywhere. "Cass, I—"

"Don't say we're not going to work out," she blurted.

He straightened and fell back a step. "I wasn't going to say that."

"You were," she said.

"I wasn't." He did start walking then, and she fell into step beside him. When they reached the end of her driveway, they went right, and Harrison breathed out. "I was going to say that Jane doesn't like me much. In fact, she doesn't like me at all. So much so that she had to drug herself to get through meeting me."

"No," Cass said.

"And that yeah, I'm not sure me bein' here is that great of an idea."

"I want you here."

"And then, Conrad's here? And you didn't tell him I was coming?" He shook that cowboy-hatted head and exhaled again. "Like he has to come sailing in to the rescue if I'm here."

"It's not that," Cass said.

"Then what is it, Cass?" Harrison paused in the shade of her huge oak tree, and Cass did too.

"I don't know," she said, her frustration building and building. "I don't know, okay? I think they're all just..." Cass gestured beyond the trees, where the house stood. "First off, Jane has been taking those gummies for who knows how long. It has nothing to do with you. Secondly, Sariah's been stressed about her new job and the apartment hunt. Once they move, they'll be fine. And Conrad's...Conrad knows you. He likes you. He spent all summer with you."

Harrison nodded, but he didn't look convinced. Cass couldn't believe she'd just made excuses for two of her children. "I don't like their behavior either, but they're adults, and they can act however they want." She slipped her hand through his arm. "It doesn't impact how I feel about you."

He looked down at her without moving his head. "Cass, they're your *kids*."

"I don't want to break up."

"I don't either, but I don't want family gatherings to be Jane passed out on pot and Conrad squinting at me like I've done something wrong, then Sariah huffing and rolling her eyes. It's so *tense* in there." He shook his head and started strolling again.

Cass swallowed, her throat so narrow. "Grief looks different for every person," she said quietly. "Sariah is overprotective of me. Conrad is worried he'll lose me like he lost his father. Jane is..." She blew out her breath in a loud, explosive sigh. "Jane is coping the only way she knows how outside of therapy. In fact, this is Jane *with* therapy. I can't even imagine what she'd be like without it."

Actually, she could imagine, because she'd tried to heal and come to terms with things on her own, and it hadn't been pretty.

"Maybe they need more time." Harrison's words floated on the air like wraiths, and Cass wanted to bat them back with her palms.

"They'll have all the time they need."

"Without me around," he said.

Cass didn't know what to say next. "I want you here," she said again, because she didn't feel like he'd heard her the first time.

He paused again, turning toward her. "Then I'll be here." He leaned down and kissed her, and Cass didn't care who saw them, who drove by, or if her kids hadn't accepted that she could move on sooner than them.

Kissing Harrison only cemented what she already knew—she wanted to be with him. She wanted him here. Everyone else would have to learn how to deal with their own emotions and feelings.

THAT EVENING, CASS LIFTED A HUGE PLATTER OF enchiladas between Jane and Sariah. "All right," she said with a grunt as she lowered it. "Everything's ready." She smiled at her daughters and went to take her seat across from them.

Harrison waited too, pulled out her chair, and then slid it in for her before taking his seat. She caught Sariah rolling her eyes, and instant humiliation and anger shot to her head. "Remember that boyfriend you had your freshman year?" she asked as casually as she could. She lifted the Caesar salad and started serving herself.

She looked across the table to Sariah, who wasn't rolling her eyes now.

"What was his name?" Cass asked, as if she couldn't remember. "Spencer?" She glanced at Harrison, as that was his brother's name. "Steven?"

"Sebastian," Sariah said.

Cass snapped her fingers, her smile instant. "Sebastian. That's it."

"You *hated* Sebastian," Jane said. She'd woken an hour ago, all apologies and bright eyes. She'd showered, and clearly, she hadn't picked up on any of the vibes around the house. That, or she didn't care. She laughed as Sariah elbowed her. "What? She did. Both she and Daddy did."

Jane looked across the table to Cass, who'd passed the salad to Harrison. She picked up a piece of garlic bread. "I didn't hate him," she said. "I simply knew he wasn't who Sariah should be with."

"Lucky for you that you get to make those assumptions," Sariah said dryly.

"I was right, though, wasn't I?"

"How do you know I'm not right about this?"

Cass looked straight at her. "Because you're not my mother."

"Have you introduced Harrison to Grammy?" Sariah challenged.

"We're going to breakfast tomorrow before his flight," she said, lifting her chin.

"Mama." The word had come out of Sariah's mouth as a plea and a gasp at the same time.

"Your brother and sister are going to help you move," Cass said. Her pulse bobbed in the back of her throat. "I don't need to be there. I can barely lift anything, and you two downsized so much to go to Taiwan." She glanced over to Robbie, who wore a wide-eyed expression as well.

"You're not going to come help us move in?" Sariah sounded like she'd inhaled helium.

All eyes landed on Cass, and she couldn't just brush

them off. They weighed so much. "Harrison is here," she said. "I haven't seen him for weeks, and my parents want to meet him."

He put his hand over hers, though they'd talked about this already this afternoon. While Sariah sulked and packed. While Jane slept. While Conrad lounged on the furniture, obviously bored to be there as he swiped over and over on his phone.

She'd finally escaped with Harrison to the beach, but they'd only had a couple of hours of respite before returning to this suffocating house.

She looked down the table at her children. "I'm listing the house on Monday. I'm flying back to Hilton Head on Tuesday. Miles is going to show the house, and it has to be in pristine condition, so no one can be living here." That last part was for Jane, as Conrad would go back to Baylor tomorrow.

Her son threw his napkin on the table. "I can't believe you're selling the house." He got up and started to leave the table.

"Sit back down," she barked at him.

She must've carried something in her voice, because Conrad faced her, his jaw tight and storming, but he sat back down. He folded his arms, and oh, that made him look like West too.

"You kids need to understand something," Cass said, not sure what else would come out of her mouth. "I have lived my whole life to be your mother. I have shielded you from as much pain and disappointment as I could. I couldn't stop your father from dying, and I haven't told you how to grieve the loss of him."

Jane watched her with wide eyes. Sariah sniffled and let her tears track down her face. Robbie had bent his head toward the table, and Conrad simply stared back at her, fire in his dark eyes.

"I have paid for everything any of you have wanted to do. I have adjusted my schedule and my needs to help you at every turn. I have gone without so you didn't have to, and I have sacrificed and sacrificed for the three of you in ways you will never understand."

She gritted her teeth, almost angry at them.

In a breath, it went away. Just floated out of her and up through the ceiling. "Because that's what mothers do for their children." She sniffled too, which brought Sariah's eyes to hers and the flame in Conrad's gaze to a simmer.

"I love the three of you dearly, but you are not my life anymore. Sariah and Robbie will do amazing things with their lives. Conrad is going to meet some fabulous woman and marry her and whisk her all over the world. Jane, I don't know what you'll do, but I have never doubted for a moment that you'll be fantastic at whatever you set your mind to."

"I want to start a business that makes backpacks out of recycled billboards," Jane said. She flicked a look in Sariah's direction and then looked at Cass again. "I've been putting together a business plan."

Cass started to cry as she nodded. "That sounds amazing, dear." She reached across the table and covered Jane's hand. This time, when she surveyed her children, she felt love for them.

She pulled her hand back and leaned into Harrison. He put his arm around her, and she took his hand in both of hers. She looked at the back of it, wondering how much his hands had seen during his time on Hilton Head, building everything from garages, to houses, to barns.

"I like this man," she said. "I know he's not your father; I don't want him to be your father. I'm not trying to replace him, and he's not trying to replace him."

She looked up at Harrison. "I'm falling in love with him, because he's good, and kind, and he treats me like a queen."

He gave her the ghost of a smile, and Cass wanted to kiss him. *Later*, she told herself. *Don't make a bigger fool of yourself than you already have.*

She faced her children again. "I'm ready to move on. I've known it for some months now. I'm sorry if you're not, and I encourage you to keep working through your feelings, your grief, and your obstacles. When you're ready to act like mature adults, you'll be welcome at my beach house on Hilton Head Island."

She nodded like that would be the end of the conversation. Silence draped the picnic table in the shade on the deck, where West had often taken his coffee in the morning after watching for the birds he loved.

"All right," Robbie said. He reached for the bowl of salad and handed it to his wife. "That sounds like a good plan to me, Miss Haslam. I know I'm going to need a break this fall." He gave a light laugh. "Starting late to in-person classes in this one calculus class." He shook his head and made a whistling noise. "I'll be glad to come to the beach for some rest and relaxation."

Sariah looked at him like he'd lost his mind. "We're not going to the beach for some rest and relaxation."

Robbie looked at her, and for maybe the first time, he

wore determination in his gaze. "Maybe you're not, but I am. I know how to act like a mature adult around your mother and Harrison."

Harrison reached for some garlic bread, took a piece, and handed the platter to Conrad. Conrad looked at it, then Harrison, then melted completely.

"The beach house is great," he said, taking the bread. "And Harrison makes a mean hamburger in his outdoor kitchen." He grinned, and just like that, the tension at the table broke. Jane smiled and said, "I'd love to come to the beach house, Mama. Can I fly out with you on Tuesday?"

Only Sariah remained a bit of a stonewall, but Cass once again recognized the grieving and acceptance process in her own daughter. She'd come around...eventually.

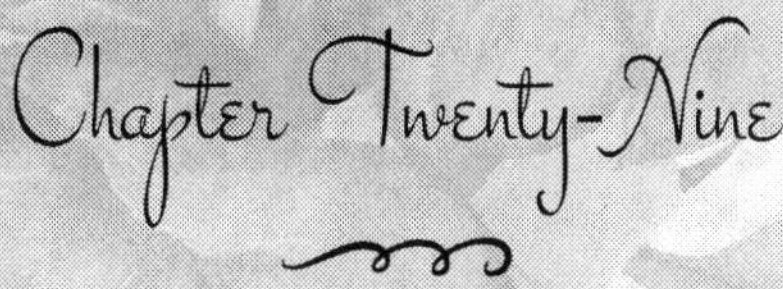

Chapter Twenty-Nine

Harrison slicked his hands down the front of his shorts, wishing he'd known about this meet-the-parents breakfast during packing time. He didn't think the khakis cut it, though Cass had assured him and reassured him several times that morning.

He wore a shirt he'd thought was pink, but Jane had informed him was "coral," and that he looked "hot" in it. He'd blinked at her in response, because he wasn't sure if he should react. And if so, in what way.

She'd laughed at him, and he did like her a whole lot more when she wasn't high or coming off a high. Sariah had given him a tense smile that morning, and Cass had swooped in to say it was time to leave before he could speak to her.

He knew she was protecting him, and he appreciated it whether he believed he needed to be protected or not. She didn't want her children to hurt his feelings or say something insensitive, so she hovered a little. He wasn't going to hold it against her.

"There they are," Cass said, and she rose to her feet. Harrison shot to his too, searching for a pair of faces Cass had only shown him on her phone last night.

He spotted her mother, and the woman exuded confidence, class, and kindness. She moved the way Cass did, and she held her head in the exact same way. She didn't stand as tall as Cass, and her height obviously came from her father.

He opened the door, his head full of white hair practically gleaming in the sunshine, and he put a big smile on his face when he saw his daughter. "Cass," he boomed, just as Cass said he would.

He doesn't speak much, she said. *But when he does, it's loud.*

She flew into her mother's arms first, the two of them wrapping themselves right up together. Cass's mother smiled and pressed her eyes closed, her graying hair falling to her chin in a neat bob, appropriate for a woman her age.

"Howdy, sir," Harrison said, playing up the cowboy angle because he wore the hat again today. He actually liked it, and as he shook Cass's father's hand, he sank into a different state of relaxation. They were just people, and yes, they loved Cass.

He smiled at her and her mother and said, "I'm Harrison Tate."

"Bob," her dad said. "My wife is Kara."

That got her to pull back from Cass, who wiped her eyes and looked up at Harrison. "I meant to introduce you."

"I know how," he said, taking her hand in his.

He did look at her mother and wait for Cass to say, "Momma, this is Harrison Tate, my boyfriend." She beamed up at him then, the tears in her eyes drying right up.

"Ma'am." He eased forward and took her in a hug, then dipped back and kissed both of her cheeks.

She blushed and said, "Well, oh my." She reached up and patted her hair.

"Harrison, my mother is Kara," Cass said. "My daddy is Robert."

"He said Bob," Harrison said.

"Call me either," the older gentleman said. He held up six fingers, and somehow that got them a table instantly. "Liz is almost here."

Cass kept her hand in Harrison's as the hostess took them back to a corner booth. She slid into the middle of it, which meant Harrison had to as well. Her parents sat on her side, and he figured he could keep her sister entertained easier than her momma and daddy.

"Harrison, look," she said. "They have breakfast hand pies." Cass tipped the menu toward him, and he felt like he was moving in slow motion. He looked where she pointed, but he barely saw the words before she moved the menu back in front of her. "I'm going to get that."

"Chicken fried steak and eggs," her dad yelled. "It's the best in the whole state."

"The whole state, Bob?" Kara asked, her voice dripping with disbelief. "How could you possibly know that?"

"I've eaten it," Bob said. "That's how I know that." He hadn't picked up his menu, and as a waitress approached, Harrison almost wanted to tell her to run.

Instead, she placed four glasses of water on the table and looked at the empty seats next to Harrison. "Expecting two more?"

"Yes," he said.

"I can take drink orders now," she said, smiling past him to the others at the table.

"We're here," another woman said, and she practically flopped onto the bench. She scooted over, and Harrison looked at a lighter version of Cass. "You must be Harrison." She grinned at him. "I'm Liz."

"My sister," Cass said on his other side. "Her husband Cole."

"Nice to meet you both," Harrison said.

"I want a mimosa," Kara said, and both of her daughters looked at her sharply.

"Orange juice now," Bob said. "Milk later. Cold milk. Put ice in it if you have to." He looked at Cass, who'd started giggling. Harrison wasn't sure if he should join her or keep staring and trying to keep up.

"Diet Coke," she said.

Harrison's turn, and he looked up at the waitress. "I want that orange-pineapple-banana smoothie I saw out front."

"You got it." She moved on to Liz, who also ordered soda pop, as did her husband.

"You're drinking this early in the day?" Liz asked casually, her eyes down on her menu. Harrison volleyed his gaze to her mother, who narrowed her eyes at her daughter.

In that moment, he felt like he'd just been trapped in another generational argument. He could just hear and see Sariah saying something like that to Cass. In fact, she *had* given Cass a casual jab only yesterday.

"She's an adult," Cass said, clearing her throat. "Daddy drove, and Momma can have a mimosa if she wants one."

That brought silence to the table, and Kara's eyes as wide

as a meerkat. Harrison wasn't sure if he should laugh, cough, or get the heck out of there. He did duck his head and smile, and when he cut a look over to Cass, she was looking at him too.

She leaned toward him, and he met her halfway so she could whisper in his ear, "Hey, at least I'm learning this lesson, right?"

He chuckled and shook his head, then secured her hand in his beneath the tabletop. It almost felt forbidden and intimate, and he looked over to her parents to find both of them watching him and Cass. His face heated, and he said, "I think I'm gonna get the chicken fried steak and eggs too, sir. It's one of my favorite things."

"What would Cass get?" Liz asked.

Harrison swung his attention toward her. "Is this a quiz?"

Her sister grinned at him and perched her head in her hand. "Yep."

He looked back at the menu, glad Cass had exhibited her excitement about the hand pies already. "Let's see..." He saw a couple of things right at the top she'd like. "She loves deviled eggs, and these come with candied bacon. I could see her ordering that."

"I—"

"You say nothing," Liz said, and Cass snapped her mouth shut.

Harrison shifted in his seat, his collar suddenly too tight. "Uh, she'd order that from the appetizer menu, and sometimes she'd eat it as a meal, depending on how long it's been since she's eaten."

He didn't look up again, and he decided to just get this

over with. If Cass liked him at all, she'd just agree with him no matter what he said. "I'd then go with the Belgian waffle with raspberries, not strawberries, and then a bacon and egg hand pie." He looked up at Liz, as she was the quiz-master.

She cocked her eyebrows and leaned forward to look at Cass.

"That's exactly what I'm ordering," Cass said. "All three of those things."

"Cole," Liz said, turning toward her husband. "Can I get three things? Cass is."

"Get what you want, sugar," he drawled at her, clearly not interested in the game being played at the table.

"We're buying breakfast," Bob said, and a couple of people at the next table over looked their way. Harrison wondered if he needed hearing aids or if he just yelled. He'd have to ask Cass.

Two days, he told himself. She'd be back on Hilton Head in two days.

"So," Kara said. "Are you two serious?"

"Momma," Cass warned. "I told you no questions like this." She glanced from her mother to Harrison and back. "We're—"

"I don't know about Cass," Harrison interrupted. "Since we're only three or four months in, but I'm pretty serious about her."

Every eye came to him, and he simply smiled. He squeezed Cass's hand under the table and lifted it to his lips, right there in front of everyone. He may have imagined it, but he thought he heard Liz sigh.

Cass ducked her head, her smile wide, and Bob grinned and grinned too.

"So," Harrison said. "Cass said you didn't like West much when you first met him." He surveyed the crowd at the table, noting the shock on their faces. "I guess I get a year to win you over?"

"You don't need a year," Liz said. "Did you guys really not like West?"

"They didn't," Cass said. "Because he was too 'stuffy.'"

"Oh, come on, baby," her father said. "West *was* a little stuffy."

Cass started arguing with her parents, but Harrison dipped his chin toward Liz. "I don't need a year?"

"Nope." She popped the P and grinned at him. "I like you a lot already, and look at my mother." She nodded across the table. "That's not only the mimosa making her smile. She likes you."

Harrison watched her, and seeing as how the drinks hadn't even arrived yet and Kara hadn't even taken a sip of alcohol yet, her smile did seem genuine.

He returned it, then tuned back into the conversation, which somehow got pointed back to him. He didn't mind, because he knew Cass's family had a lot of questions about him, his business, his life on Hilton Head, and their relationship.

To his great relief, he answered them, and by the time they'd eaten and left the restaurant, he finally felt like someone in her family had accepted him and liked him.

In Cass's SUV, finally alone, she buckled her seatbelt and looked at him. Her dark eyes shone like diamonds, and she squealed. "They loved you, Harrison." She threw her arms around him, and he leaned over into her embrace.

She'd been pretending like her children's reactions to

him didn't bother her, but Harrison had suspected they did. Now he had proof. But it didn't matter, because her parents and sister liked him.

"I'm glad you're excited," he said.

"It's not that I would've cared," she said, disentangling herself from him.

"Yes, you would've," he said. "If your momma and daddy didn't like me, you'd really think Sariah and Conrad were right."

She shook her head, but she didn't deny it again. "It's just..." She didn't finish the sentence as she pulled out of the parking lot. He gave her time to think as he watched the green hills roll by in the blue sky.

"It's just that you think I'm wonderful," he finally said. "And you're falling in love with me, and you want to share that with those you love."

"Yeah," she said.

"I'm falling in love with you too," he said very quietly. "In case I haven't said it yet."

"You haven't." She looked over to him, hope adorning her expression. "Really, Harrison?"

"Totally," he said.

She nodded, swallowing against a lump he could see in her throat. "I just want my kids to come see me," she said. "I don't want to drive them away."

"It's like you said," he said. "They just need more time than you. You're the one who stayed in the house, Cass. You were there for over a year, with just the memory of West. They weren't. They didn't get to experience that. Say goodbye to that."

She looked over to him again, a hint of surprise riding in

her eyes now. "You're right," she said. "I've been there. They weren't."

"Everyone grieves in their own way," he said. "You taught me that."

"Maybe I shouldn't have listed the house."

"Where's the strong, independent woman you once told me you once were?" he asked. He shook his head. "No, Cass. Who's going to be at the house when we get back?"

"No one," she said.

"That's right. No one." Sariah and Robbie were moving to San Antonio that morning. Conrad and Jane had gone with them to help.

"Jane's coming back," Cass said.

"For a few days," Harrison said, trying to gently remind her that Jane's gypsy soul still hadn't been healed or satisfied.

"Yes," Cass murmured. "For a few days."

"So I can kiss you when we get back to your place," he teased, and that made Cass look over to him with one eyebrow cocked. "I can't?"

"Fine," she said as if kissing him would be a great burden. "You can kiss me when we get back to the house."

A COUPLE OF DAYS LATER, HARRISON ONCE AGAIN found himself at the airport to pick up Cass. As he eased his truck next to the curb, he found the tall, lithe, gorgeous woman smiling—at him. The first time he'd met her, he'd nearly dropped her luggage. This time, he jumped from the truck and laughed as he rounded the hood.

He swept her into his arms as if he hadn't seen her a

mere two days ago, and he lowered his head to kiss her right there on the curb.

"Aw, you guys really do like each other," Jane said, and Harrison broke the kiss though it hadn't truly had room to grow yet.

He grinned at her and said, "Let me get your luggage."

"This is all I have," Jane said, patting her shoulder strap. "Everything I own is on my back."

Harrison blinked at her as she stepped around him. He'd gone on fifty-mile hikes as a Boy Scout with more stuff than Jane had in her significantly smaller backpack.

Cass, in contrast, had two suitcases, one large and one small. "You can get mine, cowboy." She patted his chest. "And then kiss me properly."

"At your house," he murmured, because he wasn't supposed to park on this curb for long, and the last thing he needed was an airport attendant yelling at him and interrupting his *welcome back* kiss again.

He wanted his next kiss with Cass to be a *welcome home* kiss anyway, and that definitely required some privacy.

"Come on, Beryl," he said to the dog. "Load up, and let's hit the road." The golden retriever jumped into the back seat with Jane, and Harrison opened Cass's door for her before going around to the driver's seat.

The closer to Hilton Head they got, the more his stomach buzzed and the tighter his fingers became on the wheel. Cass reached over and took his hand in hers. "What's got you so worried?"

"Nothing," he said, though he could name a fair few things. Her flight had come in on time, and a quick glance at the clock showed him that dinner should be getting delivered in the next five minutes.

He hadn't told her that he'd taken the whole day off of work, just so he could get into her house and make sure her welcome home party was perfect.

Bea had made a dog-diet-friendly cake just for Beryl, and Grant had promised to have all of the pastries from Gourmet Goods on display. His friend staged rentals for a living, so Harrison trusted him. He hadn't wanted to get them this morning and have them sit all day, so Grant had agreed to go this afternoon.

Harrison had spent his time cleaning the house, airing it out, spraying that peachy spritzer Cass liked, and arranging the new dog toys he'd purchased for Beryl. He'd been at the house to receive the enormous bouquet when it had been delivered, and he'd set it just-so in the middle of her butcher block in the kitchen.

He'd also set up a record player and by some miracle, had found an old record of the Osmonds to play, as Cass had told him at their one dinner-dance-date in Charleston how much she loved watching her parents dance in their kitchen...to the Osmonds.

Harrison wanted to create that same sort of safety and security for Cass, between the two of them, and he'd told Grant he'd text him when they were five minutes away from the community. Then Bea and Grant could start the record and get the heck out of the house before Harrison, Cass, and Jane arrived.

He swallowed, because he wanted everything to be perfect. For her. For him. For the two of them together.

At the point of no return—a stoplight near the grocery

store—Harrison picked up his phone while waiting at the red light. Grant had texted.

The house smells amazing, he said. *Blinds open. Dinner and dessert are waiting on the table. Those flowers? AMAZING, Harry. ETA?*

Five minutes, Harrison sent to his best friend, and then he put his phone down. He didn't want Cass to think he was planning something, and he rarely looked at his phone in the car, especially while driving.

"Almost there," Cass said, the words practically a sigh.

"Yep," he said, maybe sounding a little too upbeat. He wasn't sure. Cass looked out her window, the picture of beauty, grace, and...freedom. Harrison smiled at her, but she didn't see him.

Only minutes later, he pulled into her driveway to Jane going, "Holy Texas longhorns, Mama. This is *your* house?"

"This is it," Cass's voice carried happiness and joy. She looked at Harrison with the same emotions streaming through her. "Leave the bags. Let's go listen to the ocean."

He chuckled with her, but he couldn't get ahead of her. She practically leapt from the truck while it was still moving, despite his protests. In that moment, he had a feeling this was going to be his life moving forward.

Always a couple of steps behind Cass, trying to keep up. And he didn't mind at all. He let Cass and Jane go ahead of him, Beryl wagging his tail at their side.

He followed, and he knew the moment Cass had seen the gifts he'd put into play for her. She screamed and said, "Harrison, get in here!"

So he did just that.

Chapter Thirty

Cass couldn't believe the spread in her kitchen. She'd known something was up when the front door wasn't locked, but she hadn't commented on it. Then, right there in the foyer, she could smell the fruity-floral scent of the air freshener she loved. That definitely wouldn't still be hanging in the air after so many weeks away.

The blinds over the back windows had been raised, but Cass hadn't frozen until she'd seen the food on the dining room table. The desserts carefully laid by each plate. The giant arrangement of daisies, lilies, and roses.

That was when she'd screamed, and she turned into Harrison as he arrived at her side. "You're too good to me," she whispered.

"I wanted everything to be perfect for you," he said. "Ready to just relax for the evening."

She gazed up at him. "You cleaned my house."

"Guilty."

"You ordered dinner."

"And dessert."

She tilted her head to the side, finally realizing what that sound was. She'd been trying to locate and identify it for a solid minute. "The Osmonds are playing."

"Will you dance with me?" He took her effortlessly into his arms, and they swayed right there between her island and her dining room table, just the way her parents once had.

She closed her eyes and pressed her cheek to his chest, enjoying the warmth of his body, the scent of his clothes and skin, and the bumping of his heartbeat.

"Mama," Jane said, but Cass ignored her. "Look at this view!" She slid open the back door, and Beryl went barreling out.

"I got him a new ball," Harrison said. He stepped away from Cass for a moment to hand the toy to Jane. "He loves to chase it in the water."

"Be back soon!" Jane yelled as she left, and Harrison once again wrapped Cass in his arms.

"She seems to like the beach house more than your other kids," he murmured.

"Yes." Cass snuggled into him, so many things storming and then quieting within her. They danced, but after one song, she knew she had to say something. She looked up at Harrison, finding such softness in his eyes. Kindness and love—for her.

"Cass," he said, tension flying into his face. "I know it's fast, and I know it's early, and you don't need to say anything, okay?" He took a breath. "I love you. I'm in love with you. I know you don't want to rush things, and that's fine. I just wanted to...tell you." He visibly relaxed, his smile making a reappearance.

She smiled up at him too. "Okay, good," she said. "Because I love you too."

He kissed her then, and that was all the answer she needed to what he'd said, to what she'd said, to this puzzle that had become them in the past couple of months.

CASS SIGHED AS A FLURRY OF TEXTS CAME IN RIGHT as Lauren opened the door to her house. "Hey," she said, and she looked downright domestic in a fifties-style dress with a white apron tied around her waist.

"Evening," Bea said evenly. Then she broke into a squeal as she high-stepped it into the house. Several others had clearly already arrived as more screams met Cass's ears.

She stepped out of the doorway and over to Lauren's porch railing, for she'd just received no less than eight texts from Sariah.

The house hasn't sold, Mama.

Robbie and I are talking to a loan officer.

Can we maybe talk to you about it? We might need some help with the mortgage. A loan or a partial loan or something.

Mama?

Oh, you're flying for Supper Club. I forgot. Call me when you land.

Cass obviously hadn't called, as she hadn't gotten any of these texts until this moment. Sariah's next three weren't as nervous or as nice.

I know you're there now. I can see your pin. Why aren't you answering?

Mama, don't be like this. It's just a house to you, but it means something to me.

Fine. Be like that. I won't answer when you call anyway. See how you like it.

That was her last message, and Cass looked up from her device. Indecision raged inside her as she took in Lauren's pristine lawn. She too paid for a groundskeeping service, and it showed.

"Cass?" she said. Cass turned toward her and gave the best smile she could. Lauren didn't return it. "What's going on?"

"My daughter." She handed Lauren the phone. "Same as always."

Lauren took the phone and frowned at the texts from Sariah. She gave the phone back to Cass, and together, they leaned against the railing and looked over Lauren's lawn.

"She's a good woman," Cass said. "But I don't think she understands what it'll take to keep that house in the shape it's in. She's teaching eighth grade. Does she think she's going to be able to come down and do the yard work?"

"Or pay someone to do it?" Lauren gestured to her lawn. "This isn't cheap, and it's year-round."

Cass nodded, thinking of other duplicate bills. "I don't feel comfortable selling it to her."

"Then don't."

That sure was easy for someone else to say. Cass worried that Sariah would never forgive her if she sold the house when her daughter didn't want her to. Then what?

She wanted to move on from the grief, the lonely nights at home alone, the constant physical reminders of West. Of course she had all of her memories, which were fond and furious in her mind all the time. She wasn't trying to forget about him or replace him.

She was simply ready to move on from the past chapters of her life.

"Cass," Joy said, and Cass turned away from the current situation. Joy wore a wide smile on her face, and Cass stepped into her embrace, really sinking into it. They'd gone to lunch last week, and Cass had told her all about her troubles with her kids then.

"You okay?" Joy asked, her grip on Cass tight.

"Yes." She stepped back and brushed her hair out of her face. "Yes, I'm fine."

She exchanged a glance with Lauren, who thankfully said nothing. Cass caught the look, and she handed her phone to Joy. "Will you answer Sariah for me?"

"Answer her?" Joy took the phone, her brows furrowed. She read the texts too, then jerked her gaze back to Cass. "Yeah, I've got this."

She turned and went into the house, leaving Cass's pulse vibrating as she watched her friend leave.

"Well, I've got to see what she says," Lauren said. She brushed by Cass, adding, "I'm not cooling the state of Texas, Cass. Come inside."

She did and closed the door behind her, sealing in the cool air and shutting out the heat. Bessie and Bea stood in Lauren's gourmet kitchen at the back of the house, laughing about something. Cherry sat at the bar, also giggling with them. None of them looked to the huddle in the living room which Cass joined.

"There." Joy handed the phone back to Cass, and she

held it so she and Lauren could see the screen. Sage stood from the couch and leaned into the group too.

I don't think that's a good idea, dear. You and Robbie are so busy with so many things, and I don't feel comfortable adding the house and yard and everything else to your load.

"Perfect," Cass said. The message also testified of how well Joy understood and knew Cass.

I know this will upset you, the second message said. *Think of how much work your apartment is, then multiply that by a five-bedroom house on almost an acre of land.*

I'm at Supper Club now, so I'll call you tomorrow. I love you and Robbie.

That was it, and Cass looked up. Tears formed in her eyes, and she gave her phone to Sage so she could hug Joy. "Thank you, Joy. It's exactly what I wanted to type but couldn't get my fingers to do."

"All right," Lauren said. She stepped away from the women in the living room and clapped her hands. "Dinner is ready, and I ordered from *Chez Françoise*. The first course is French onion soup, and everyone knows it's not good if the cheese is too cold."

Cass stepped away from Joy, turned to Sage and hugged her hello too. She took her phone and shoved it into her purse, which she then left on the couch before joining her friends in the kitchen.

She hugged Cherry and Bessie, and then she was in very real danger of angering Lauren if they didn't all sit down to eat, so she did that. After all, the last thing she wanted was to lose her friendships from this Supper Club. They definitely needed to continue into her new chapter of life, and Cass resolved right then to make sure she stayed an active member of this Supper Club—because that would ensure she stayed in touch with these ladies she loved so much.

"This is it," Cass said. She didn't get out of the rental car though Harrison had come to a stop. The house in front of her didn't look the same as it usually did this close to Halloween.

It did, and it didn't. The dark brown brick was the same. The front door stood tall and sturdy. The lawn had just been clipped, and all of the bushes and flowers had been pruned in anticipation of the somewhat cooler winter months.

But the house didn't boast a wreath from the front door like usual. Cass loved autumnal wreaths, and the house felt lifeless.

The yard usually held fall plants and flowers, which Cass loved to plant and cultivate. But this year, she'd wanted it as clean as possible. Presentable. Perfect curb appeal—which the house possessed.

But it had no spirit.

"One last walk through?" Harrison said, and Cass nodded.

She drew in a breath and hitched up her courage. "My parents will be here soon." She got out of the car then, left her purse behind, and only took her phone.

When she met Harrison at the front of the car, she handed her device to him. "Will you take my picture here?"

"Sure," he said easily.

She paced away from him and posed, put a smile on her

face, and waited for him to tap to take the pictures. She wasn't sure why she wanted them, only that she did.

The new owners of the house would take possession of it on November first, only six days from now. Cass had come this weekend to get everything else out of it that wasn't staying, and her parents had agreed to store a few things in their shed. It was six boxes of West's things that Cass hadn't needed with her on Hilton Head. Some of his case files. His bird-watching manuals. His notes on their vacations, finances, and his word puzzles.

He wasn't a hoarder, but he loved to write everything down, and Cass didn't need his notes. She'd kept his journals, his personal thoughts, and that was enough for her.

She'd sold all the furniture. Someone in the family had taken anything she hadn't moved to South Carolina, like a tea set or the bath towels she'd replaced in more oceany colors for her beach house.

"Are the kids coming?" Harrison asked.

Cass shook her head. "Jane's in Italy. Sariah is up against a term deadline, and Conrad just started that second job."

Her son had been amazing since the mini-intervention several weeks ago. He'd called Cass and thanked her for all she'd done for him. He'd said he didn't want to keep taking her money, and he'd been working hard to make enough to pay his own bills.

Sariah had taken some time to come to terms with the fact that no, she and Robbie were not in a position to pay for the house and then take care of it. She texted or called Cass every day too, and Cass loved talking to her children as adults. They still needed a parent, and she was happy to be that for them too, just in a different way.

Jane had gone back to her world traveling, and Cass still paid for what she needed. She had noticed that her daughter's conversations had changed, however, and she had hope that Jane would soon return to the US and her college education. Maybe. Cass was trying to have an open mind when it came to Jane, as well as provide any help she could for her daughter.

Tires crunched over the gravel at the end of the driveway, and Cass turned back to see her parents pulling in. She smiled at their arrival and went to greet them.

They adored Harrison, and they had from the very beginning. Honestly, without their positive assessment of him, Cass might have broken up with him. She simply couldn't see what her children did—and thankfully, her parents couldn't either.

"Momma." She embraced her mother, and then went to greet her daddy. "It's only a few things."

"Take your time," Momma said. "I can make tea, and we can just enjoy one last moment here."

Cass nodded. Once upon a time, she'd thought she'd live in this house forever. She took Harrison's hand and said, "West and I bought this place intending to raise our family here, retire here, die here."

Happy memories flooded her mind then, and it wasn't so hard to go up the steps. "It was kind of a wreck when we first moved in. I picked out this door, and West widened the frame so it would fit."

She ran her hand along the wood. She punched in the code for the automatic lock, and when it disengaged, she went inside.

All of the furniture had been removed. The windows

sat bare, curtain-less. "I picked out the carpet in here just a few years ago. I liked to constantly be updating things, you see."

Harrison's hand tightened in hers. "I had no idea you did that," he said dryly.

She laughed with him and her parents. "I would've remodeled the kitchen last year. The cabinets are too dark now."

"Probably why the house sat on the market for a full month," he joked next.

It had taken a week or two to get buyers into the house, but once the showings had started, the offers had come in. Cass had selected one that had come in above her asking price, for a couple with two small children. They wanted to raise their family with the outdoors right at their fingertips, and Cass had felt a connection to their letter, though she'd never met them.

She'd never given Harrison a tour, but she did now. She took him down the hall and said, "This was Conrad's bedroom. The girls wanted the basement, and after they moved out, Conrad didn't feel the urge to move." This room still held boxes, but she continued on. "This was West's office."

Only his desk remained, as the couple had requested it to stay with the house. Apparently, the woman worked from home, and she'd loved the office with the big window looking into the front yard—and that desk.

Cass walked over to it and placed her palm against the top of it. She could almost feel West's presence when she did that, and she closed her eyes.

She breathed in, seeing him sitting at this desk in the

morning and evening. He was organized and deliberate, and going through his office had been easy.

"He was such a great investigator," she whispered. Her mother's arm came around her shoulders, and Cass let her eyes burn with tears. She wiped them away and looked at her mom. "I'm not sad."

"I know." Momma nodded, her own expression soft and tense at the same time. "Sometimes happy memories are laced with tears. That's all."

Cass nodded and turned to leave the office. "The master suite," she said. The room was huge, as she'd had a reading nook in here, complete with a loveseat and a recliner, which had once stood sentinel around the window and a couple of bookcases.

She and West had had individual dressers, bathroom sinks, and sides of the massive master closet. A king bed would fit easily, and once, during a Texas hurricane, all five of them had crowded into this room to survive the night.

She told the story quickly, and then walked back down the hall. It wasn't as hard to turn her back on everything that had happened here in this house as it had been when she and Conrad had packed the truck and driven to South Carolina.

She knew why, and that was because she was confident in her choice. There was no coming back and deciding later. Not this time.

She skipped the tour of the basement, which was just more bedrooms, bathrooms, paint and wallpaper she'd picked out, and empty space.

With the four of them, getting the half-dozen boxes out of the house took minutes. She ran the vacuum in the bedroom where they'd been, and that was it.

Her parents left the house, and Harrison waited for her by that widened front doorframe.

She tucked the vacuum into the closet and faced him. She smiled, and then she turned in a full circle, drinking in this place one last time.

She breathed in and out, feeling pure peace and contentment fill her with her next lungful of oxygen.

She pushed all the air out and met Harrison's eye again. "Ready." She crossed to him and let him wrap her into his arms. "Thank you for coming with me to do this."

"I wouldn't be anywhere else," he whispered. When they separated, they smiled at one another, and Cass took his hand and led him out of the house.

She locked the door behind him and feeling lighter than she had in twenty months, she practically skipped down the front steps.

"Lunch?" her father yelled, and Cass nodded.

"Yes," she said to him. "We'll follow you." She got back in the passenger seat, buckled her seatbelt, and waited for Harrison to back out of the driveway.

She kept her eyes on the house as he did, but when he drove away, she didn't look back.

She wasn't doing that anymore. Her future lay in front of her, with the man driving at her side, and she wanted to be present for anything that came their way.

Five Months Later

Harrison pushed open the door leading into Cass's house, noting the still silence inside. He definitely didn't want her to come home to this.

Or maybe he was being over-sensitive to what today was like for her.

The anniversary of West's death.

She'd scheduled an appointment with AnnaMae Hank at the Highmarshall Country Club today, so maybe she was fine. Harrison still didn't want her to come home alone or feel alone at all today.

None of her children were coming to town for this, as Spring Break was in another three weeks, and they were all coming then. Even Jane, who hadn't been in the country since Christmas.

Harrison opened the fridge and slid the blackberry cheesecake inside. That done, he returned to the truck and grabbed the six-pack of the peach-cranberry iced tea she loved. That went in the fridge too, and he'd poured one into a tall glass with ice for her before she got here.

He'd taken the afternoon off from the construction site so he could shower and be here for her, as her meeting should've ended ten minutes ago. The drive from the Highmarshall Plantation would take her a half-hour, and Harrison went back outside one more time.

The flowers went in the middle of her dining room table, and she'd kept the record player and the Osmond nine-track, and they'd danced to the music several times since her return to Hilton Head last September.

It felt kind of cheesy to have the same things now as then, but Harrison didn't need to reinvent the wheel. Cass had said she didn't want to go out to dinner tonight. She wouldn't want the noise or the hassle of getting ready.

He'd never seen her when she didn't look like a million bucks, and if she had a meeting with an important client today, she'd have gotten ready.

"The flowers," he said, marking things off verbally. Cass loved flowers, and she'd started customizing her front and back yard this year already. Before long, it would be the envy of every house on this lane.

She loved her treats, the tea, and dancing. And hopefully, she'd love that he was here so she didn't have to think about West by herself.

"You're here," he said to Beryl as the golden retriever finally deemed him worthy enough to get off the couch for. He gave the dog a pat and then let him outside to take care of his business.

Just as he let Beryl back inside, Harrison heard the garage

door start to lift, and he hurried to get out a glass and fill it with ice.

He'd just popped the lid on the iced tea as Cass came in, and she met his eyes. "Harrison." She carried a feminine briefcase bag with her, which she promptly put down on the narrow countertop immediately inside the door.

She sighed as she kicked off her heels. She didn't ask him what he was doing there, and he poured her tea and handed it to her as she joined him at the counter. "Thank you."

He put his arm around her waist and let her lean into him while she took a drink. "I love this stuff."

He smiled and dipped his head, so his mouth sat closer to her ear. "I was hoping you'd say you loved coming home to me in your house."

She turned toward him, and their eyes met briefly. "That too," she murmured just before she kissed him.

Harrison loved kissing her and being kissed by her, and he easily took her into his arms and held her against his chest. When they parted, he said, "I didn't want you to be alone today."

"Thank you," she said again. She started the dance this time, despite the silence in the house. Beryl came to say hello to her, but she ignored him as they swayed back and forth.

Without her heels, she wasn't as tall as him, and Harrison felt like the anchor in Cass's life he really wanted to be. "Dinner will be here in an hour," he said. "We can eat here or at my place. I just have to text Lindsey and tell her where to deliver."

"Your place." Cass stepped out of his arms and gave him a soft smile. "I'll change, and we can lay in your hammock." She lifted her eyebrows, and he nodded.

She finally bent to greet her dog, and Beryl trotted after her as she went through the living room and down the hall to her bedroom.

Harrison sent the evening manager of the restaurant where he'd ordered dinner a text, and then he sank onto Cass's couch. She took her time in the bedroom, but he didn't mind.

When she came out, she wore a pair of loose, navy pants that brushed the floor with wide pantlegs, a pale pink blouse that made Harrison's mouth water, and her hair all piled up on her head.

"Ready," she said.

He got to his feet and drew her toward him again. "You are my favorite person in the world," he whispered. "I love you."

"Mm." She smiled at him and tipped her head back. "I kinda like you too."

He grinned at her. "Two years without West. How are you feeling?"

She exhaled slowly, in measured beats. "Better than last year. Better all the time."

He waited for her to go on, but she didn't. They'd talked a lot about this day in the past couple of weeks leading up to it, and maybe she'd said all she needed to.

"I don't want to celebrate this day," she said.

"That's not what this is."

"No, I know," she said, placing one hand on his chest. She smoothed it around to the back of his neck. "This is you taking care of me on what you know is a hard day."

"Yes," he said. "That's what this is meant to be." He

tilted his head and looked at her. "You've been thinking about him all day."

"Yes," Cass admitted. "All the good things, like a celebration, and that's not what I want this day to be."

Harrison took a few moments to think. "You wouldn't want to remember the bad things. Or just ignore it, I wouldn't think."

"No," she murmured.

"So just some self-care," he said. "Which I'm happy to provide for you."

Cass nodded, her smile back. "Okay, cowboy. Take me to your place, please."

"There's more tea in the fridge," he said as he stepped back. "And cheesecake for later."

Her face lit up. "Cheesecake? Tell me it's the blackberry one from Stroud's."

He grinned at her. "It's the blackberry one from Stroud's."

"I'm so glad you're mine," she whispered just before kissing him again. Hey, he'd take it. If bringing her a cheesecake made her kiss him like this, he'd do it every day.

Harrison was running late, and he hated the anxious, fluttery feeling in his chest. He couldn't control some aspects of his job, and he'd already texted Cass to let her know that he'd be about a half-hour late to dinner at her house.

Her children were all on-island for Spring Break, and while he'd visited with them over the holidays, they hadn't been back to South Carolina since Christmas. Three months was a long time, and Harrison didn't want to leave a bad taste in anyone's mouth.

It's okay, Cass said. *You're still getting the buns?*

Yep, he sent off quickly, and then he got back to work. Their electrical on this last building had been wired wrong, and he'd been dealing with the rewiring for three days now.

"Done?" he asked Jeff. The man looked up from the dustpan where he'd been sweeping up various bits of colored plastic that had come off the electrical work. "This is it," he said.

"Perfect." Harrison sighed in relief. "Thanks for stepping in last-minute."

"Happy to do it." Jeff smiled and continued with the clean-up. Harrison had put as many people on electrical—including the clean-up—as he thought he could without being annoying, and tomorrow, they'd get back to their usual duties.

Back to normal.

He hoped. In all honesty, his version of normal changed on a daily basis.

Over the past ten months, the only thing that had been constant was this build. And since September, when Cass had stood up to her children, him and Cass.

He saw her every day. Took her pastries every day. Kissed her every day. Told her he loved her every day.

And tonight, with her family here, he wanted to see if she'd agree to become his wife.

He respected and appreciated that she needed time to come to a place where she was ready to get married again.

They'd talked about it off and on over the past five months, more and more in recent weeks.

He'd bought her a plain gold band, because as trendy as Cass wanted to be with her interior designs, she was traditional when it came to weddings and marriage. So not white gold, she'd told him. Regular yellow gold.

He hadn't wanted to get the diamond until she could choose it herself, and he'd bought from a jeweler who could do any setting she wanted on the band.

His heart jumped and thrashed against his ribs, and then he managed to calm it. He wanted to ask her the question; he could live with whatever answer she gave.

"You can," he muttered as he jogged toward his truck. "Even if she says no, it's not a no forever. It's a *not right now.*"

He hurried to pick up the buns she wanted for dinner, and he left them in his truck while he ran inside to shower. Finally fresh and presentable, he drove around the curve to Cass's house.

He knew by the number of cars in her driveway that more than her children had come to town. She and Bea had hosted Supper Club at her house in November, and she normally didn't have to host again for six more months.

This wasn't Supper Club night anyway, and Cass hadn't told him her friends would be there. So it couldn't be them.

Still, there were far more cars than needed for her three kids, two of whom had flown in together.

He'd find out soon enough. He grabbed the bag of buns and headed for the front door. He normally knocked and entered at the same time, and he did the same tonight. No one would've heard him anyway, as plenty of chatter and laughter filled his ears the moment he opened the door.

He closed it behind him, feeding off the energy here in Cass's beach house. Grant's voice stood out, so he and Bea were here. That was one extra car.

Lauren came around the corner from the kitchen, and she lit up at the sight of him. "It is Harrison." She continued toward him, her loose beach clothes billowing as she walked. "Hey, Harrison."

He hugged her and said, "Hey, Lauren. I didn't know you'd be here."

"It was a surprise." She stepped back and smiled at him, and Harrison could appreciate her beauty without being attracted to her.

"Did you all come?"

"Yes," she said, grinning. "I think Cass is a bit overwhelmed." She started back toward the kitchen. "Come on. She'll want to see you, but she's chained to the stove, making caramel with Bessie."

"Caramel?" Harrison followed Lauren at a crisp clip. "I didn't know she knew how to make caramel."

Lauren laughed. "She doesn't. That's why Bessie won't let her step away from the stove."

In the kitchen, Harrison could only stand out of the way. Bea and Joy worked on something at the counter, their heads bent together. Cherry—the newest addition to their Supper Club—wrapped corn in aluminum foil, passing the packages to Sariah, who put them in a bin.

Cass stood at the stove, her upper half shaking as she whisked violently. Bessie stood next to her, giving directions.

Life and love lived here, and Harrison smiled around at

everyone. "Howdy." He moved over to Conrad and shook the young man's hand. "How was the flight?"

"Good," he said. He stood and hugged Harrison. "How's the build?"

"Going," Harrison said. "Trouble with wiring this week, but it's all sorted now."

"Mama says only one more building to go."

"Yep." He turned to include Robbie in the conversation. "Almost done with school." He gave him a quick hug too. "Cass and I can't wait to come to commencement."

Robbie grinned at him. "Thanks, Harrison. I can't wait either."

"Tell them about the job interview," Sariah called from the kitchen, and Harrison looked at her. He lifted his hand in a wave to her, and she smiled and nodded at him.

"Job interview?" Harrison looked at Robbie.

He seemed nervous as he swallowed and shifted his feet. "I didn't mention it, because it's such a long shot."

"But I can pray anyway," Harrison said.

"It's with a big law firm in Denver," Robbie said. "They sometimes hire people who do family law, and they have one opening right now. They have hundreds of candidates."

"It's his third interview," Sariah said. "He's being modest."

Harrison grinned at Robbie and leaned a little closer to him. "Nothing wrong with modesty, son. But they must see something they like."

Robbie swallowed again. "We'll see. I have another interview next week—in Denver."

Harrison nodded. "Keep us informed." He loved including himself with Cass, and it felt natural to do so.

Jane joined the group, and Harrison shifted to make room for her too. "Grammy wants more tea," she said.

"Oh, is your grandmother here?" Harrison scanned the crowd and didn't see her. "Was that a surprise too?"

Jane looked at Conrad blankly, and Conrad shrugged. "I don't know," they said together.

Harrison hadn't known Cass's parents would be there, but he didn't want to say that. Instead, he put his arm around Jane and said, "It's good to see you."

She grinned up at him and said, "You too."

"Where are you off to after this?"

Jane looked over to her mother, and Harrison followed her gaze. He wanted to go help her, kiss her, and whisper how he couldn't wait until they could be alone. She seemed a little frazzled, and Harrison would've never surprised her with eight extra mouths to feed. That just wasn't how Cass was built. She could plan a big party, and do so gladly. But she wouldn't like planning for six people and then suddenly have to add eight more to it.

In that moment, he decided tonight would be a bad time to ask her to be his wife. It would be one too many surprises, and she'd reject him in front of everyone.

Thankfully, he'd told no one about his plans—which was really to simply pull out the ring in the moment before dinner started, with everyone seated at the table, and proclaim his love for her one more time before he asked her if she'd marry him.

The ring sat in his pocket, and there it could stay...for now.

"I can't wait to see your outdoor kitchen," Jane said. "It's all Conrad talks about."

"That's not true," Conrad said with a healthy roll of his eyes. "But it's pretty cool."

"I'm hosting a barbecue on Thursday," Harrison said. "Y'all can see it then." He nodded to Bea and Joy. "How long are the ladies staying?"

Sariah joined the group, wiping her hands on a towel. "They're leaving Thursday morning," she said. "So your barbecue will just be us."

"And your grandparents?"

"Yes, them too." Sariah moved into him and gave him an awkward side-hug. She cleared her throat and stepped back. "So eight of us."

Just the fact that she included him in the "us" was far more than she'd done before. The hug too.

"Great," he said. "I'm ready for eight of us." He looked over to Cass. "I'm going to go see what Cass needs." He extracted himself from the conversation and went into the kitchen, nodding and saying hello to the people he went past. He still didn't see Cass's parents, so they must be outside.

"Hey." He arrived at Cass's side and slid his hand along her waist, a thrill moving down his spine as he did. "You smell like sugar." He chuckled as she leaned into him.

Her exhaustion bled into him, and he held it for her so she didn't have to. "Eight extra people showed up," she said. "I was ready until the doorbell rang."

"They're your friends," he said under his breath. "You love them, and they love you. No big deal."

She met his eyes and searched his face. "You're right. This isn't that big of a deal."

"They're your best friends," he said. "They miss you."

"Maybe I should go to Texas more often," she said.

"Then *I'll* miss you." He grinned at her, because she had gone to Texas twice for her Supper Club. His gaze landed on the caramel. "This looks amazing."

"It goes on popcorn," she said, and Bessie squeezed in between them.

"Oops, sorry Harrison. Cass, we're ready." She glanced at Harrison, her eyes blue and deep and pretty.

"Howdy, Bessie." He backed up. "I'll get out of the way unless one of you gives me a job. Just wanted to say hi to Cass."

"If you have any single friends as nice as you, I'd love for you to pass out my number." Bessie gave him a flirty smile, and the three of them laughed.

"What's going on over here?" Lauren demanded. "If this is all we're waiting on, can we get started?" Her dark eyes blazed at Cass. "Your momma just told me she might faint from hunger."

That only made Cass laugh harder, and Harrison joined her. As he quieted, he said, "I'll take care of Kara, Lauren. Okay?" He looked between Cass and Lauren, and both women wore gratitude in their eyes.

"Take her this," Bessie said, pressing a wrapped caramel popcorn ball into his hand.

"Yes ma'am." He went to do that, because he wanted Cass's life to be joyful and happy, and he'd do what he could to make it that way.

Outside on the patio, he found Kara and Bob. "Kara," he said. He extended the popcorn ball toward her. "Look what I found for you."

She took it with the words, "Thank goodness someone around here knows it's far past suppertime."

He grinned at her and sat down at the patio table. They wouldn't all be able to sit out here, but it had been set for eight. "So," he said. "When did you get in?"

Chapter Thirty-One

Cass walked through Harrison's house with the package of cheese he'd asked her to get and bring. She caught sight of him working outside, in his kitchen there, and he wasn't wearing a shirt.

Her pulse picked up the pace, though she'd spent several days at the beach with him, shirtless, in the past. She couldn't help that she found him sexy and desirable, and she was actually glad she did. It would be a fairly boring relationship if she wasn't attracted to him.

"Hey," she said as she opened the door. She let Beryl go out ahead of her, and Harrison threw them both a smile.

"Hey." He lifted the lid on the smoker, and a billow of the stuff puffed out. "Sorry, I'm right in the middle of this."

"It's fine," she said. "I have the cheese here."

"Put it by the burgers." The raw patties sat on the stone countertop, and Cass put the cheddar next to them. "You haven't started these yet?"

"They're fast," he said. "These au gratin potatoes are

giving me fits." He squinted through the smoke and did something with the tongs in his hands.

She moved over to his hammock and collapsed into it with a long sigh. "Remember when you made me my first hamburger here?"

He chuckled but otherwise didn't answer, and when he closed the smoker, he came over to her. He leaned down and kissed her. She wanted to fist her hands into his collar and pull him into the hammock with her, but he wouldn't be able to stay for long.

"I remember," he murmured. "That was a great first date."

"At least my foot isn't dripping this time," she teased. "And it's just me tonight. Everyone's on their way home." She'd been entertaining her friends and family at her beach house for a week. She wouldn't complain about it. She absolutely would not. She wanted everyone to come spend time with her on the island, especially her children. She just wished they'd have told her, because she hadn't had enough food, and she'd spent a lot of the evening trying to work out the sleeping situation.

Harrison had stepped in and taken her parents to his house, along with Conrad, Jane, and Bessie and Joy. He had extra bedrooms, same as her, and he didn't mind if he then took a week or two to put the house back together.

Cass minded, and she'd probably spend tonight after this dinner with Harrison doing laundry and remaking beds so they were ready for the next time she had company.

"Good," he said. "It was a fun week, but I'm tired."

"And yet, you're cooking for me."

"I'd be cooking for me anyway," he said, straightening.

"You're just a bonus." He grinned at her and went to put the hamburgers on the grill. Cass closed her eyes and listened to the hissing-sizzle as the raw meat touched the hot grill. She loved resting while Harrison bustled around and prepared dinner, as West hadn't been much of a cook, and this was a new experience for her.

Several minutes later, he said, "Ready, sweetheart," and Cass had to heave herself out of the hammock.

She did willingly, and she went into the kitchen with Harrison. She wrapped her arms around him from behind and laid her head against his back while he chuckled.

"Rough day?" he asked.

"Not really," she said. "I just like you."

He said nothing, and when he scooped the burgers from the grill and turned, she released him. He put the plate on the small table-for-two in the shade and took her into his arms again.

"I love you," he said. "So any answer is okay, all right?"

"Any answer?"

Harrison dug into his pocket and lifted a ring to her eye level. "I know you need time, and I'm willing to give you whatever you need. If you're not ready to be engaged, fine. But if you are, and you want to put the wedding off for another year, that's fine with me too. Or if you want a short engagement, I'm okay with that too. I just want you to be mine, and I want to be yours."

"You are mine," she whispered. She pulled her gaze from the ring and looked at him. "And I'm yours."

He nodded, his throat moving as he swallowed. "I want to get married. Will you marry me?"

Cass hadn't had any problem saying yes to West when

he'd proposed. She wouldn't have a problem telling Harrison yes either.

But was she ready to get married again?

She didn't have to say "I do" today. Today was just him asking if she could say that to him one day—sooner or later.

"Yes," she said.

Harrison's eyes widened, and his grin multiplied. "Yes?"

Cass laughed and backed up so she could hold out her hand. "Yes. I love you, and I want to marry you too."

He slid the plain band on her her finger. "It's plain purposefully. I'll take you to pick out your setting, and Gavin will keep the ring for a week or two to get it how you want it."

"How I want it," Cass echoed, once again realizing how well Harrison knew her. How perfectly he took care of her. She did want to pick her wedding ring, and he knew that and had given her the chance to do so.

"So I can't tell anyone yet," she said, admiring the look and feel of the ring on her finger.

"Why not?" he asked.

She raised her eyes to his. "Because I want to show everyone the perfect ring you picked for me, and it's not ready."

"Or maybe it is," he said. "Because the perfect ring for you is one you get to design yourself." He gathered her close again and bent his head to kiss her. "I love you." He touched his mouth to hers, and Cass was the one to accelerate the kiss this time.

"I love you too," she said after he broke their kiss.

"All right," he said. "The food is getting cold, and we can talk about a date while we eat."

THE FOLLOWING DAY, CASS HELD OUT HER LEFT hand and took a hand selfie. She attached it to a text to her three kids. Then one to her Supper Club. Then one to her parents and Liz.

They each got the same message with the picture.

Harrison and I are engaged! We've set a date for July sixth, as a lot of you expressed interest in coming to the island for the Fourth. No formal invitations will be sent. This is me inviting you to the wedding and the island for fireworks and a barbecue, hosted at Harrison's house. Between the two of us, we have plenty of beds for everyone. Let me know if I should plan on you or not! Love you all.

Once the last message had gone out, Cass put her phone facedown on the table and left it there. "Come on, Beryl," she said to her dog. "Harrison should be walking by any minute."

They went out onto the back patio and then down the steps to the beach. Sure enough, they'd barely cleared the taller beach grasses before Harrison whistled.

Beryl perked right up and then took off as a golden streak down the beach toward Cass's fiancé.

Her *fiancé.*

She tilted her head back and let the sunshine flow through her. "I love you, West," she said. "And I love how the human heart has an unlimited capacity to love."

To her, that was one of the best parts of being human, and when she reached Harrison and kissed him, she said, "I love you, Harrison," and meant it completely.

"Love you too, baby," he said. "How'd the news go

over?"

"I left my phone inside," she said, grinning at him. "But I'm sure they'll all be happy for me." At the very least, she wouldn't hear about it if someone wasn't happy about the forthcoming nuptials. "What did you have planned for dinner, because I saw that the Crusted Crab is open now..."

"The Crusted Crab," Harrison said, chuckling. "I just need to kiss you one more time."

And he did just that.

Keep reading for a sneak peek at **THE SEASIDE STRATEGY,** the next book in this romance and friendship fiction series. It features Lauren Keller and her journey toward discovering what really matters to her...

I hope you enjoyed Cass, Harrison, Lauren, Blake, Bea, Grant, and everyone else in *The Paradise Plan*! **Please leave a review for the book if you did.**

Scan the QR code below to preorder THE SEASIDE STRATEGY, the next book in the series.

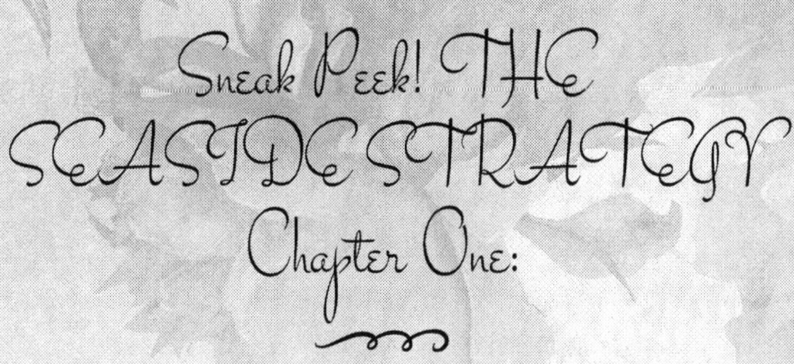

Sneak Peek! The Seaside Strategy Chapter One:

Lauren Keller used the remote on the larger of her two monitors to turn it off. She still had work to do, but she had to draw a line somewhere. Otherwise, she'd work twenty-four hours a day. She'd allowed herself to go down that path before, but not this summer.

No, this summer was about finding balance. Accepting things as they stood. Being more patient with herself—and those around her.

She sighed as she stretched both hands high above her head and held the position. Sitting at a desk wasn't the best for her shoulders and back, and Lauren stood and went through a few simple exercises that should help the knot in the back of her neck.

What she really needed was a good masseuse, and she'd ask Cass who to go to here on Hilton Head when she made it downstairs.

She left her bedroom-slash-office on the second floor of

Cass's beach house and went down the hallway. She'd be moving out next weekend, but she wouldn't be going far. When she'd first decided to come to the island for the summer—as she had last year—she'd secured a rental.

Cass had thrown a fit. A major, royal fit, and she'd insisted that Lauren take the bedroom where she'd stayed last year. Cass had wanted help with the wedding, and Lauren didn't need bad Supper Club mojo on her hands. So she'd been living with Cass, Conrad, and Joy for about seven weeks, and the three of them got along splendidly.

Conrad once again worked for the outdoor tour company he'd been with last year, and Cass had plenty to keep her busy with her interior design clients. The house was cool and quiet, and Lauren loved everything about it.

So much so, that she'd started looking at properties here on Hilton Head too. If she was going to live here for five or six months out of the year, she figured she should have her own place.

Everything she did came with a strategy; she couldn't help it. Her job as a marketing analyst, team leader, and corporate strategist had the label in the title. She barely got dressed without a routine, a strategy to get the most done in the least amount of time.

Right now, however, she set aside her strategies and went into the kitchen. No one else lingered, and she reasoned that it was five o'clock somewhere. Almost here, as a glance at the clock told her. So she popped the top on her Diet Coke and emptied the can into a tall glass.

Cass didn't own any dishware that was plastic, and Lauren actually liked that about her. It made Lauren feel less like a diva for the nice things she enjoyed. She splashed in an ounce of rum, stirred her drink, and took a healthy sip.

The alcohol warmed her mouth and throat, almost burning as she swallowed. She sighed and relaxed her hip against the countertop, then put away the bottle and took her drink out to the patio.

She sat in the rocking bench and looked out to the ocean, letting her mind come and go the way the waves did as they washed ashore. She could hear them chattering, even as far away as she was, and she wondered what they said to each other. She wondered why she found them so soothing to her soul. She wondered how she could make them part of her permanent reality.

Coming downstairs or out of an office to a drink and the sound of the ocean? That was heaven to Lauren, and she flicked on her phone and started a familiar search for property here on the island.

Her biggest obstacle was price. Oceanfront property wasn't exactly cheap, and it wasn't infinite. She earned a good salary, and she didn't really have anything or anyone keeping her in Texas.

Yes, her corporate headquarters were there, but they had branches and offices all over the country. All over the world. She was, in fact, assigned to the Miami office right now, and Lauren traveled for about a third of her working hours anyway.

She thought of Joy, Bessie, and Sage back in Sweet Water Falls. Cherry Forrester too, now that the woman had joined their Supper Club. Joy would especially be upset if Lauren made the move to Hilton Head permanent.

"It's not permanent," she murmured to herself. "It's a few months out of the year."

Her phone chimed, nearly deafening her, as she'd forgotten to turn down the notification volume when she'd turned off her computer screen. Thankfully, it wasn't from anyone on her team. No one needed help. There was no crisis.

This text had come from Harrison Tate, Cass's fiancée. The man she'd marry in just another week's time.

Lauren's heart bobbed around inside her body, nearly bursting through her ribs when she finished reading. *MaryLou just called*, Harrison had said. *They approved your rental. You can move into my place while Cass and I are on our honeymoon.*

"Thank you, Dear Lord." Lauren pressed her phone to her chest and smiled up to heaven. She'd always anticipated finding somewhere else to live once Cass and Harrison tied the knot. She'd secured two other rentals—and they'd both canceled on her. She'd been scrambling for a week now, and Harrison hadn't put his house up for sale yet.

He too was scrambling to finish the last building in a huge construction project he'd been working on for over a year. He wanted it done and signed off before the nuptials got said, and he hadn't had time to call a realtor, clean up his place, and get it listed.

Cass had put a lot of time and energy into her house, and she was quite particular about the yard, the house, the textiles, all of it. Harrison had readily agreed to move in to her house once they were married, and he'd have his outdoor kitchen transplanted over here once they returned from Bora Bora.

Lauren took another sip of her drink and looked at her phone again. She'd been about to search for property here on the island, and she decided to go ahead and do that. Not rentals, though.

Something to buy.

She swiped and tapped, read about floorplans, and leafed through pictures. There were some really gorgeous homes here on Hilton Head, but nothing that truly spoke to her soul. Her eyes started to blur, and she lowered the phone once again.

"There you are," Joy said, bringing up Lauren's head.

"Hey." She smiled up at her friend. "How was work?"

"Great." Joy exhaled as she sat down next to Lauren, the bench swaying wildly as it accommodated for the extra weight. "I called you. Harrison said the HOA approved his rental. We can move in there."

"I got his text," she said. Her tongue felt a little thick, and her brain a tiny bit fuzzy. Maybe she'd splashed in a little too much rum. Or maybe it was just so warm and gorgeous here on this patio. The swaying of the bench. Something.

"I'm relieved," Joy said. "I actually looked at a long-term hotel this morning." She shook her head and bent to take off her shoes. She worked as a classroom aide in an elementary school back in Texas, but she'd come to Hilton Head this summer too. She'd been here for almost a month now, and she'd gotten a job as a technician at an optometrist office. She wore scrubs to work every day, and she seemed to really enjoy interacting with patients and the rest of the staff there.

"Can you imagine?" Lauren asked. They laughed together, and then Lauren looked at her phone again. "Oh, I missed a call from my boss." She got to her feet, and she didn't wobble too much. She also had no idea how she'd missed a call from Mark. Had she fallen asleep after looking at real estate?

Probably.

She walked to the edge of the patio and tapped to call Mark Apgood, the man who'd been her boss for about a decade now. She worked directly beneath him, and there wasn't really anywhere else for her to go. Another company, perhaps, but she enjoyed the work she did now, as well as the people she worked with. Most of the time, anyway.

"Lauren," he said crisply when he picked up.

"Mark," she said back. No excuses. She missed calls sometimes, and it was after working hours. She didn't have to call him back until tomorrow if she didn't want to.

"Can you be on a plane to Texas tonight?"

"Wha—? I—" Lauren turned around and looked at Joy. She'd leaned back in the swinging bench and closed her eyes. "Why?"

"There's some serious stuff going down, and I need you here."

"How long?" Lauren asked, already moving back to the house. She could pack and be on the road to the airport in twenty minutes. Whether they had a flight or not, that was a different story. "Cass is getting married in six days, Mark."

"Not that long." Something banged on his end of the line. "I can guarantee you won't miss her wedding."

"I can't," Lauren said. "I won't."

"You won't," he assured her. "I'll see you when you get here."

"Your office?" True surprise wove through her as she

strode through the living room toward the stairs. "Tonight? You're not going home?"

"Not until this is settled," he said. "See you soon." The call ended, and Lauren dashed up the steps to the second floor. She had no idea what was going on—Mark had been very light on the details.

To her credit, she wore professional clothes to sit at the table in her bedroom, so she didn't have to change. She threw a couple of extra outfits in a bag, sat at the computer, and looked for a ticket. She had toiletries and everything else at her place in Sweet Water Falls. Truth be told, she had clothes there too. Plenty of clothes.

A flight left Atlanta at ten-forty, and Lauren booked herself a ticket. Then she grabbed her purse, her bag, and her laptop and headed for the door.

Whatever was happening better get resolved quickly, because Lauren would not miss Cass's wedding. Oh, no, she would not.

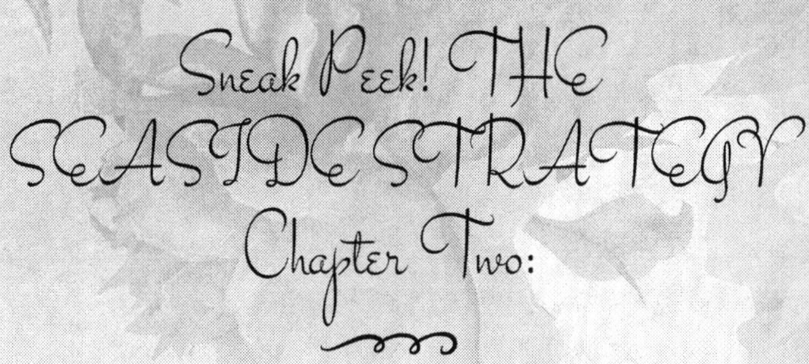

Sneak Peek! THE SEASIDE STRATEGY Chapter Two:

Lauren pulled up to the office building where she'd put in the last fifteen years of her life, catching sight of the top row of windows. Lights burned there, and while only one other vehicle sat in the lot—a big F-350 truck—it sure seemed like she'd find more people inside than just Mark.

Her anxiety had been quietly doubling since she'd boarded the plane, almost four hours ago now. It was almost one-thirty in the morning, Texas-time, but that didn't seem to matter. She'd slept a little bit on the plane. How, she wasn't sure.

She pulled into her reserved parking spot, as if that mattered right now, gathered her purse and keys, and headed inside. She normally wore heels to work, but such footwear wasn't practical for airports or driving, and her loafers didn't make quite the same clicking noises as her pumps usually did.

The elevator took her to the twelfth floor, and the *ding!* of her arrival seemed to screech through the empty building.

She stepped onto the floor she'd known so well, almost pushing through the doors because they opened so slowly.

She immediately froze. Nothing currently being digested by her eyes was right.

A long, chest-high counter usually greeted guests who came to the twelfth floor. No one could get into the offices behind them without checking in with either Sheila or Reginald. Lauren didn't expect to see them here tonight, but to have the counter completely gone?

She blinked, wondering if she'd gotten off on the wrong floor.

Cubicles took up the left half of the floor, but the six-foot dividers had been pushed against the walls. Some of them, at least. Some lay in a heap, like a giant had picked them up, broken the hinges, and flung them back to earth.

"What is going on?" she wondered aloud.

She saw no computers. No desk chairs. No papers. No filing cabinets. The right side of the floor held a column of meeting rooms encased in glass. Four conference rooms, usually, that had to be booked through Sheila and Reginald, who of course, couldn't do that anymore. Angry marks on the industrial carpet where their workstation had been glared back at Lauren.

Her throat finally remembered how to swallow, and she did that while her pulse raced through her veins. She gripped her purse tighter, not sure if she should proceed toward Mark's office or leave immediately.

"Lauren." Mark's voice echoed strangely in this now-open space, and she jerked her attention toward him. He wore what she usually saw him in: a white shirt, a tie knotted tightly at the throat, and a pair of black slacks. He didn't look like he'd been working for almost twenty-four hours, or that he was responsible for the complete chaos on the twelfth floor.

"Mark." Lauren moved toward him, somehow wanting to run into his arms and be reassured that she was simply dreaming. She even jogged a couple of steps, and he did catch her against his chest. "This is awful. What's going on?"

She'd had a normal day of work. Meetings with two clients. Her team, both in the morning and the afternoon. She'd gone over marketing specs that had come in from the accounts team, and she'd approved the initial mocks to be shown to a client, for which a meeting was set for next week.

She'd had a drink, a chat with her friend, and everything had been so perfectly...normal.

Nothing here was normal. At least not for her memory.

"Are you guys closing this office?" That made no sense, as this was the corporate headquarters. She stepped back and looked up at Mark. He suddenly did wear age and exhaustion on his face.

"We're in trouble," he said. He gestured for her to follow him to his office, which she did. His sat in the back corner, the one with two walls of windows. Hers still stood next to his, but as she walked by the great glass walls, where the blinds had been raised, she could see that they now sat empty, like big fish bowls waiting to be filled with water.

She shivered, the thought of sharks entering her thoughts.

Her office door sat closed, and Lauren had the greatest itch to go inside. She hadn't brought her laptop in from the car either, and she clutched her purse even tighter as if someone might jump out from the wall and take it from her.

The art had been cleared out. The potted plants. Everything. Absolutely everything.

Her stupor deepened as she entered Mark's office. It looked like he'd tossed a bomb inside, then waited in the hall with the door closed until it had gone off. All of the papers, files, and furniture she'd expected to see out on the main floor did live in here. In heaps. In tatters. At odd angles.

Somehow, he sat in a chair that was positioned slightly behind his desk. Lauren only took three steps into the office before she stalled. "Mark," she said, and it sounded like a child's voice. She shook her head. She needed to get a grip on her composure and figure out what was going on.

For it sure didn't look like she had a job anymore. Or, if she did, it had morphed and changed in a single second the moment she'd stepped off the elevator.

"Mark," she barked. The man looked at her now, his dark eyes surrounded by pinched lines and...sadness.

"I messed up," he said feebly.

Lauren's normally dormant maternal side reared up. She wanted to tell him it couldn't be that bad. That she'd help him iron everything out and they'd find a solution to whatever he'd done. He'd always been a highly capable and approachable boss. This couldn't be all that bad.

She indicated the floor beyond his open door without looking in that direction. "Yeah, it looks like it," she said. This was why she hadn't been able to find a nice man to settle down with. She told herself Mark wasn't her boyfriend, or even a friend, really. He was her boss, and if he'd messed up, she'd probably have a price to pay.

"Start at the beginning," she said.

"Yes," another, deeper voice said.

Lauren cried out and jumped to her right—away from the sound of the voice. Two men entered the office, and they looked perfectly refreshed, with their hair combed to the side just-so, and black suit coats buttoned neatly. Honestly, if it wasn't two o'clock in the morning and she'd walked onto a normal twelfth floor, she'd think they'd shown up for a cocktail party.

"Lauren Thelma Keller," one said, and he wasn't asking. "You're under arrest for the embezzlement of corporate funds."

"What?" she demanded. "No, I'm not." She looked over to Mark, who hadn't moved. In fact, the man wept. He *wept*, the tears making slow tracks down his face while he didn't make any sound at all.

"I'm afraid we have to take you in."

Mark finally got to his feet. "I told you she had nothing to do with it." He took a few steps and positioned himself between Lauren and the federal agents. Lauren suspected that was who they were, at least.

"You just want me."

The two men appraised him. Looked at her. Then one another. "We went through her computer?" one asked.

"Yes, sir," the other said.

"Her office?"

"Every inch."

"Where's the laptop?"

"Digital forensics connected to it the moment she touched down in Corpus Christi, sir."

"What in the world is going on here?" Lauren demanded. "I get a call after hours from my boss, telling me I better get on a plane and get here quick. That there's some 'serious stuff' going down. So I do, and I show up to some... some...apocalyptic scene in my office building."

Her chest hurt from the lack of oxygen, and Lauren hated how manic she sounded as she sucked in a breath. She tried to hold it, but it wouldn't stay in her lungs.

"You can't stay here, ma'am," the agent said who'd been reporting to his boss. "If you'll come with us, we'll lay it out for you."

"You'll interrogate me," Lauren said, shying further from them. "I'm exhausted. I've been flying for three hours, terrified of what I'd find here, but it wasn't *this*."

"I'm Agent Toledo," the taller man in charge said. "Come next door with me, please." He indicated the open doorway behind him, and Lauren had no idea what to do. She looked at Mark, plenty of pleading silently thrown in his direction.

"Go," he said. "You'll be okay, Lauren. It's my fault. It's all my fault." The slow weeping started again, and Lauren really didn't know what to make of that. She'd seen Mark angry plenty of times. So angry, he'd throw a tape dispenser or the nearest object he could get his hands on. But weeping?

Never had she seen him do that.

She held her head high and stepped past him. She told herself she could answer any question set to her, and do so truthfully. She didn't know why there would be two federal agents at Simple Solutions, and Agent Toledo had sounded like she had an office to go into.

She did that, flanked by both suited men. The lights came on as she entered, the way they usually did. They didn't illuminate total chaos like she'd seen out on the main floor, but there had definitely been a crew of people in her personal space.

On her computer. In her files. Accessing her laptop the moment she landed in Corpus Christi. She started to turn numb, her mind going blurring along the edges of her thoughts.

"Ma'am," the agent who hadn't identified himself said. "I'm Agent Bell, and we've been investigating an embezzlement scheme here at Simple Solutions for the past nine months."

She blinked. "What?"

"Please sit down," Agent Toledo said, and Lauren did. Her sleek, shiny black leather couch still sat against the wall, though the framed picture of the ocean she kept above it had been removed. As she stared across her office to her desk, she found the majority of the artwork from the office standing against the far wall. The one she shared with Mark.

"I don't have a job anymore, do I?" she asked.

"We've frozen everything inside Simple Solutions," Agent Toledo said. "Mark Wellington, as well as at least three others, have been siphoning money from corporate funds to the tune of seven-point-three million dollars." He perched on the edge of her desk and picked up a black pen. One of her really nice gel ones, as Lauren wouldn't sign documents with anything else. "And ma'am, you'll forgive me, but as closely as you two worked, I'm finding it hard to believe you didn't know."

He looked up, his eyebrows adding a silent question mark to the statement.

"I didn't." Lauren swallowed and cut a look to Agent Bell. "I only work out of the office about half the time. I'm not over any corporate budgeting. I get told from the accounting team how big the individual account budgets are, but even that I don't touch. I'm in charge of design, communication, and quality assurance for our clients."

Their clients.

She took a long breath in through her nose, trying to calm down. "What about our clients?"

The two agents exchanged a glance. "We can't comment on them at this time," Agent Bell said. He took a seat next to her on the couch and touched her knee. "Miss Keller."

She swung her gaze to him, surprised he was there. Lauren felt outside of herself, and she didn't like it. "I think you should get on home," he said, and these federal agents were definitely Texas-based. She could hear the twang in their accents. Why her brain seized on that, she didn't know, but it did make her feel more comfortable with them.

They knew how things ran in Texas. They understood Texas manners.

"We'll drive you, as we've confiscated your car," Agent Toledo said.

"My car?" Lauren asked.

"Truth be told," Agent Toledo said. "I was hours away from putting your name out to Interpol and launching a nation-wide manhunt for you and your car." He gave her a smile that wasn't meant to be happy.

A *smile.*

Lauren sucked at the air then, full-blown panic descending on her. She'd been holding it back since she stepped into the wasteland that was now the twelfth floor, but there was no stemming it now.

"Jack," Agent Bell chastised, and then Lauren passed out.

ROUGHLY EIGHT HOURS LATER, LAUREN CLUTCHED a piping hot mug in her hands. She wrapped her icy fingers around it, trying to infuse some warmth into herself though the Texas July heat was brutal that day.

Not inside this police station, it wasn't. Her house had been likewise chilled with air conditioning. She'd bundled up in a pair of jeans and a mustard-yellow sweater to come with the agents to give her testimony.

Her *testimony*.

Lauren had never done anything of the sort, and she had no idea what her life had come to. Agent Bell had taken her phone last night, and Lauren hadn't seen hide nor hair of it since. The only thing they'd allowed her to keep after going through it was her purse.

She felt violated on a level she'd never even considered, and she knew that everything in her home was currently being examined too.

Seven-point-two million dollars. Gone.

Six named thieves.

The company name of Simple Solutions all over the news.

She knew the full story now, and she found it hard to believe. Sheila had always been professional and kind at the same time. She'd calmed irate clients, had a London fog at the precise temperature Lauren liked on her desk each morning, and never missed a memo.

She'd become a grandmother last year, and Lauren pressed her eyes closed so she wouldn't be staring at the cold, white wall. She wasn't sure how long she'd been here. The gray tea she'd been brought was half-gone and cold by the time someone came into the room.

Agent Bell put her phone on the table, and the level of relief shooting through Lauren couldn't be quantified. She wasn't sure why, but she felt connected to the outside world with that phone. She had no idea if anyone had tried to get in touch with her, but she suspected both Joy and Cass had.

At least she hoped so. How pathetic would it be if she had no missed calls? No texts from anyone?

She could literally be arrested, detained, experience a debilitating panic attack and be anywhere in the world by now, and she didn't have one person who cared.

She didn't reach for her phone immediately, but after several seconds, she couldn't resist the pull of it. "Thank you," she murmured.

"We can't find anything to hold you," Agent Bell said. He smiled at her. "This is good, Lauren. You're cleared. You can go."

Go? she wanted to rage at him. Where was she to go? Back to her house, which had been filled with strangers? Strangers touching all of her belongings?

Lauren had seen crime dramas, and she had no desire to return to her house. Not right now, and not alone.

She could call Bessie and see if she could get off of work and go with her. Then she'd have to tell someone about the past several hours, and she had no desire to do that. She closed her eyes again, this time just in a long blink.

Pure humiliation pulled through her, filling her to the

point of choking. There was no way she could tell any of her friends about this.

"Come on," Agent Bell said, standing. "Let's get you processed and out of here."

Processed. Like she was some kind of meat.

Lauren stayed numb and silent through the rest of the process, and when she finally found herself sitting behind the wheel of her car, the doors all closed and locked, and the engine running so she didn't fry in the heat, she leaned her head down and started to sob.

THAT EVENING, LAUREN SAT ALONE ON THE outdoor patio of her favorite restaurant in Corpus Christi. She'd once dated a chef at the resort here, and she loved the deviled eggs with *chicharróns*, as well as the fried green tomatoes.

She'd only ordered her favorite appetizers, and the three plates sat half-eaten as the sun went down in the west, painting the Gulf of Mexico in pinks, purples, and golds.

The strategy she'd started on after she'd stopped sobbing in her car sat on the table in front of her, anchored in the wind by her coffee mug. She had some savings, and she'd be okay until she found another job.

She'd sell her house here and move to Hilton Head Island permanently. Her thoughts jumbled here, because Bessie, Joy, Sage, and Cherry were so important to her. She'd put stars out to the side of "Sell your house and move to SC" and written, *Can fly in for Supper Club or video chat like Bea has before.*

She couldn't lose her friends, not when so many other things in her life had crumbled.

At the same time, nowhere on her strategy was the note to tell her friends and family what had happened. Not yet, anyway. Lauren liked to keep things to herself for a while, because it took her a long time to process them in such a way that she could then make sense of them and talk about them.

Every time she closed her eyes for longer than a blink, she saw Mark weeping. She saw the toppled cubicle dividers. She saw the fish bowl conference rooms.

She had received several texts from people today. At least thirty or forty from former employees of Simple Solutions. They'd all lost their jobs, so Lauren wasn't the only one. Still, that didn't make it sting any less.

Cass, Joy, Bessie, and Bea had texted her, and as she sat at the table and lifted her first and only glass of Prosecco to her lips, another message came in. This one bore Cherry's name, and it said, *How does this dress look for Cass's wedding? I've asked a few other people, but I really trust your opinion.*

Lauren smiled as the picture came in, and Cherry looked stunning in a bright red dress that hugged all of her curves. She was six or seven years older than Lauren, and she and Jed Forrester had no children either. Lauren had seen how blissfully happy they were, and she'd started to see that she didn't need to be a mother to be filled with joy.

She told Cherry, *You look like a million bucks. Wear that for sure.*

Cass won't be outshined?

Not at all.

With this talk, Lauren remembered the wedding. She'd

been fine to attend alone before, but now the thought made her shoulders sag and her heart sink to her feet.

Joy said you're in Sweet Water Falls? Cherry asked. *Want to do lunch tomorrow or are you leaving? Too busy at work?*

Lauren didn't answer, because she didn't have a flight booked, nor would she be sleeping in her house. She'd taken out a room at the resort here, on the highest floor they'd give her, so she could witness the Gulf as far as her eyes could see.

She picked up her black gel pen and wrote on her strategy outline. *Get a date to Cass's wedding.*

The words swam in her vision, and she blinked and went to her phone. Now, to find a date.

She scrolled through her contacts, stalling very early in the alphabet.

The B's, in fact.

Blake Williams.

Her heartbeat stalled. Could she ask him to be her date? Would he be there anyway? He was one of Harrison's good friends.

Without planning or strategically outlining her message, her fingers flew across the screen. *Hey, Blake. It's Lauren Keller. Do you have a date to Cass's and Harrison's wedding? If not, I'd love to hang on your arm for the evening. No strings attached.*

Without even reading over it again, she sent the message. She felt wild, impulsive, and oh-so-desperate. But if she could keep the news of her company's failure, her lost job, and her complete and utter humiliation off her friends' radar until after the wedding, she would.

She didn't want Cass worried about her on her honeymoon. She didn't want Bessie texting her every evening. She didn't want Joy to look at her with mournful eyes.

And she absolutely didn't want to attend the wedding alone.

She checked her phone, but Blake hadn't texted back. An hour passed, and Lauren had her food boxed and she took it up to her room.

He still hadn't answered, and she wondered if she'd shocked him into silence with her invitation. They hadn't exactly been on the best of speaking terms prior to this. The last time they'd truly talked, he'd offered her a job, and she'd laughed and told him no.

"A job," she whispered to herself, wondering if Blake could possibly A) be willing to let her hang on his arm at the wedding and B) still have a job opening.

She wouldn't know until he texted back, and her phone stayed stubbornly silent all the way until she went to bed, and Lauren disliked the unsettled feeling of having something on her list that she'd started but which hadn't been finished.

Oh, what is Blake going to say? Will he be ready for another try with Lauren? Is *she* ready to look past her career in favor of finding true love?

Preorder THE SEASIDE STRATEGY now! Scan the QR code to get it on any retailer.

Books in the Hilton Head Romance series

The Love List (Hilton Head Romance, Book 1): Bea turns to her lists when things get confusing and her love list morphs once again... Can she add *fall in love at age 45* to the list and check it off?

The Paradise Plan (Hilton Head Romance, Book 2): When Harrison keeps showing up unannounced at her construction site, sometimes with her favorite pastries, Cass starts to wonder if she should add him to her daily routine... If she does, will her perfectly laid out plans fall short of paradise? Or could she find her new life *and* a new love, all without any plans at all?

The Seaside Strategy (Hilton Head Romance, Book 3): Lauren doesn't want to work for Blake, especially not in strategic investments. She's had enough of the high-profile, corporate life. **Can she strategically insert herself into Blake's life without compromising her seaside strategy and finally get what she really wants...love and a lasting relationship?**

Books in the Sweet Water Falls Farm Romance series

Cross Cowboy, Book 1: He's been accused of being far too blunt. Like that time he accused her of stealing her company from her best friend... Can Travis and Shayla overcome their differences and find a happily-ever-after together?

Grumpy Cowboy

Grumpy Cowboy, Book 2: He can find the negative in any situation. Like that time he got upset with the woman who brought him a free chocolate-and-caramel-covered apple because it had melted in his truck... Can William and Gretchen start over and make a healthy relationship after it's started to wilt?

Surly Cowboy

Surly Cowboy, Book 3: He's got a reputation to uphold and he's not all that amused the way regular people are. Like that time he stood there straight-faced and silent while every-one else in the audience cheered and clapped for that educational demo... Can Lee and Rosalie let bygones be bygones and make a family filled with joy?

Salty Cowboy

Salty Cowboy, Book 4: The last Cooper sibling is looking for love...she just wishes it wouldn't be in her hometown, or with the saltiest cowboy on the planet. But something about Jed Forrester has Cherry all a-flutter, and he'll be darned if he's going to let her get away. But Jed may have met his match when it comes to his quick tongue and salty attitude...

Books in the Hope Eternal Ranch Romance series

Hopeful Cowboy, Book 1: Can Ginger and Nate find their happily-ever-after, keep up their duties on the ranch, and build a family? Or will the risk be too great for them both?

Overprotective Cowboy, Book 2: Can Ted and Emma face their pasts so they can truly be ready to step into the future together? Or will everything between them fall apart once the truth comes out?

Rugged Cowboy, Book 3: He's a cowboy mechanic with two kids and an ex-wife on the run. She connects better to horses than humans. Can Dallas and Jess find their way to each other at Hope Eternal Ranch?

Christmas Cowboy, Book 4: He needs to start a new story for his life. She's dealing with a lot of family issues. This Christmas, can Slate and Jill find solace in each other at Hope Eternal Ranch?

Wishful Cowboy, Book 5: He needs somewhere to belong. She has a heart as wide as the Texas sky. Can Luke and Hannah find their one true love in each other?

Risky Cowboy, Book 6: She's tired of making cheese and ice cream on her family's dairy farm, but when the cowboy hired to replace her turns out to be an ex-boyfriend, Clarissa suddenly isn't so sure about leaving town... Will Spencer risk it all to convince Clarissa to stay and give him a second chance?

Books in the Hawthorne Harbor Romance series

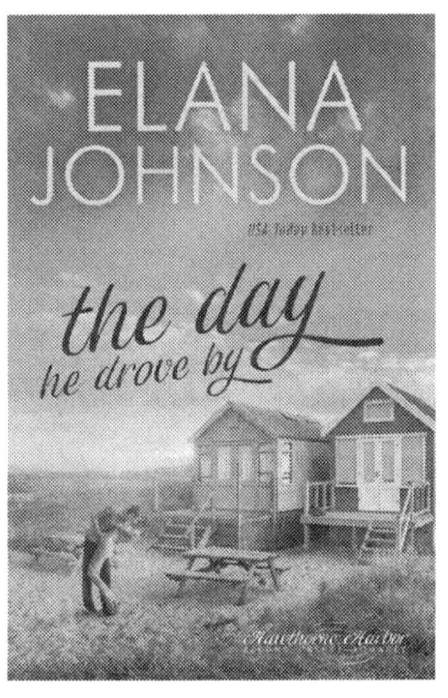

The Day He Drove By (Hawthorne Harbor Second Chance Romance, Book 1): A widowed florist, her ten-year-old daughter, and the paramedic who delivered the girl a decade earlier...

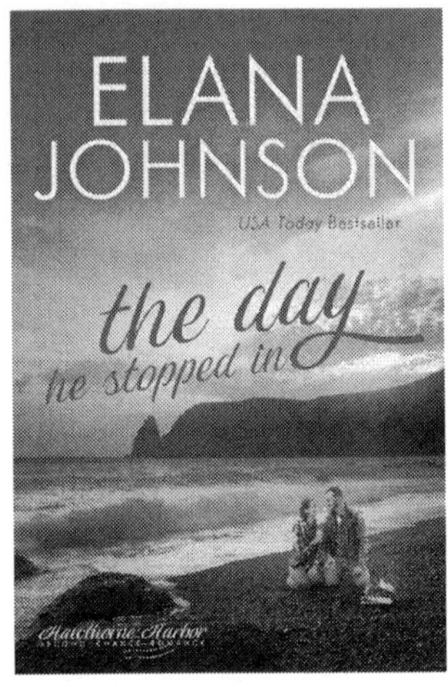

The Day He Stopped In (Hawthorne Harbor Second Chance Romance, Book 2): Janey Germaine is tired of entertaining tourists in Olympic National Park all day and trying to keep her twelve-year-old son occupied at night. When longtime friend and the Chief of Police, Adam Herrin, offers to take the boy on a ride-along one fall evening, Janey starts to see him in a different light. Do they have the courage to take their relationship out of the friend zone?

The Day He Said Hello (Hawthorne Harbor Second Chance Romance, Book 3): Bennett Patterson is content with his boring firefighting job and his big great dane...until he comes face-to-face with his high school girlfriend, Jennie Zimmerman, who swore she'd never return to Hawthorne Harbor. Can they rekindle their old flame? Or will their opposite personalities keep them apart?

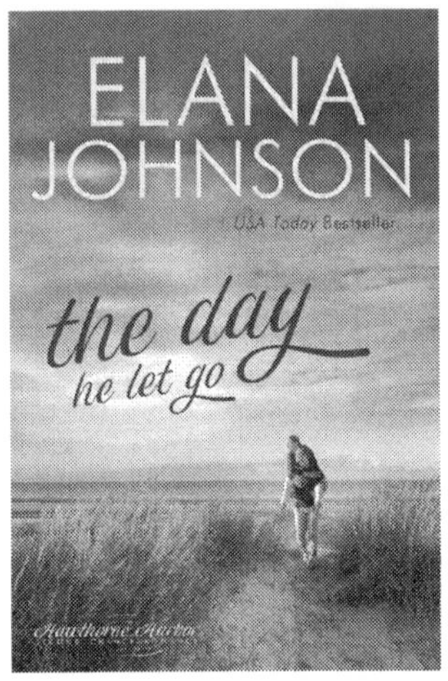

The Day He Let Go (Hawthorne Harbor Second Chance Romance, Book 4): Trent Baker is ready for another relationship, and he's hopeful he can find someone who wants him and to be a mother to his son. Lauren Michaels runs her own general contract company, and she's never thought she has a maternal bone in her body. But when she gets a second chance with the handsome K9 cop who blew her off when she first came to town, she can't say no... Can Trent and Lauren make their differences into strengths and build a family?

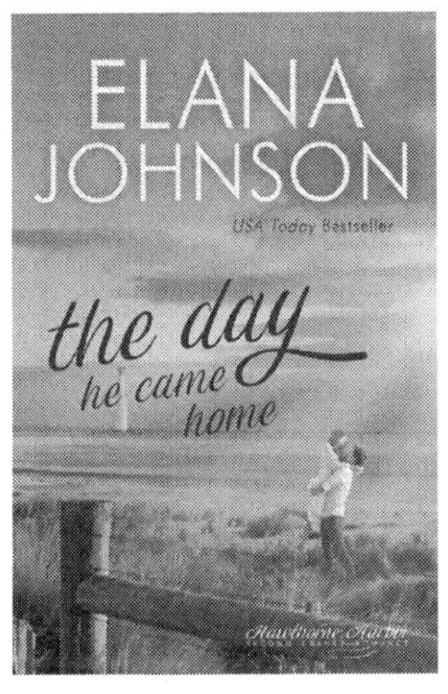

The Day He Came Home (Hawthorne Harbor Second Chance Romance, Book 5): A wounded Marine returns to Hawthorne Harbor years after the woman he was married to for exactly one week before she got an annulment...and then a baby nine months later. Can Hunter and Alice make a family out of past heartache?

The Day He Asked Again (Hawthorne Harbor Second Chance Romance, Book 6): A Coast Guard captain would rather spend his time on the sea...unless he's with the woman he's been crushing on for months. Can Brooklynn and Dave make their second chance stick?

About Elana

Elana Johnson is the USA Today bestselling and Kindle All-Star author of dozens of clean and wholesome contemporary romance novels. She lives in Utah, where she mothers two fur babies, works with her husband full-time, and eats a lot of veggies while writing. Find her on her website at feelgoodfictionbooks.com.

Made in the USA
Middletown, DE
29 November 2022

16355354R00267